Microeconomics

an introduction to theory and applications

Microeconomics

an introduction to theory and applications

David King

Lecturer in Economics, University of Stirling

Ronald Shone

Senior Lecturer in Economics, University of Stirling

Edward Arnold

© D.N. King and R. Shone 1987

First published in Great Britain 1987 by
Edward Arnold (Publishers) Ltd, 41 Bedford Square, London WC1B 3DQ

Edward Arnold (Australia) Pty Ltd, 80 Waverley Road, Caulfield East, Victoria
3145, Australia

Edward Arnold, 3 East Read Street, Baltimore, Maryland 21202, USA

British Library Cataloguing in Publication Data

King, David N.
  Microeconomics: an introduction to theory
  and applications.
  1. Microeconomics
  1. Title   II. Shone, R. (Ronald)
  338.5   HB172

ISBN 0-7131-6479-4

Text set in 10/11½ pt English Times Roman
by Colset Private Limited, Singapore
Made and printed in Great Britain
by Richard Clay plc, Bungay, Suffolk

Contents

Preface

This book is written principally for students in their first year at universities and colleges who are taking an introductory course in microeconomics. There are many other textbooks available to accompany these courses, most if not all of them concentrating on presenting the same basic theory in much the same way. We have written a rather different sort of book. This covers fairly succinctly much the same theoretical ground that is found at length in these books, and it concentrates most of it into four key chapters, namely chapters 1, 6, 10 and 16; these four chapters are necessarily rather long. The remaining chapters are shorter and show a number of ways in which the basic theory can be applied. Of course, most texts contain some applications as well as theory; it is the balance between the two which is different here.

There are three reasons why we have adopted this approach. The first and most important is a conviction that encouraging first-year students to concentrate a little more on how to apply economic theory and rather less on some of the more abstract parts of the theory itself makes for a better grounding in economics as a discipline. In our judgement, a student who has, for example, seen supply and demand curves used in the analysis of fixed exchange rates will get a firmer feel for this branch of economics than one who has been busily computing point and arc elasticities; the student who has considered an application of indifference analysis to labour supply will probably have acquired a deeper understanding of the theory of household behaviour than the student who has contemplated the probable non-existence of Giffen goods; the student who has looked at the effects of taxes and subsidies on firms is likely to have a fuller appreciation of the theory of the firm than the student who has always dealt in an abstract way with fixed and variable costs; and the student who has considered why wages differ in different occupations will have a greater knowledge of the behaviour of labour markets than the student whose study of input markets has been confined to a discussion of marginal revenue products and the demand side alone.

Our second reason concerns motivation. We believe that the pure theory approach which dominates so many texts leaves students with a feeling that economics may be stimulating for people who like geometry and algebra, but has little to say about the real world. This is perhaps more of a danger in microeconomics than in macroeconomics where throwing in the words 'unemployment' and 'inflation' from time to time may help to sustain interest.

We hope that students who see how elementary theory can produce insights into tariffs, criminal behaviour, learning curves and the effects of trades unions on wage rates will realize the wide-ranging value of microeconomics.

Thirdly, we feel our approach is particularly valuable for two (partly overlapping) subsets of students who make up a large proportion of those whom we teach. One group comprises those who claim to have 'done it all before' either for their A-Levels or, in Scotland, for their Highers. Colleges and universities often try to sweep this problem under the carpet by belittling the value of economics done at school. However, we accept that these students do have a problem. True, they will find they have not already covered everything they meet in their first year, but they can still get bored. We hope that this book will suit them by taking them into new territory. The other group comprises those students who will do economics for just one year in higher education. We hope that the necessarily modest amount of microeconomic theory they will learn will be of more value to them if they can see different ways of applying it.

Once we had decided to write a book on these lines, we had to give much thought to what applications to include. In the end, we tried to select topics which met two criteria. First, did they really apply the theory? Secondly, were they likely to interest students? It may be helpful to see how we used these criteria by considering two applications that we initially thought of including but eventually decided to exclude. We decided against a chapter on agriculture chiefly because there does not seem to be a great deal to learn from basic microeconomic theory about agriculture policy in the EEC, except that the quantity supplied will exceed the quantity demanded if the authorities fix a price above the equilibrium level. We decided against a chapter on the virtues of a tax on the rent from land because any theoretical advantages it might have seem to us to be outweighed by its manifest unfairness to those who have invested their savings in purchases of land rather than in purchases of other assets; this objection tends to reduce or eliminate any interest students might otherwise have in such a proposal.

We did not seek to apply a uniform length or standard of difficulty to the applications. Some, like the one on criminal behaviour, are fairly long and challenging; others, like the one on subsidies versus cash handouts, are short and straightforward. Students are heterogeneous, and we hope that their varying tastes and needs will be catered for by this variety of presentation. Moreover, we hope that students who move rapidly through some of the easier applications will then be inspired to tackle some of the harder ones.

We have four debts to acknowledge. First, to our students at the University of Stirling on whom we have experimented with many different applications in recent years. Secondly, to Mrs Catherine McIntosh who typed the first draft of the manuscript and then made countless changes, and to Mrs Ann Cowie for assistance at the final stages. Thirdly, to Mrs Shirley Hewitt, who prepared with great care all the diagrams ready for publication. And, fourthly, to our publishers for waiting so patiently for a typescript which they were told was 'very nearly ready' over a remarkably long period of time.

Introduction

Economics is frequently regarded as having two broadly separate parts known as macroeconomics and microeconomics. This distinction is certainly useful at the introductory level, though students will find that it becomes more blurred in more advanced work. Broadly speaking, macroeconomics is concerned with the performance of national economies taken as a whole. In the UK, therefore, macroeconomics would be used to help explain why, in 1984 for example, there were over three million people registered as unemployed, why the level of prices faced by consumers was growing at around 5 per cent, why average wage rates were rising by a little more than prices, why the total output of goods and services rose only slightly, why interest rates rose, and why the total value of exports rose more slowly than the total value of imports.

However, this book is concerned with microeconomics. In contrast to macroeconomics, microeconomics is concerned with individual parts of the economy, and, in particular, with individual markets. The word market applies to the transactions of any item which is bought and sold. In some cases, such as second-hand sales of shares in ICI, these transactions may be confined largely to a single building, in this instance the stock exchange in London. In other cases, such as washing-up liquid, transactions may take place in countless locations up and down the country. Nevertheless, economists regard anyone who buys or sells ICI shares as being active in the market for them, and anyone who buys or sells washing-up liquid as being active in the market for it.

There are two main aspects of the market for any individual item which are of particular interest to economists, and these are the price of the item and the quantity which is traded in any given period of time. However, it is important to be clear about the nature of economists' interest in these aspects. The critical point to grasp is that economists are not especially interested in discovering what the prices and quantities of individual items are, but rather in the factors which determine those prices and quantities. Thus it is not the dream of economists to have an up-to-date list of the prices and quantities of all traded items; rather, it is to understand what factors determine these prices and quantities, what events could cause them to change, and how sensitive the prices and quantities are to the events concerned.

It is clear that in any country there will be markets for thousands of different items. However, most of these numerous markets fall into one or other of five main groups of markets, as follows:

1 Markets for new goods and services bought by households (or consumers) from producers (or businesses).
2 Markets for new capital goods purchased by producers from other producers. These goods include industrial plant, buildings, vehicles and machinery. It is noteworthy that market groups (1) and (2) cover the bulk of the output of finished goods and services bought from a country's producers, at least if purchases of exports by foreign households and producers are excluded. However, they do not, of course, cover the output of producers whose products are not sold, such as the output of many charities (like Oxfam) or government departments (like the ministry of defence), for their products are not dealt with on any markets.
3 Markets for intermediate products purchased by producers from other producers. These products include items such as raw materials, energy, transport, advertising and insurance. They differ from capital goods in that they are rapidly used up in the process of producing and selling, whereas capital goods are likely to have a life of several years at least.
4 Markets for the many different types of labour which are supplied – or, as it is often said – hired by households to producers. In these markets, the term wage rate is generally used instead of price.
5 Markets for second-hand products. Many of these, such as houses and cars, are bought and sold chiefly by households. Others, such as second-hand capital goods, are traded between producers. Yet others, such as second-hand securities, may be bought and sold by both households and businesses, especially financial companies.

This list is not exhaustive. There are markets for many items which do not fall into any of these groups. For instance, there are markets in new securities, which are generally sold by businesses in an attempt to raise money to purchase new capital; there are markets for loans of money, where money itself is borrowed and lent under various repayment conditions for various 'prices' known as rates of interest; there are markets for foreign currencies; and there are markets for different types of land, such as rough pasture and building plots.

It is a major proposition of microeconomics that the price and quantity in any particular market are determined by the demand for and the supply of the item concerned. Accordingly, much of microeconomics is concerned with the analysis of supply and demand. Part I of this book examines the way in which supply and demand determine the price and quantity in any market in which there are many buyers and many sellers of a particular product. Strictly speaking, its analysis applies only if a number of stringent conditions are met, especially that the buyers and sellers are all dealing in identical or homogeneous products and that they are all perfectly informed about the market. Whilst these conditions might be fulfilled in a few cases – second-hand shares in ICI being a possible example – they are probably not fulfilled in many markets. In the case of washing-up liquid, for instance, prices of similar bottles may vary from shop to shop. For example, a village shop may be able to sell bottles at higher prices than those charged for similar bottles in the supermarket of a distant town, for its bottles are more conveniently located to villagers, and so may not be regarded as wholly equivalent in its customers' eyes; and supermarket A may manage to sell quite a lot of bottles at a higher price than supermarket B down the street if A's customers are ill-informed about B's prices. For such reasons, it is not wholly satisfactory to talk about 'the' price of most commodities. Nevertheless, it is perhaps fair to say that the discussion in Part I provides a useful – if not strictly precise – view of how the general level of prices and the quantity are determined in many markets.

If prices and quantities are determined by supply and demand, then it is clear that economists will be interested in turn in the factors that cause supply and demand to change. The more important factors are mentioned in Part I, but they are examined in greater depth in later parts. Thus Part II considers the theory of household behaviour which can be used to throw some light on what causes household demands for goods and services and household supplies of labour to alter. Part III considers what is often called the theory of the firm, which looks at the factors which determine the supplies of goods and services made by producers, and Part IV looks at the factors which determine the demands made by producers, especially for intermediate products and labour. Part III also looks at markets where there are many producers each producing rather different products, and at markets where there is just one producer; and Part IV also looks at labour markets where the presence of trades unions means that certain types of labour are effectively supplied by single bodies rather than by many quite separate individual workers.

Part I

Market equilibrium

1

The elements of supply and demand

Introduction to supply and demand

How the equilibrium price and quantity are determined

This chapter, along with the other chapters in Part I, is concerned with the determination of both the price and the quantity traded in a period of time in any market where a (more or less) identical product is bought and sold by many buyers and sellers. In this introductory chapter, a basic supply and demand framework is presented which shows how the price and quantity might be determined in a typical market of this type; it is supposed that there is no government intervention in the market concerned. Later chapters consider in turn some of the ways in which governments might intervene in certain markets and some of the effects of their intervention, and also adjustments which need to be made to analyse atypical or unusual markets.

As it happens, an attempt to select a typical market is every bit as difficult as it would be to try and select a typical person or country. However, the market for fresh trout will serve as well as any. It will be supposed, for simplicity, that all trout are sold to customers by fish farms at the farms themselves; in practice; many fish will be sold indirectly via shops, an arrangement which makes the situation rather more complex but which is unlikely to affect the principles on which the general level of trout prices and the quantity traded are determined. One way in which the demand for and the supply of fresh trout could be summed up is shown in Table 1.1. The first column here shows a range of possible retail

Table 1.1 The demand and supply of fresh trout

Price per kg £	Quantity demanded per week (tonnes)	Quantity supplied per week (tonnes)
10	58	118
9	70	113
8	84	107
7	100	100
6	118	92
5	138	83
4	160	73

prices at which fresh trout might sell; in principle, it could sell for a higher price than the highest shown (£10 per kg) or for a lower price than the lowest shown (£4 per kg), but, as will become clear, these extreme possibilities are unlikely to apply and so are of little interest.

The second column of Table 1.1 shows the total quantity of fresh trout which consumers might between them wish to buy each week at each possible price. The figures shown are purely illustrative and are not intended to reflect the actual situation in any particular country. This column suggests that there would be a greater quantity demanded at lower prices than at higher ones; in principle, this situation might not be true for all markets in all countries, but it seems highly probable, and no exceptions are known to exist.

The third column shows the total quantity which suppliers might between them wish to produce for sale at each possible price. Again, the figures shown are not intended to reflect the actual situation in any particular country. This column suggests that more would be supplied at higher prices than at lower ones. This situation is likely to apply in most, if not perhaps all, markets. For example, if trout prices rise then trout farmers might find that it becomes profitable initially to sell slightly smaller fish and then to step up their breeding programmes. They might also find it profitable to import foreign trout, despite the transport costs involved, and they might offer more money for wild trout caught in rivers which would encourage anglers to put more effort into catching them on their behalf. Note that the figures in this column might rise or fall according to the time of year.

Suppose, for a moment, that the price in one particular week is £5 per kg. At this price, consumers want to buy more trout (138 tonnes) than suppliers wish to sell (83 tonnes); this situation is called one of excess demand, the excess here being 55 tonnes (138 tonnes less 83 tonnes). Consequently, one can imagine sizeable queues at trout farms. As a result, suppliers are likely to raise their prices, and they will be tempted by these higher prices to supply more trout. It follows that if the price is ever at a level where the quantity demanded exceeds the quantity supplied, that is below £7 per kg, then the price is likely to rise.

Conversely, suppose the price in one particular week were £9 per kg. At this price, suppliers want to sell more trout (113 tonnes) than consumers wish to buy (70 tonnes); this situation is called one of excess supply, the excess here being 43 tonnes (113 tonnes less 70 tonnes). Consequently, one can imagine trout farms cutting their prices in an attempt to sell more trout, and simultaneously reacting to the lower prices by reducing the amount of trout which they supply. Similar action would be expected at any price which produced an excess supply, that is at any price above £7 per kg.

The upshot of the analysis in the last two paragraphs is that if the price of trout is ever above £7 per kg then it will fall, whilst if it is below £7 per kg, then it will rise. Accordingly, it should eventually settle at £7 per kg, and this price is known as the equilibrium price. It is useful to realize that there is only one equilibrium price in this case (and indeed in virtually all markets) because there is only one price which ensures that the resulting quantity supplied equals the resulting quantity demanded; at any price other than the equilibrium, one quantity will be demanded and another different quantity supplied. In other words, there is only one price at which the resulting desires of suppliers and consumers are compatible. In some markets, the movement of the price towards a settled equilibrium may occur very quickly – perhaps in minutes in the case of second-hand securities – but in others it may occur very slowly. Note that the forces of supply and demand determine not only the equilibrium price, but also the equilibrium quantity of trout, 100 tonnes per week, which will be supplied and demanded at the equilibrium price.

Illustrating supply and demand on a diagram

Although the forces of supply and demand can be illustrated with numbers, as in Table 1.1, it is usual in economics to illustrate them on a graph, as shown in Figure 1.1. The vertical axis shows the possible prices and the horizontal axis indicates quantities of trout per week. The demand curve shows the quantity of trout demanded at each price, and the supply curve shows the quantity of trout supplied at each price. Like the figures in Table 1.1, these curves show the total quantity demanded and the total quantity supplied in the market at each price, and they should strictly be termed the *market* demand curve and the *market* supply curve; this would distinguish them clearly from the *individual* demand

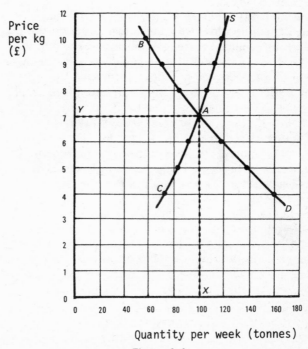

Figure 1.1

curves and *individual* supply curves met in some later chapters which show how much individual buyers demand at each price and how much individual suppliers want to supply at each price. The curves in Figure 1 intersect at the point A, which is at the level of the equilibrium price (£7), the only price where the quantity demanded equals the quantity supplied, and this point A also shows the equilibrium quantity (100 tonnes).

If the price exceeds the equilibrium price, then there will be an excess supply, shown by the gap between the curves at the price concerned. Thus at a price of £9 per kg, the excess is 113 tonnes less 70 tonnes. In this case, the actual quantity sold will be the lesser of the two, 70 tonnes, since suppliers cannot force consumers to buy more at this price. If the price is below the equilibrium price, then there will be an excess demand, shown by the gap between the curves at the price concerned. Thus at a price of £ 5 per kg, the excess is 138 tonnes less 83 tonnes. In this case, too, the actual quantity sold will be the lesser of the two, 83 tonnes, since consumers cannot force suppliers to sell more at this price. In short, the actual amount which would be sold at each possible price is shown by the kinked line BAC. An interesting consequence of this is that if the actual price is not the equilibrium one, then the quantity actually traded will always be below the equilibrium quantity. As the price moves towards the equilibrium, whether up or down as the case may be, the actual quantity sold will rise.

A similar result may be expected in most markets, though temporary exceptions can occur with products like frozen shrimps, which can be stored for long periods. With storable products, it is still true that if the price is above the equilibrium, then the quantity sold will equal the quantity demanded, and that this will be below the quantity which would be demanded at the (lower) equilibrium price; in these circumstances, more is supplied, or produced, than is sold and stocks will rise. The rise in stocks here would be one factor encouraging producers to reduce their prices and produce less for sale. However, if the price is below the equilibrium, so that the quantity produced is less than the quantity demanded, then suppliers might be prepared to sell more than they produce by running down their stocks. If stocks were sufficiently large, then suppliers might even be able to meet the entire quantity demanded, and might certainly be able to sell more than the quantity which would be demanded at the (higher) equilibrium price. Of course, they could sell more than they produce only for as long as stocks last. The fall in stocks here would be one factor encouraging producers to raise their price and produce more for sale.

One further feature of Figure 1.1 should be noticed, and this is that it is possible to show on it the amount of money that will change hands each week once the equilibrium price and quantity have been reached. This amount is £7 per kg times 100 tonnes, or £7 per kg times 100,000 kg, which is £700,000, and this is represented in Figure 1.1 by the area of the rectangle OXAY; for the area of this rectangle equals its height (shown as £7 per kg) times its length (shown as 100 tonnes or 100,000 kg).

How the equilibrium price and quantity change

Since the equilibrium price and quantity in the typical market is determined – at least in the absence of government intervention – by the forces of supply and demand at the point where the demand and supply curves intersect, it follows that the equilibrium positions can change only if one or other of the curves shifts. Essentially, there are four possibilities, and these are shown in Figures 1.2 to 1.5, where the initial demand and supply curves are labelled D and S respectively.

In Figure 1.2, there is what is termed an increase in demand, shown by a rightward shift in the demand curve from D to D'. An increase in demand occurs when there is an event which means that there would be a higher quantity demanded at each possible price. The chief types of event concerned are considered later, but on this occasion it could be that there has been a rise in consumers' disposable incomes, perhaps as a result of a fall in income tax rates. The initial equilibrium price and quantity are shown by P_0 and Q_0. The price P_0 may continue to be set for a while after the demand curve moves from D to D', but, if so, there will be an excess demand of $(Q_2 - Q_0)$. As explained earlier, excess demands result in price rises, and the price will continue rising until it reaches P_1; at this price, the equilibrium quantity will be Q_1.

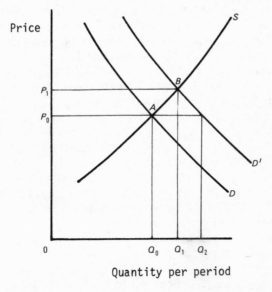

Figure 1.2

Figure 1.3 illustrates the effects of a fall in demand, shown by a leftward shift in the demand curve from D to D'. This fall means that less would be demanded at each possible price, a consequence perhaps of a fall in consumers' disposable incomes following a rise in income tax rates. The initial equilibrium price of P_0

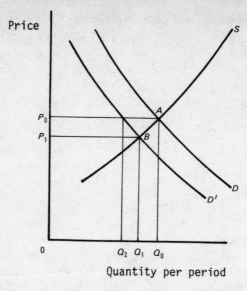

Figure 1.3

may persist for a while, but, if so, there will be an excess supply of $(Q_0 - Q_2)$. This will put downward pressure on the price which will continue to fall until it reaches P_1. The initial equilibrium quantity was Q_0, and the final one is lower at Q_1.

In Figure 1.4, there is what is termed an increase in supply, shown by a rightward shift in the supply curve from S to S'. An increase in supply occurs when there is an event which means that there would be a higher quantity supplied at each possible price. A number of possible events are considered

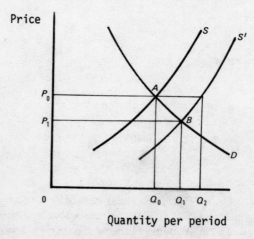

Figure 1.4

later, but one possibility is the invention of a fertility drug for trout which makes trout breeding cheaper and so encourages producers to supply more. The initial equilibrium price and quantity are shown by P_0 and Q_0. The price P_0 may persist for a while after the supply curve moves from S to S', but, if so, there will be an excess supply of $(Q_2 - Q_0)$. This will put downward pressure on the price which will fall until it reaches P_1; at this price, the equilibrium quantity will be Q_1 which is higher than the original Q_0.

Figure 1.5 illustrates the effects of a fall in supply, shown by a leftward shift in the supply curve from S to S'. This fall means that less would be supplied at each possible price, a consequence perhaps of a rise in the price of trout food. The initial equilibrium price of P_0 may persist for a while but, if so, there will be an excess demand of $(Q_0 - Q_2)$. This will put upward pressure on the price which will continue to rise until it reaches P_1. The initial equilibrium quantity was Q_0, and the final one is lower at Q_1.

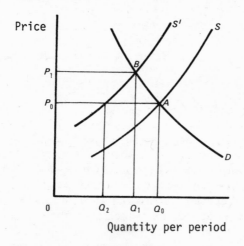

Figure 1.5

It will be noticed that Figure 1.2 indicates that a rise in demand raises not only the equilibrium price (from P_0 to P_1) and quantity (from Q_0 to Q_1) but also the equilibrium amount of money going from buyers to sellers. This rise can be seen by comparing the original amount of money, shown by the rectangle $0P_0AQ_0$, with the new amount, shown by the rectangle $0P_1BQ_1$. Conversely, Figure 1.3 shows that a fall in demand reduces not only the equilibrium price (from P_0 to P_1) and quantity (from Q_0 to Q_1) but also the equilibrium amount of money changing hands. This can be seen by comparing the original amount, shown by $0P_0AQ_0$, with the new amount, shown by $0P_1BQ_1$.

By contrast, Figure 1.4 shows that a rise in supply reduces the equilibrium price (from P_0 to P_1) and raises the equilibrium quantity (from Q_0 to Q_1). In principle, the equilibrium amount of money changing hands beforehand, shown by $0P_0AQ_0$, could be either less or more than the amount changing hands afterwards, shown by $0P_1BQ_1$. Conversely, Figure 1.5 shows that a fall in supply raises the equilibrium price (from P_0 to P_1) and reduces the equilibrium quantity (from Q_0 to Q_1); again, the equilibrium amount of money changing hands beforehand, shown by $0P_0AQ_0$, could in principle be less than or more than (or even just equal to) the amount changing hands afterwards, shown by $0P_1BQ_1$.

Price elasticity

Price elasticity of demand

The effects on the equilibrium amount of money changing hands caused by shifts in the supply curve depend on what is known as the price-elasticity of demand. Demand is said to be price-elastic if a fall in price would raise total spending while a rise in price would reduce it, and demand is said to be price-inelastic if a fall in price would cut total spending while a rise in price would raise it.

Economists sometimes seek to measure the price-elasticity of demand for a particular item, and they do so by considering what happens to the quantity of the item demanded if its price changes. Its elasticity can be calculated from this formula:

$$\text{Price elasticity of demand} = \frac{\text{Percentage change in quantity demanded}}{\text{Percentage change in price}}$$

This formula indicates that the elasticity of demand of an item actually measures the responsiveness of the quantity of it demanded to changes in its price. Thus if a 5 per cent fall in price led to a 10 per cent rise in quantity demanded, then the elasticity of demand would be 10 divided by -5, that is, -2; in this case, total expenditure on the item would rise, so demand is elastic, and indeed demand is elastic whenever the elasticity is less than -1. Had the 5 per cent fall in price led to a rise in quantity demanded of just 2 per cent, then the elasticity would have been 2 divided by -5, that is -0.4; in this case, total expenditure on the item would have fallen, so demand would be inelastic, and indeed demand is inelastic whenever the elasticity is greater than -1.

It is possible to explore calculations of elasticity of demand in much more detail than is given here (as explained in many microeconomics texts). However, such detail is seldom necessary for students, and is not necessary in the remainder of this book. There is one important point which should be noted, though, and this is that elasticity is generally different at all points on a demand curve, even if it is a straight line. This can be readily explained with the help of the demand curve (D) in Figure 1.6. At a price of P_1, none of the item concerned is demanded and there is no expenditure on it, though if price fell to P_2, then some units (A) of the item would be sold, so some money would now be spent on it; demand on this part of the demand curve is clearly elastic.

Conversely, if the price were P_3, then there would be substantial sales (B) and hence money would be spent on the item, though if the price fell to P_4 (that is

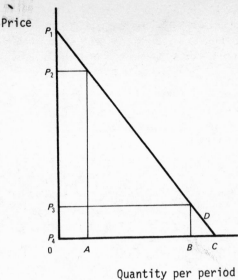

Figure 1.6

zero), then consumers might demand a lot (C) but they would spend nothing on it as it would now be free; demand on this part of the curve is clearly inelastic. This analysis shows that elasticity is not the same at each point and so it cannot be estimated for a given point simply from the slope of the curve at that point, for the slope here was the same at each point! It should be remarked, though, that it is possible to have demand curves where the elasticity *is* the same at each point. There are two important cases: a horizontal demand curve, where elasticity is infinite at each point (for a minute fall in price would have a huge effect on quantity demanded) and a vertical demand curve, where elasticity is zero at each point (for a large fall in price would have no effect on quantity demanded); these are referred to respectively as situations of perfectly elastic demand and perfectly inelastic demand.

Price-elasticity of supply

Economists also have a term price-elasticity of supply, which measures the responsiveness of the quantity of an item supplied to changes in its price. It can be found from the following formula:

$$\text{Price elasticity of supply} = \frac{\text{Percentage change in quantity supplied}}{\text{Percentage change in price}}$$

Thus if a 5 per cent rise in price led to a 15 per cent rise in quantity supplied, then the elasticity of supply would be 15 divided by 5 which is 3. Supply is said to be elastic if the elasticity exceeds one and inelastic if it is less than one. The elasticity of supply is generally different at each point on a supply curve, even if the curve happens to be a straight line. However, the elasticity would be infinite at each point on a horizontal curve, a case of perfectly elastic supply, and zero at each point on a vertical one, a case of perfectly inelastic supply.

Some further observations on shifts in curves

Distinguishing shifts of curves from shifts along curves

The preceding paragraphs have indicated that economists regard supply as changing only when an entire supply curve shifts. It follows that a change in demand, as shown in Figures 1.2 and 1.3, will not alter the supply curve, and hence will not alter what economists term supply, even though the actual equilibrium quantity supplied changes in each case from Q_0 to Q_1; the equilibrium merely moves from one point A to another point B on an unchanging supply curve. Similarly, economists regard demand as changing only when an entire demand curve shifts. It follows that a change in supply, as shown in Figures 1.4 and 1.5, will not alter the demand curve, and hence will not alter what economists term demand, even though the actual equilibrium quantity demanded changes in each case from Q_0 to Q_1; the equilibrium merely moves from one point A to another point B on an unchanging demand curve.

This analysis suggests that changes in equilibrium prices and quantities can generally be attributed to changes in demand and supply curves. Not surprisingly, much of microeconomics is concerned with identifying factors which cause these curves to shift. Some of the main factors will be noted shortly. It must be realized that the factors which apply to households' demand curves (for consumer products such as gin or Siamese cats) are rather different from those which apply to producers' demand curves (perhaps for labour or for raw materials such as steel for cars or old horses which are used in the production of dog meat) so these two types of demand curve will be considered separately; of course, some products such as glue may be demanded by both producers and consumers, and the total demand for these items can be affected by any of the factors mentioned in the following two sections. Likewise, the factors which apply to households' supply curves (for various types of labour such as supermarket cashiers) are rather different from those which apply to producers' supply curves (for products such as cattle to be used for beef) so these two types will also be considered separately.

Before considering why demand and supply curves might shift, it is worth noting one factor that will not shift the demand or supply for any item, and that is a change in the item's own price. This important point can be seen in Figure 1.1. A rise in the price of trout from £5 per kg to £7 per kg will discourage buyers and will reduce the quantity demanded from 138 tonnes to 100 tonnes; and it will encourage producers and increase the quantity supplied from 83 tonnes to 100 tonnes. However, these changes are reflected in the different points of the demand and supply curves shown. These curves themselves do not shift in this instance.

Why households' demand curves may shift

Consider, first, the demand curve for a product demanded by households. This shows the total amount which would be demanded by households at each possible price. It will shift only if there is a change in the population, which alters the number of households interested in buying the product concerned, or if there is an event which changes the amount which individual households would want to buy at each possible price. Perhaps the three events most often cited are changes in disposable incomes, changes in the prices of other items (especially substitutes and complements) and changes in tastes. Thus the demand for Siamese cats could rise in a period when wages are rising (or at least rising faster than the cost of living); it could rise if the price of Persian cats rose or if the price of cat-food fell; and it could rise if it became more fashionable to own cats with blue eyes.

The term income elasticity of demand is used to describe the responsiveness of the quantity demanded by households to changes in disposable income. It may be defined as follows:

$$\text{Income elasticity of demand} = \frac{\text{Percentage change in quantity demanded}}{\text{Percentage change in income}}$$

Thus if a 5 per cent rise in incomes led to the quantity of gin demanded rising by 1 per cent of its present level, then the income elasticity of demand for gin would be 1 divided by 5, or 0.2. A rise in incomes may lead to a rise in the quantity demanded for most items, but there will be a fall in the case of some items, such as minced beef perhaps, for which there are more expensive but more appealing substitutes. Thus a 5 per cent rise in incomes could lead to a 2 per cent fall in the quantity of minced beef demanded giving it an income elasticity of −2 divided by 5, that is −0.4. Items like this, with their negative income elasticities, are known as inferior goods, whilst items with positive income elasticities are known as normal goods. Some items may have positive elasticities as incomes rise to a certain level, and then have negative ones; for instance, veal might be a normal good in a poor country, where a rise in incomes causes people to switch from mince into veal, and yet inferior in a rich country, where a rise in incomes causes people to switch from veal into rump steak. There are also some items, such as salt perhaps, which have income elasticities close to zero since income changes have negligible effects on the quantity demanded.

It should be noted that it is possible for an item to be normal over all possible income levels but not possible for an item to be inferior over all possible income levels. This can be seen by considering what might happen to the consumption of gin and minced beef if incomes fell steadily each year until they were zero. Each year's fall in income could be accompanied by a fall in the quantity of gin demanded and, if so, this would be a normal good throughout. As for minced beef, initial falls in income could certainly cause the quantity demanded to rise, and whilst this happened minced beef would be an inferior good. Eventually, though, there would come a time when further income falls did start causing a fall in the quantity demanded, and eventually, therefore, minced beef would be a normal good; this result must occur because, of course, if incomes fall to zero then eventually no minced beef at all would be demanded.

The term cross (or cross-price) elasticity of demand is used to describe the responsiveness of the quantity demanded by households for one item when the price of another changes, and it may be defined as follows:

$$\text{Cross price elasticity of demand for A with respect to B} = \frac{\text{Percentage change in quantity of A demanded}}{\text{Percentage change in price of B}}$$

The quantity of any given item demanded will be most sensitive to changes in the prices of substitutes and complements. Suppose the quantity of Siamese cats demanded would rise by 2 per cent of its present level if either the price of Persian cats rose by 10 per cent or the price of cat-food fell by 20 per cent; then the cross elasticity of demand for Siamese cats with respect to Persian cats would be 2 divided by 10, or 0.2, whilst with respect to cat-food it would be 2 divided by -20, or -0.1. Cross elasticities are positive for substitutes and negative for complements. Borrowed money can be seen as a complement for some purchases, such as cars or houses, and a rise in the price of borrowing, that is in interest rates, can cause a fall in the quantity demanded for these items.

There are a number of further factors which can affect the demand curves by households for particular products. For instance, the introduction of a substitute for an existing item could cause the demand for the existing item to fall; an example of this would be the fall in the demand for blankets when duvets were introduced. In contrast, the introduction of a complement for an existing item could cause the demand for the existing item to rise; an example of this would be the increase in the demand for milk following the widespread introduction of breakfast cereals. Insofar as loans can be regarded as a complement for some purchases, the demand for such items as houses and cars could be sensitive to the terms on which loans were made available; governments have at times been inclined to influence these terms by imposing rules (or changing the rules) about how much can be borrowed and for how long. In addition to these factors, the demand for many products can be affected by expected price changes; for instance, the demand for petrol may rise one week if a rise is expected in the following week, though such changes in demand are generally only temporary.

Why producers' demand curves may shift

Consider, next, the demand curve for a product demanded by producers as an input. This shows the total amount which would be demanded by producers at each possible price. It will shift only if there is a change in the number of producers wishing to buy the input or if there is an event which changes the amount which individual producers would want to buy at each possible price. Three major sorts of event can be mentioned, namely changes in the demand for the outputs of the producers concerned, changes in the prices of other items (especially of substitute inputs and complementary inputs) and changes in the productivity of the input concerned – that is, in the amount of output which can be obtained from each unit of input.

These factors can be illustrated in the case of the demand by dog-food manufacturers for old horses. For instance, a rise in the demand for dog-food will raise its price and so the profit which its makers can earn from processing each horse, and so in turn it will increase the number of horses which the makers will want to process at each possible price of horses. A rise in the price of a substitute input, such as old donkeys, will cause dog-food producers to buy fewer donkeys: this will initially cause a sizeable reduction in the amount of dog-food produced so raising its price which in turn makes processing old horses more profitable and so leads to an increase in the demand for them. Likewise, a fall in the price of horse-processing equipment will make processing horses more profitable and so raise the number which producers wish to process.

A rise in the productivity of horses, caused perhaps by a discovery which enables previously unusable parts of horses to be converted into dog-food, has less certain effects. Initially, it will make using horses more profitable and tend to increase the number processed; but if more horses are processed and if more dog-food is produced from each horse, then dog-food prices will fall, and this will reduce the profitability of horses again and so reduce the number of horses demanded. The net effect could be either an increase or a fall in the quantity of horses demanded. By analogy, any general improvement in the productivity of a given sort of labour, brought about perhaps by improved working practices, could in some cases raise and in other cases reduce the number of people sought by employers for the work concerned.

It may be added that for some inputs, particularly capital goods, borrowed money can be regarded as complementary so that the quantity of inputs demanded will fall if the price of borrowed money, that is interest rates, rise. Also, there may be a temporary rise in the demand for storable inputs if price rises are expected shortly.

Why households' supply curves may shift

Turning to factors affecting supply curves, consider first the supply curve by households for labour in a particular labour market such as cashiers in supermarkets in a large urban area. Such a supply curve will have the normal upward sloping form, as show in Figure 1.7. The vertical axis shows the possible prices of this item, expressed as possible wage rates for an hour's work, and the horizontal axis shows the quantity in terms of the total number of hours supplied in a period of time, here a week. This supply curve will shift only if the (working) population of the area changes or if an event occurs which changes the number of hours which (at least some) individual citizens are prepared to work at each possible wage. As with changes in household demands, the main events concern changes in incomes, the prices of other items and tastes. In the case of incomes, for instance, a rise in child benefits or student grants might reduce the extent to which some people wished to work at all and, in turn, reduce the supply of labour as cashiers. The supply might also fall if the wage (or price)

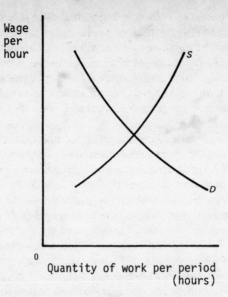

Figure 1.7

of other types of labour such as post office clerks were to rise. The supply of cashiers, and indeed of many types of labour, could also be affected by a rise in the general level of prices faced by consumers, though such a rise could move the supply curve either way; the point is that some people might react by seeking to work longer hours in an attempt to maintain their previous living standards, whilst others might react by working fewer hours on the grounds that work would become less worthwhile if each pound earned bought less. (The identical situation would arise, if, instead, income tax rates had risen, for this too reduces the value of the income from each hour worked. It follows that cuts in income tax rates might also shift supply curves to the left or to the right.) Finally, the supply of labour as cashiers might fall if, for instance, changing tastes resulted in fewer people seeking sedentary occupations.

Why producers' supply curves might shift

Next, consider the supply curves of producers. Each such curve shows the total amount of a particular product which would be supplied at each possible price, and it will shift only if there is a change in the number of producers making the product concerned or if there is an event which changes the amount which individual producers want to sell at each possible price. The main events concerned include changes in the prices and the productivities of the inputs used in production. Thus the supply of beef cattle by farmers to the meat industry would fall if cattle-food prices rose, thereby making cattle production less profitable, and it would rise if improved high meat-yielding breeds of cattle were introduced which made it more profitable. It should be emphasized, though, that (for reasons explained in Chapter 10) a change in an input's price will not affect the supply of an output it helps to produce until producers are able to vary the amount of the input they can use. Accordingly, the supply of beef cattle may react quickly to a change in cattle-food prices, as farmers can quickly change the amount they feed to their herds (and, indeed, the size of the herds) but it will not react quickly to changes in the price of buildings for storing cattle over the winter months, for farmers cannot quickly change the amount of buildings they have available for use.

A further factor which can affect the supply of products applies only to those that are in what is termed joint production with other products, and this is a change in the price of the other product produced along with them. Now beef can be regarded as, to some extent, in joint production with milk, and hence the supply of beef will also be affected by the price of milk. For instance, a rise in milk prices makes those breeds of cow used for both meat and milk production more profitable; thus it could lead to farmers wanting more cows like this and so eventually lead to an increase in the supply of beef when their cows' male calves were slaughtered. Producers' supply curves can be affected by an array of other factors. For instance, the supply of crude oil may fall if many tankers are destroyed in the Iran–Iraq war, the supply of fresh foods generally varies according to the time of year, the supply of many crops will be affected by weather conditions, and supplies are often reduced, temporarily at least, by industrial disputes.

2

Government intervention in markets

The theory of supply and demand outlined in Chapter 1 showed how prices are determined in markets where there are many buyers and sellers of a homogeneous product. One assumption in that theory was that the markets were free from government intervention. This chapter is concerned with markets where this assumption does not hold.

It is perhaps helpful to realize that governments can intervene in markets – and so affect the equilibrium prices – in a variety of ways. For instance, governments act as buyers in a number of markets. Thus the central government in the UK buys parachutes for paratroopers, sheets for hospitals and sausages for prisoners whilst local governments buy chalk for schools, fuel for fire engines and land for cemeteries. These purchases reflect demands which are included in the market demand curves for the products concerned. A change in public spending levels could change governments' demands for these items; in turn, market prices could be altered if the governments' share of market demand was relatively large, as might apply to parachutes and chalk but not to sausages or fuel.

Alternatively, governments can affect prices more directly by means of taxes and subsidies. There is a wide array of taxes and subsidies which governments can use. For instance, a tax on labour (such as, in effect, national insurance contributions) would raise firms' costs and would shift the market supply curve to the left, thereby raising the equilibrium price of their output. Conversely, a labour subsidy (such as the present temporary employment subsidy) effectively cuts costs and shifts supply curves to the right; wage subsidies are considered further in Chapter 18. Taxes on profits (such as corporation tax) and subsidies on purchases of capital equipment (such as investment grants) are a little harder to analyse, but are discussed further in Chapter 11.

The present chapter looks at taxes and subsidies on the actual products sold by suppliers. It also considers how governments may seek to affect market prices with price controls. Where a government particularly wishes to raise the price of a particular product, it is more likely to use either a tax on that product or a price control than it is to use any other sort of tax or to start buying (more of) the item concerned, though the EEC does purchase many agricultural products in order to raise the prices received by farmers; and where a government wishes to reduce the price of a particular product, it is more likely to use either a subsidy on that product or a price control than it is to use other sorts of subsidy or to buy less. Of course, taxes on products often stem more from a desire to raise revenue than a feeling that the prices of the taxed products are too low, though taxes on items such as alcoholic drink and tobacco can be at least partly explained by a desire to raise prices and restrict consumption.

Specific taxes

To see the effect of a tax on a particular product, consider Figure 2.1. Suppose, initially, there is no tax, and that the market price and quantity have settled at the equilibrium levels given by the intersection of the demand curve (D) and the supply curve (S) so that the price is £3 and the quantity is 40 units per week. Now S indicates that whilst producers would produce 40 units a week if they received £3 for each, they would produce only 10 units a week if they received just £2 per unit, and they would produce 70 units a week if they received £4 per unit. Suppose the government imposes a tax of £1 per unit and requires producers to hand over in tax £1 for each unit sold. Such a tax, expressed as so much per unit sold, is termed a *specific* tax. Its effect is, in fact, to produce a new supply curve (S'). To see how S' is derived, consider how much producers would now wish to supply each week at two possible consumer prices, namely £3 and £4.

If the price paid by consumers stayed at £3, then producers would end up with £2 per unit for themselves (after tax) and would now want to produce only 20 units per week. If, however, the price paid by consumers was £4, then producers would receive £3 each for themselves and would wish to produce 70 units per week. S' shows, for example, that with a consumer price of £3, producers would wish to produce 10 units a week, and that with a consumer price of £4, they would produce 40. It will be seen that the new supply curve is parallel to the old one and that the vertical gap between them equals the amount of tax.

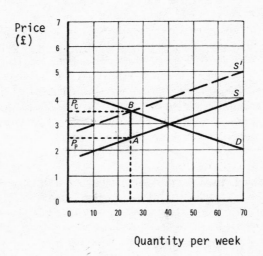

Figure 2.1

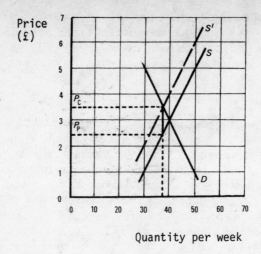

Figure 2.2

The new equilibrium will be where S′ cuts D (at point B), at a consumer price (P$_c$) of £3.50 and an output of 25 units per week. The price eventually received by producers (P$_p$) is £1 less than the one paid by consumers, and it can be found by looking on S at the new output level (at point A). With 25 units being sold each week, and £1 paid in tax on each, it follows that the tax revenue for the government is £25 per week. This is indicated by the rectangle P$_p$ABP$_c$.

In this case, supply and demand were both elastic at the initial point. Indeed, it could be shown that they were equally elastic. In these circumstances, the tax affects consumers and producers equally in that the £1 tax on each unit results in consumers paying 50p more per unit (£3.50 instead of £3.00 as before) and producers receiving 50p less (£2.50 instead of £3.00); thus the *incidence* of the tax falls equally on consumers and producers. A similar result would arise if both supply and demand had been (equally) inelastic in the pre-tax position. Such a case is shown in Figure 2.2 where, once again, equilibrium price and output were initially fixed at £3 and 40 units by S and D, and where a tax of £1 per unit produced the new supply curve S′ (which, like S′ in Figure 2.1, is parallel to the original curve in a position where the vertical gap between the two curves equals the amount of the tax). The tax results in the new consumer (P$_c$) and producer (P$_p$) prices of £3.50 and £2.50 respectively. Note, though, that output now falls by less (in fact to 37.5 units per week) than in Figure 2.1.

However, the incidence of a tax is not always shared equally. Figure 2.3 shows a case where supply was initially more elastic than demand. The result of a £1 per unit tax here is to drive the consumer price up by 80p (from £3.00 to £3.80) and to cut the producer price by a mere 20p (from £3.00 to £2.80), so in this case the incidence falls chiefly on consumers. Had demand been perfectly inelastic (as with a vertical demand curve) or supply perfectly elastic (as with a horizontal supply curve) then it is easy to show that the incidence would have fallen wholly

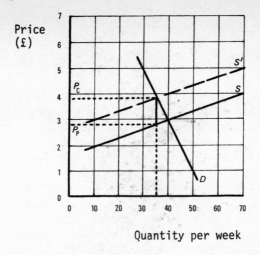

Figure 2.3

on consumers whose price would rise by the full amount of the tax whilst the producer price would remain at its initial level.

In contrast, Figure 2.4 shows a case where supply was initially less elastic than demand. The result of a £1 per unit tax here is to drive the producer price down by 80p (from £3.00 to £2.20) and to raise the consumer price by a mere 20p (from £3.00 to £3.20), so in this case the incidence falls chiefly on producers. Had supply been perfectly inelastic (as with a vertical supply curve) or demand perfectly elastic (as with a horizontal demand curve) then it is easy to show that the incidence would have fallen wholly on producers whose price would fall by

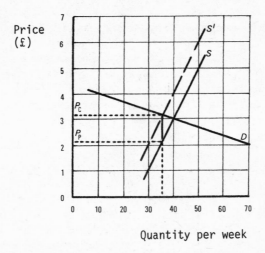

Figure 2.4

the full amount of the tax whilst the consumer price would remain at its initial level.

Ad valorem taxes

Figures 2.1 to 2.4 have considered what is termed a *specific* tax where the tax is stipulated as a fixed amount per unit sold. The UK's taxes on alcoholic drink, tobacco and motor fuel are all specific taxes. However, some taxes, such as value added tax, are termed *ad valorem* taxes, for here the tax is set at a percentage of the producers' final (post-tax) price. Figure 2.5 shows an example of an ad valorem tax of 50 per cent. Initially, the supply curve (S) and demand curve (D) determine an equilibrium price of £5.00 and quantity of 50 units per week. Now S shows that producers would be willing to produce 50 units a week if the price were £5. S shows also, for example, that producers would produce 20 units a week if the price were £2. Now suppose a 50 per cent tax is levied. In order to receive £2 per unit, producers would have to charge consumers £3 so that they could keep £2 and pay an amount equal to 50 per cent of what they keep, that is £1, to the government. Accordingly, a total price of £3 would now be needed to persuade producers to supply 20 units per week, a fact indicated by point A on the new supply curve S′. Also, to receive £5 per unit producers would now have to charge consumers £7.50 so that they could keep £5 and pay 50 per cent of this, £2.50 to the government; point B on S′ shows that consumers would now have to pay £7.50 a unit in order for producers to be able to keep £5 and so be persuaded to supply 50 units per week. Likewise, point C on S′ shows consumers would have to pay £9 per unit to persuade producers to supply 60 units per week, for producers would keep £6 per unit and pay £3 to the government. In short, the new supply curve is higher than the old one, as in earlier figures, but is not parallel to it.

The new equilibrium consumer price (P_c) £6, and quantity, 40 units per week, are determined by the intersection of S′ and D. The new producer price (P_p) is found at the point on S vertically below B, and is £4. The 50 per cent tax means the tax is 50 per cent of P_p (not, incidentally, 50 per cent of P_c) or £2 per unit. In this example, the tax ends up at £2 per unit (50 per cent of P_p) and the incidence of this £2 is divided equally between consumers (whose price rises by £1 from £5 to £6) and producers (whose price falls by £1 from £5 to £4). As with a specific tax, however, the incidence need not be shared equally; the extent to which it falls on consumers and producers depends once again on the relative elasticities of the demand and supply curves.

Taxes paid by consumers

All this analysis has assumed that the tax is paid to the government by producers. It is easy to show that identical results would arise if it were paid directly by consumers. This situation is unusual, though it does occur with the rates paid directly by tenants to their local authorities, for these are (in principle anyway) set as a percentage of the rent value of their houses. The equivalence of

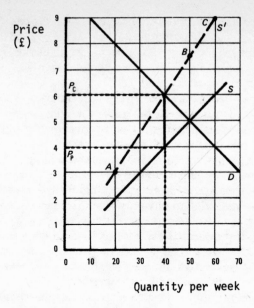

Figure 2.5

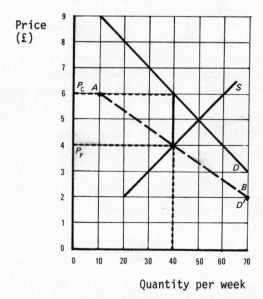

Figure 2.6

a tax on consumers and one on producers is often of help in the analysis, as for instance in Chapter 11. To see this equivalence, consider the ad valorem tax referred to in Figure 2.5 but suppose it had to be paid by consumers. Figure 2.6 reproduces S and D from Figure 2.5 to show the initial equilibrium price and quantity of £5 per unit and 50 units per week. D shows, of course, that buyers will be persuaded to buy 50 units a week if they have to spend £5 on each. It also shows, for instance, that they would be persuaded to buy only 10 a week if they had to spend £9 on each, and that they would buy 70 a week if they had to spend just £3 on each. Initially, all the money consumers spend goes to producers, but suppose, now, they had to pay a tax to the government equal to 50 per cent of what they paid to producers. In this case, the relationship between various possible producer prices and the amounts consumers would buy would no longer be shown by D but would be shown by the new curve D'.

To understand D', suppose, first, producers set a price of £6 per unit. In this situation, consumers would have to spend £9 a unit (paying £6 to producers and £3 to the government) and it has been seen that if they have to spend £9 a unit then they will be persuaded to buy only 10 units a week; so if producers set a price of £6, then buyers would now buy 10 units a week, a fact shown by point A on D'. Likewise, if producers set a price of £2, then consumers would have to pay £3 a unit (£2 to producers and £1 to the government) and it has been seen that if they have to spend £3 a unit they will buy 60 units a week; point B on D' shows that 60 units will be bought each week if producers set a price of £2.

The market equilibrium is where D' intersects S. This shows that buyers will buy 40 units a week off producers and will pay the producer price (P_p) of £4 on each; of course, consumers will also have to pay a tax equal to 50 per cent of this (£2) and the total consumer price of £6 (P_c) can be found from the point on D vertically above the equilibrium position on D'. It will be seen that P_p (£4), P_c (£6) and the equilibrium quantity (40) are identical to those found in Figure 2.5 when the tax was levied on producers. Perhaps this is not a very surprising result, but it is a very useful one; for it means that either type of diagram can be used in economic analysis, irrespective of whether the tax is in fact paid by the producer or the consumer. Incidentally, if the approach of Figure 2.6 were used for a specific tax, then the new demand curve would be parallel to the old one, and would be below if by the amount of the tax per unit.

Subsidies

This section is concerned with the effects of subsidies on particular items. The effects are the same irrespective of whether the subsidy is paid to the sellers whenever they sell the product, as happens with dentists offering dental treatment under the National Health Service, or to buyers whenever they buy it, as happens with certain wage subsidies paid to employers. For convenience, it will be assumed that the subsidy is paid to sellers of a certain product. Consider the market concerned in Figures 2.7 and 2.8 which will show respectively the effects of a specific subsidy and an ad valorem subsidy. The initial demand and supply curves, D and S, fix the initial equilibrium price of £3, and quantity of 40 units per week.

S shows, for example, that in the absence of a subsidy producers would supply 20 units per week if they could get £2 a unit from consumers and 60 if they could get £4 a unit. Suppose the government offers a specific subsidy of £1 a unit. In

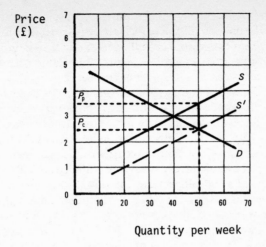

Figure 2.7

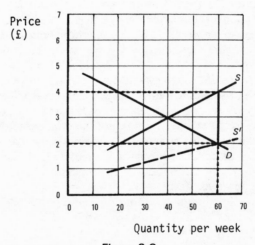

Figure 2.8

that case, producers would be willing to supply 20 units for a price of £1 to consumers (as the government would bring the revenue from each unit up to £2 by adding the £1 subsidy) and 60 units for a price of £3 to consumers (as the government would bring the revenue from each unit up to £4 by adding the £1 subsidy). The new supply curve S′ in Figure 2.7 reflects this information; it is parallel to S, the gap between S′ and S equalling the value of the subsidy. It intersects D to show the new equilibrium price of £2.50 to consumers (P_c) and quantity of 50 units per week. The new price for producers (P_p) is £2.50 plus the £1 subsidy, that is £3.50, and can be found from the point on S vertically above the intersection of S′ and D.

Suppose, instead, the government had introduced an ad valorem subsidy to producers of 100 per cent of the amount they obtain from consumers. This would produce the new supply curve S' shown in Figure 2.8. This subsidy would also mean that producers would be willing to produce 20 units a week at a price to consumers of £1 (as the government would add 100 per cent of that – that is another £1 per unit – to bring the revenue from each unit sold up to £2); but now they would need only £2 per unit from consumers to be persuaded to supply 60 units a week (as the government would add 100 per cent of that – that is £2 per unit – to bring the revenue from each unit sold up to £4). The new supply curve S' in Figure 2.8 reflects this information; note that it is not parallel to S. S' intersects D to show the new equilibrium price of £2 to consumers (P_c) and quantity of 60 units per week. The new price for producers (P_p) is £2 plus the subsidy which (in the case of a 100 per cent subsidy) equals the price paid by consumers, that is £4 in all; this can be found from the point on S vertically above the intersection of S' and D.

In the examples shown in Figures 2.7 and 2.8, the incidence of the subsidies fell equally on consumers and producers, for both groups had equal price improvements in each case. The reader may care to draw a series of figures (analogous to Figures 2.1 to 2.4) to show that the incidence will be chiefly on consumers when supply is relatively elastic compared with demand, and chiefly on producers when demand is relatively elastic compared with supply.

Price controls

When a government wishes to reduce the price in a particular market, it may prefer a price control – in the form of a mandatory maximum price imposed at a level below the initial level – to a subsidy since this will save the expense on the subsidy. Also, when it wishes to raise the price in a particular market, it may in some cases prefer a price control – in the form of a mandatory minimum price imposed at a level above the initial level – to a tax even though the tax would have raised some revenue.

Consider, first, a maximum price control. Such controls are often used in an attempt to reduce rent levels for housing. Suppose the initial equilibrium rent level and quantity of space (in square metres) let for housing in one area of the country are respectively R and Q as determined by the demand curve (D) and supply curve (S) in Figure 2.9. The government might then intervene and rule that in future rent levels should not exceed R'. The result will be an increase in the quantity of housing demanded (up from Q to Q_A) and a fall in the quantity supplied (down from Q to Q_B); in turn, this leads to an excess demand or shortage (of Q_A less Q_B) as more is demanded than supplied. The rent control has mixed results. Those who rent the (Q_B) property that is still let gain as they now pay a lower rent (R' instead of R). Those who are evicted – or who would have been able to find accommodation in the absence of the control – clearly lose (these people would like to occupy the area Q less Q_B). In addition, some people will look in vain for housing (amounting to an area Q_A less Q) who at the previous rent would not have been looking, and looking in vain is a loss to them. Finally, of course, landlords also lose.

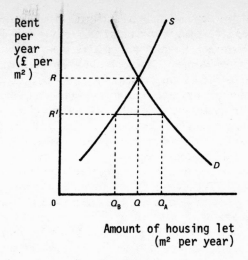

Figure 2.9

Consider, next, a minimum price control. Such controls are often advocated and sometimes used in attempts to raise wages in low wage rate occupations. Suppose the initial equilibrium wage and employment levels for one type of worker are respectively W and N as determined by the demand curve (D) and supply curve (S) in Figure 2.10. The government might intervene and rule that in future wage levels for this type of worker should not be below W'. The result will be an increase (from N to N_A) in the number of people wishing to take up this sort of work and a fall (from N to N_B) in the number which employers wish to engage; in turn, this leads to an excess supply (of N_A less N_B) as more people want work than there are posts available. Again, the price control has mixed

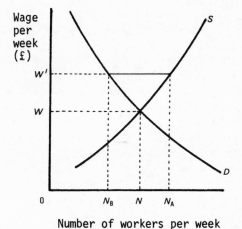

Number of workers per week

Figure 2.10

results. Those who still have jobs gain as their wage is higher (W' instead of W). Those who are laid off – or who would have found work in the absence of the control – clearly lose (these people would fill N less N_B jobs). In addition, some people now look in vain for jobs (in fact N_A less N people) who at the previous wage would not have been looking, and looking in vain is a loss to them. Finally, of course, employers are likely to find profits falling, and buyers of whatever product the workers make are likely to find its price rising.

3

Tariffs and quotas

Tariffs

Tariffs are no more than a tax on imported goods, and usually they take the form of a specific tax on each unit imported. There are many reasons for imposing a tariff – such as to protect home industries from foreign competition, obtain revenue, to restrict imports and to improve the balance of payments. The economics of tariffs differs from the economic treatment of taxes considered in the previous chapter in two respects: first, the home market must be distinguished from the overseas market; and, second, the tax applies only to imported goods. The home and foreign goods, of course, could be identical except with regard to where in the world they are produced.

The situation can be seen in terms of Figure 3.1. Consider a commodity which can be produced at home and abroad. The home market is shown on the right-hand side by the home demand curve, D^H, and the home supply curve, S^H. If the country did not trade then D^H and S^H would determine the equilibrium price and quantity, namely an equilibrium price of £4 and an equilibrium quantity of 4 units. If, however, the same commodity is also produced abroad the situation is quite different.

Suppose the home country is small relative to the world market so that on international markets the world price is determined by world demand and

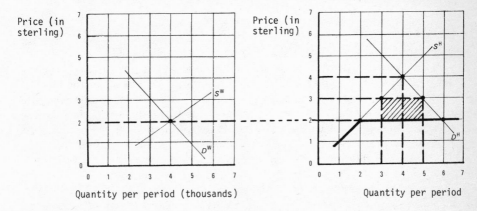

Figure 3.1

supply, as shown on the left-hand side by D^W and S^W, determining a world equilibrium price of £2. As far as the home country is concerned it must accept the world price $P^W = £2$. In other words, the world price is fixed for the home market and hence the supply curve becomes infinitely elastic at this price, as shown by the heavy line in Figure 3.1.

If the world price is below the home country's equilibrium price, as shown in Figure 3.1, then trade will take place. To see this, it needs only to be observed that domestic residents will not purchase the same good *above* the world price of £2. Hence, the supply curve becomes infinitely elastic at the world price. Given the home demand curve D^H then the home quantity demanded is 6 units. Of this 2 units are supplied by home producers and 4 units are imported. The degree of *import penetration* is measured by the ratio of imports to total home demand, i.e.,

$$\text{Import penetration}\ \frac{\text{Imports}}{\text{Home demand}} = \frac{4}{6} = \frac{2}{3}$$

Suppose a tariff is now imposed on all imports of this commodity. Let the tariff be £1 per unit. Since the world price remains constant at £2, then domestic consumers will face a price for imports of £2 plus £1 tariff, i.e., £3. As can be seen in Figure 3.1, at this new higher price of £3 the total quantity demanded falls to 5 units. Futhermore, the home quantity supplied *rises* to 3 units and imports *fall* to 2 units (5−3). By implication, import penetration falls to 2/5.

Notice that the tariff revenue is shown by the shaded rectangle. This is because the tariff only applies to the actual volume of imports. Since imports are 2 units and each unit is taxed by an amount of £1, then total tariff receipts are £1 × 2 = £2, which is no more than the shaded rectangle.

It would be possible to impose a *prohibitive tariff* which would restrict imports altogether. In this case the tariff must be such as to raise the tariff-inclusive price enough to make it equal or exceed the equilibrium price £4, determined by home demand and home supply; this means that the tariff must be at least £2 per unit.

Quotas

In Figure 3.2 a similar situation is shown to that discussed in the previous section. The world price is £2 for each unit. It is clear that at a price of £1 set by home suppliers that only one unit will be supplied, regardless of the level of home demand. Furthermore, at the price of £1 there will be no imports because these can only be purchased at the higher price of £2. However, if domestic suppliers set a price of £2 then they would be willing to supply 2 units at this price. Consumers, on the other hand, would like to purchase 6 units at a price of £2. The additional 4 units can be imported since the price on the world market is also £2. Since the world price is set at £2, and is determined by demand and supply on the world market, as illustrated in the left-hand drawing of Figure 3.1, then the price at home cannot exceed £2. Why is this? If domestic suppliers set a price of £3 they would be willing to supply 3 units. But domestic residents would not purchase these goods. They would, on the contrary, purchase them from importers at the cheaper price of £2.

Given a world price of £2, therefore, imports will be at a level of 4 units (6 − 2 = 4). Suppose for some reason, such as the reduced level of employment at home, that the government considers 4 units of imports too high, and that it imposes a quota of 2 units. In other words, the government stipulates that regardless of the price, imports cannot exceed 2 units. Let the quota be denoted $Q^* = 2$. One way to enforce such a quota is for the government to issue licences, so that only those companies who hold such a licence are eligible to import the good in question. If licences are issued which allow 1 unit to be imported, giving a total of 2 licences, then either one company can import if it holds both licences or else two companies can import each holding one licence and importing 1 unit.

It has already been established that at a price below the world price the available supply is that provided by home suppliers. But consider available supply at prices at £2 and above with the aid of Figure 3.2. At the price of £2 home supplier are supplying 2 units and a further two units are supplied by the company (or companies) holding the import licences. At a price of £3 home suppliers would be willing to supply 3 units which means total supply is 3 plus the quota of 2 giving 5 units. At a price of £2 and above, therefore, total supply is the home supply plus the quota, and is denoted by $S^H + Q^*$ in Figure 3.2. Hence, the supply curve in the presence of a quota is shown by the heavy line in Figure 3.2. Home demand is still represented by D^H. It is now possible to establish the equilibrium price and quantity. Given the supply curve $S^H + Q^*$ and the demand curve D^H, competition at home will force the price up to £3, since at £3 the quantity demand is equal to the quantity supplied, that is 5 units. The quantity demanded at home is 5 units and the quantity supplied is composed of home supply (3 units) plus the quota (2 units).

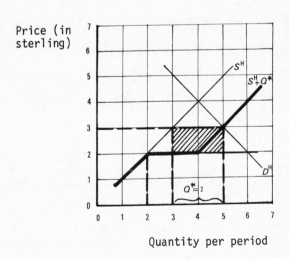

Figure 3.2

In this example the *price effect* of a quota is the same as that of the tariff, for in both cases the equilibrium price rises to £3. Also the effect on domestic production, a rise of 1 unit, and domestic consumption, a reduction of 1 unit, is the same for both a tariff and a quota. The main difference between a tariff and a quota is in terms of the *redistribution effect*. In the case of a tariff consumers pay the higher price, although the tariff receipts (shown by the shaded area in Figure 3.1) would doubtless benefit consumers as a result of the increased government spending. The effect of a quota is more complex and depends on the allocation procedure adopted for issuing import licences. For instance, if they are auctioned among importers then the competitive bidding by importers would result in a price of £1 per licence. The receipt from the sale of such licences is represented by the shaded area in Figure 3.2. This would be received by the government and means the effect of the quota would be formally identical to the effect of the tariff. On the other hand, the licences could be offered on a first-come, first-served basis. In this case the gain would go to those importers who receive the licences. The important point, however, is that there is a different redistributional effect between a tariff and a quota.

Tariffs and consumer and producer surpluses

A demand curve represents the *maximum* price that consumers are willing to pay for a particular quantity of a commodity. In Figure 3.3, for example, consumers are willing to pay £5 for the first unit, but only £4 for the second unit. If quantity is taken to be perfectly divisible then the total amount of money consumers are willing to pay for a particular quantity is the area under the

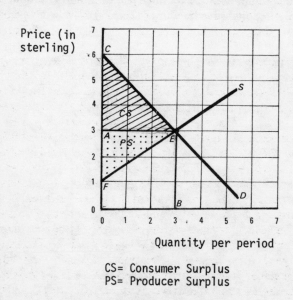

CS= Consumer Surplus
PS= Producer Surplus

Figure 3.3

demand curve up to that quantity. For example, if consumers wished to purchase 3 units of this commodity, then they would be willing to pay an amount represented by the area under the demand curve between 0 and 3 units; this is shown by the area OBEC and is approximately equal to £13.5. Of course what consumers do pay is based on the equilibrium price. It can be seen from Figure 3.3 that the market determines an equilibrium price and quantity of £3 and 3 units respectively. Hence, the three units are purchased for only £9 (as shown by the rectangle OAEB). The excess of what consumers are willing to pay over what they actually pay, is called the *consumer surplus*. In the present example, then, the consumer surplus is the area below the demand curve and above the price line, as shown by area ACE and it has a monetary value of approximately £4.5.

Consider now the situation from the point of view of suppliers. A supply curve represents the *minimum* price that suppliers are willing to accept for a particular quantity supplied of a commodity. In Figure 3.3, for example, producers are willing to supply one unit for a price of £1.67, but would be willing to supply a second unit only if it fetched a price of £2.33 (as explained in Chapter 10, this is because marginal costs rise as more units are supplied). Again, if quantity is taken to be perfectly divisible, then the total monetary cost of what is supplied is the area under the supply curve up to that quantity. For example, if suppliers were wishing to supply 3 units of this commodity, then the cost of supplying these three units would be represented by the area under the supply curve between 0 and 3 units (as shown by area OFEB) and is approximately equal to £6. However, what the suppliers actually receive for the three units is represented by area OAEB and is equal to £9. The excess of what suppliers receive over what it costs them to supply a particular level is called the *producer surplus*. In the present example, the producer surplus is the area above the supply curve and below the price line; it is shown by area AEF and is equal to £3.0.

The concepts of consumer surplus and producer surplus just outlined are very useful in discussing the welfare implications of policy. In other words, it is possible to use consumer and producer surpluses to assess the gains and losses arising from a particular policy change. To see how, it is necessary to reconsider the imposition of a tariff in terms of such gains and losses.

Figure 3.4 is a re-drawing of the home country situation as indicated in the right-hand-side of Figure 3.1, but highlighting the welfare implications.

Consider first the *change* in the consumer surplus which results from the tariff. Consumer surplus is *reduced* by the area (a + b + c + d). This suggests that a tariff makes a country's citizens worse off. A tariff does in fact do this, but the loss in consumer surplus does not accurately reflect the total loss to society of the tariff. For one thing, a tariff produces a *gain* in producer surplus, namely area a. Furthermore, there is the tariff revenue denoted by area c. When the government spend this income, consumers benefit from the increased government spending. In the present analysis it is assumed that the monetary value of the gain by consumers equals the amount of money raised by the tariff. Thus, the following situation prevails:

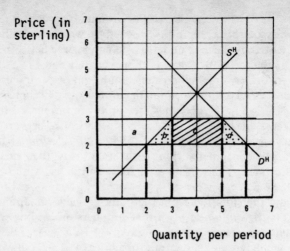

Price (in sterling)

Quantity per period

Figure 3.4

	Area
Loss of consumer surplus	a + b + c + d
Gain in producer surplus	a
Tax Revenue	c
Net loss	b + d

Area d, which equals £0.5 if it is assumed that the area can be represented by a triangle (for it equals $(1/2) \times 1$) is a net loss arising from the fact that consumers must now pay a higher price than they did before the tariff was introduced. Area b, equal to £0.5 (that is $(1/2) \times 1 \times 1$) represents a loss because the extra output is being supplied by a higher cost source of production. In the present example, therefore, the monetary value of the welfare loss of the tariff is £1.0.

4

Fixed and flexible exchange rates

Demand and supply theory is a very useful tool in analysing the exchange rate for a country's currency, irrespective of whether the country's government decides to have a fixed exchange rate or a floating exchange rate. The exchange rate is the price of one currency in terms of another. The price of a loaf of bread is the money which has to be given up for one loaf. So the price of one dollar is the amount of sterling which must be given up for one dollar. Alternatively, the price of sterling in terms of dollars is the amount in dollars that must be given up for one pound. Immediately it can be noticed that it is possible to define the price of sterling in terms of any currency. The Deutschmark price of sterling is the amount in deutschmarks that must be given up for one pound, the Yen price of sterling is the amount in yen that must be given up for one pound, and so on. Under a fixed exchange-rate system, which was used by most Western countries until 1971, most currencies were quoted in terms of the dollar. This meant that countries defined the price of the dollar in terms of domestic currency. Thus, in 1969 the French franc was pegged to the dollar at FF5.554 = \$1; the German deutschmark was pegged at DM3.66 = \$1; and the Japanese yen was pegged at Y360 = \$1. On the other hand, the British pound was pegged to the dollar at \$2.40 = £1. Such pegged rates, called *parity exchange rates*, referred only to official transactions by Central Banks. The *market exchange rate* could, however, fluctuate within a narrow band. For example, the dollar/sterling exchange rate could fluctuate between \$2.38 = £1 and \$2.42 = £1, approximately ± 1% either side of the parity rate. Under floating exchange rates, which have operated in most Western countries since 1973, only the market rate is quoted. Thus, on Wednesday 19 March 1986, the dollar/sterling exchange rate was \$1.4750 = £1; which means that anyone demanding £1 on the foreign exchange market must supply in exchange \$1.4750, while anyone demanding \$1 on the foreign exchange market must supply in exchange £1/1.4750 = £0.678.

What determines the demand curve for sterling? Consider a British firm exporting, say, Sheffield steel hacksaw blades. Suppose such blades are priced at £100 per box. Suppose further that the exchange rate is £1 = \$2. In America this box of blades would be priced in dollars at \$200 per box. Now the British company does not particularly want dollars. Certainly, British workers want to be paid in sterling. Therefore, if the American importer wants Sheffield steel blades he must obtain sterling to pay for them. Effectively, he would go to his bank in the US and supply $200 asking his bank to obtain £100 on the foreign exchange market. Consequently, British *exports* lead to a *demand* for sterling.

Now consider an American who wishes to invest in the UK. He may, for example, wish to purchase Treasury Bills issued by the UK government. Of course, the UK government want sterling in exchange for their Treasury Bills. This means that the US investor will need to exchange dollars for sterling on the foreign exchange market. In other words, a *capital inflow* also leads to a *demand* for sterling.

Similarly, the UK importer of, say, an American microcomputer will need to pay for this in dollars. To obtain such dollars the UK importer must supply sterling in exchange. Hence British *imports* lead to a *supply* of sterling. Furthermore, a UK resident who wishes to invest in the US, say who wishes to purchase US Treasury Bills, will require dollars and have to supply sterling in exchange. Hence, a *capital outflow* leads to a *supply* of sterling.

To summarize so far, UK exports and capital inflows lead to a demand for sterling while UK imports and capital outflows lead to a supply of sterling. But what shapes are the demand curve of, and the supply curve for, sterling?

Return to the UK exporter of Sheffield steel blades. Suppose the exchange rate falls to £1 = $1.50. If the UK exporter leaves his sterling price at £100 per box, then the price in dollars *falls* to $150 per box. The fall in the dollar price will lead to a rise in the quantity demanded for steel blades by US companies. This is shown in Figure 4.1. In this figure the quantity demanded for steel blades rises from 10 to 20 boxes. Since the sterling price remains £100 per box, the increase in the quantity demanded leads to an increase in the quantity demanded for sterling. This means that there is an inverse relationship between the dollar price of sterling and the quantity demanded of sterling.

Turning now to imports, it is assumed that their dollar prices are fixed so that

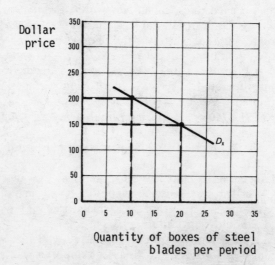

Quantity of boxes of steel
blades per period

Fig 4.1

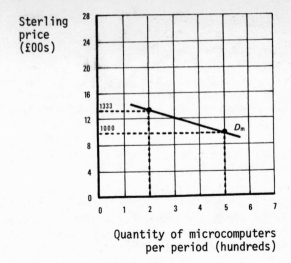

Figure 4.2

a fall in sterling's exchange rate will raise the sterling price of imports. For example, a microcomputer priced in the US at \$2000 would sell for £1,000 in the UK if the exchange rate is £1 = \$2; if the exchange rate was £1 = \$1.50, then the sterling price would be to £1,333. The quantity of sterling supplied, however, depends on the total sterling receipts (price × quantity). Thus, at the lower sterling price of £1000, the quantity of sterling supplied in payment for the import of 500 microcomputers is 1,000 × 500 = 500,000. At the *higher* sterling price of £1,333, the quantity of sterling supplied in payment for the *lower* level of imports of 200 microcomputers is 1,333 × 200 = 266,600. This is shown in Figure 4.2.

In this example the amount of sterling supplied falls from £500,000 to £266,600. The reason for this fall is that the percentage fall in the quantity of imports is greater than the percentage rise in the price, in other words, because the demand for imports is price elastic – a concept discussed in Chapter 1. (In the present example, the *arc price elasticity* of imports for the two observations just referred to is [(500 − 200)/350]/[(1,000 − 1,333)/1,166] = − 3.) Put another way, when the dollar price of sterling falls the quantity supplied of sterling also falls, given an elastic demand curve for imports. Thus, under the present assumptions, there is a positive relationship between the dollar price of sterling and the quantity of sterling supplied.

The two relationships are shown in Figure 4.3. On the vertical axis is measured the dollar price of sterling and on the horizontal axis the quantity demanded and supplied of sterling. It is important to realize that these curves are denoting *private* transactions. Government transactions will be dealt with later. The market exchange rate is where the demand curve for sterling intersects the supply curve of sterling. In Figure 4.3 this is at the rate of £1 = \$2.

Before continuing it will be useful to clarify the meaning of certain exchange

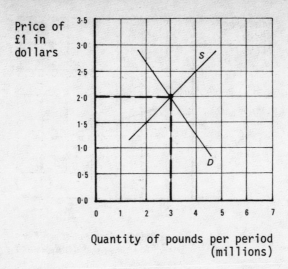

Price of
£1 in
dollars

Quantity of pounds per period
(millions)

Figure 4.3

rates. The *spot exchange rate* denotes the price of one currency in terms of another for immediate delivery (in practice within two working days). It is to be distinguished from the *forward exchange rate*, which denotes the price agreed now for the future purchase or sale of one currency for another. The *parity rate*, which applies only under a fixed exchange-rate system, is the rate at which a country's Central Bank agrees to buy and sell dollars in terms of its domestic currency. In the case of the United Kingdom, the rate was the number of dollars the Bank of England would officially exchange for £1. For example, from 1967 until 1972 the parity rate stood at £1 = $2.40. On the other hand, the market exchange rate for spot sterling, determined by the forces of demand and supply, could fluctuate within the band £1 = $2.38 to £1 = $2.42.

Fixed exchange rates

Suppose the United Kingdom government agrees on a parity exchange rate of £1 = $2.40. What happens when the market equilibrium exchange rate is different from this official parity rate? (In this discussion, the fact that the market rate could fluctuate in a band around the parity rate is ignored.) Two situations can be analysed, as shown in Figures 4.4 and 4.5. In Figure 4.4 the equilibrium exchange rate is below the officially agreed rate, for the equilibrium exchange rate is £1 = $2 while the parity rate is £1 = $2.40. If private transactions were allowed to operate freely (in other words, if trade flows were not restricted and capital controls did not apply), then the exchange rate would fall to £1 = $2. If the official exchange rate is pegged at £1 = $2.40 then the market rate will equal this parity rate only if the government step in and demand sterling. In other words, if the exchange market were free to operate then the exchange rate would fall to £1 = $2. The only way the market exchange rate could be made to equal

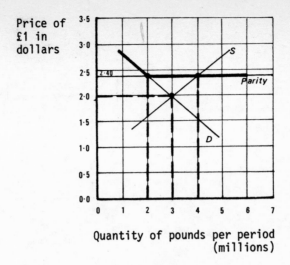

Figure 4.4

the parity rate would be for the Bank of England to demand sterling. In fact, the Bank of England must take steps to ensure that the *demand* curve in Figure 4.4 becomes infinitely elastic at £1 = \$2.40, as shown by the heavy line in Figure 4.4. Given the supply curve of sterling, the government, or strictly the Bank of England acting on behalf of the government, must in this example demand £2 million of sterling (that is £4 million minus £2 million). But what must it give up in exchange for sterling? It must give up some of its dollar reserves (or gold reserves) in exchange for £2 million of sterling; in fact, it must give up \$2.40 × 2 million = \$4.8 million.

Consider next what must happen if the equilibrium exchange rate is above the official parity rate. This is shown in Figure 4.5 where the equilibrium rate is £1 = \$3. In this situation, the Bank of England would have to take steps to make the *supply* curve infinitely elastic at the parity rate, as shown by the heavy line in Figure 4.5. Only then will the market exchange rate equal the parity rate. In this case the central bank will now supply £2 million (£4 million minus £2 million) of sterling. It will receive in exchange 4.8 million dollars (or gold) which will be placed in the country's foreign exchange reserves.

The analysis can be extended still further. If, for simplicity, capital flows are ignored, then the demand curve for sterling represents the sterling value of UK exports while the supply curve of sterling represents the sterling value of UK imports. In terms of Figure 4.4, therefore, the sterling value of UK exports is £2 million and the sterling value of UK imports is £4 million. Consequently, there is a deficit on the balance of payments on current account (where the current account is taken here to denote exports of goods and services less imports of goods and services), to the tune of £2 million. On the other hand, Figure 4.5 shows a current account surplus of £2 million.

The conclusion, therefore, is that under a fixed exchange rate a deficit on the

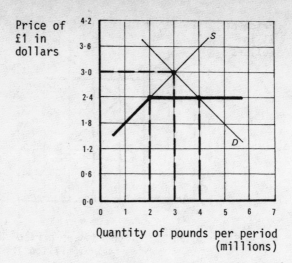

Figure 4.5

balance of payments leads to a fall in the country's reserves of gold and foreign currencies. Similarly, a surplus on the balance of payments, as shown in Figure 4.5, leads to a rise in the country's reserves.

Floating exchange rates

Since 1973 most countries have floated their exchange rates. In other words, they have allowed the exchange rates of their currencies to be determined (more or less) by the forces of demand and supply. The United Kingdom, in fact, began to float sterling in June 1972. Under a freely floating exchange-rate system the exchange rate is determined wholly by market forces. In terms of Figure 4.3 the exchange rate is determined by the intersection of the demand and supply curve of sterling. The mechanics of a freely floating exchange rate are illustrated in Figure 4.6. The initial equilibrium is given by £1 = $2, where D and S intersect. Now suppose there is an increase in the demand for British exports which causes the demand curve for sterling to shift to D_1. If the initial exchange rate of £1 = $2 persists for a while, then there will now be a surplus of £2 million on the balance of payments, the value of exports (£5 million) exceeding the value of imports (£3 million). This means foreign exchange dealers will find US (importing) citizens demanding more sterling from them than US (exporting) citizens are supplying to them which will put pressure on the price of sterling: sterling will *appreciate* against the dollar. The appreciation of sterling will stop when, once again, the demand for sterling is equal to the supply of sterling; in this example it is when the market exchange rate is £1 = $3.

A rise in the demand for imports by UK residents would result in a shift in the supply curve of sterling to the right, as shown in Figure 4.7. In this case there will be a £2 million deficit on the balance of payments at the original exchange rate

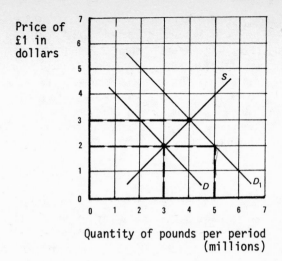

Figure 4.6

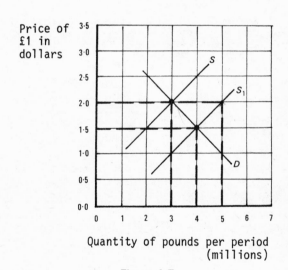

Figure 4.7

of £1 = $2.00. This means that importers in the UK are supplying more sterling to the foreign exchange market (in order to buy the dollars they need) than exporters are demanding in return for the dollars obtained (selling their exports). So there will be downward pressure on the price of sterling: in this example, sterling will *depreciate* against the dollar until £1 = $1.50.

Notice in each case illustrated in Figures 4.6 and 4.7, that the exchange rate will appreciate or depreciate respectively until the quantity demanded and the quantity supplied of sterling are brought into equality. In such situations there is no reason, in theory, for the country's reserves of gold or dollars to alter. However, in practice exchange rates do not freely float. Central Banks do intervene, which is why the present system is sometimes referred to as 'dirty floating'. In the case of the United Kingdom, the Bank of England steps in to the foreign exchange market to iron out excessive movements in the exchange rate. Thus, if the market exchange rate is (temporarily) rising too much, then the Bank of England will *sell* sterling which will reverse the upward movement; if the market exchange rate is falling too much, then the Bank of England will *buy* sterling which will push up the exchange rate. This is called 'leaning against the wind'.

Floating exchange rates and capital flows

It is pointed out earlier that a capital inflow led to a demand for sterling while a capital outflow led to a supply of sterling (a demand for dollars). What, however, gives rise to such capital flows? One major reason is interest rates at home and abroad. If interest rates rise from 10 per cent to 15 per cent in the US, other interest rates remaining fixed, then this will attract capital into the US because it can now get a better return. But this must have an impact on the exchange rate. The situation is shown in Figure 4.8(a). The supply curve for sterling will shift to the right (because there is a rise in the demand for dollars) and the market exchange rate will fall in this example from £1 = $2 to £1 = $1.50; thus sterling will depreciate against the dollar. This was exactly the situation in 1984 when US interest rates were kept high.

On the other hand, a rise in domestic interest rates from 10 per cent to 15 per cent would lead to an appreciation of sterling, as shown in Figure 4.8(b). What

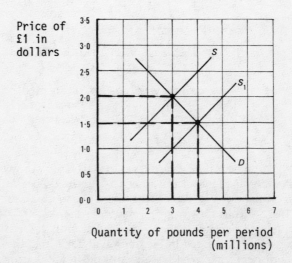

Figure 4.8(a)

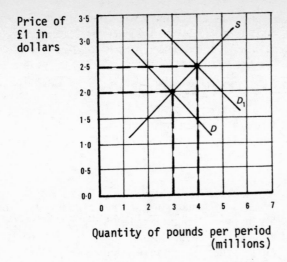

Quantity of pounds per period
(millions)

Figure 4.8(b)

can be seen in Figure 4.8 is an interdependence between the two economics arising from capital flows. This means that one country's monetary policy will have an effect on other countries.

5

Markets for second-hand goods

Stocks and flows

The analysis of supply and demand in Chapter 1 explained how the equilibrium price and quantity in a typical market were determined by the forces of supply and demand. It follows that a detailed analysis of any particular market requires some understanding of the supply and demand conditions in that market. This chapter is concerned with one group of markets, namely those in second-hand items. These markets relate to items such as second-hand (but fairly new) cars as well as vintage and veteran cars, second-hand houses, second-hand securities such as shares in ICI, and markets in collectors' pieces like Stradivarius violins and Spitfire fighters.

It is useful to begin by considering the supply curve for one such item, perhaps shares in ICI. It is tempting to suppose that as the stock of those shares is fixed (except on the rare occasions when ICI sell some new ones) then the supply curve must be vertical, as shown in Figure 5.1. In turn, it may be supposed that this is intersected by a demand curve to give the price. On a day when the price was, say, £6.00, the demand curve might be like the one shown in the figure. However, this diagram does not produce one piece of information which the supply and demand curves of Chapter 1 gave, namely the equilibrium quantity of the item concerned that is traded in a particular period of time. Indeed, the quantity axis of Figure 5.1 shows only the stock of shares in existence and does not refer to a time period at all.

For this reason, Figure 5.1 is certainly an unusual supply and demand curve diagram, and it is tempting, therefore, to conclude that it should be rejected in favour of one like Figure 5.2. This has a supply curve which shows how many shares would be offered for sale on a given day at each possible price, and a demand curve which shows how many would be demanded and bought at each possible price. These curves are much closer in spirit to those of Chapter 1, and their intersection should indeed indicate not only the equilibrium price, but also the equilibrium amount traded in a given day.

However, Figure 5.1 need not be discarded as wrong or irrelevant. As it happens, the two figures are closely related, and it is possible to show that they inevitably indicate the same equilibrium price. Figure 5.1 arrives at this price by considering what is known as the *stock supply curve* – which shows the total amount of shares in existence – along with the related *stock demand curve*. Thus, the stock supply curve denotes how much would be supplied at different

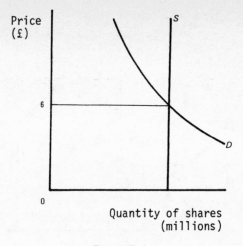

Figure 5.1

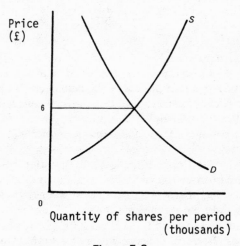

Figure 5.2

prices at a *point* in time; while the stock demand curve denotes how much would be demanded at each price at a *point* in time. Figure 5.2 arrives at it by considering what is known as the *flow supply curve* – which shows the number of shares offered for sale in each *period* of time at different possible prices – and the related *flow demand curve*.

Relating stocks and flows

The relationship between the flow supply and demand and the stock supply and demand for a particular item is shown in Figure 5.3. For simplicity, this relates to the shares in an imaginary company which has sold 100,000 shares during its

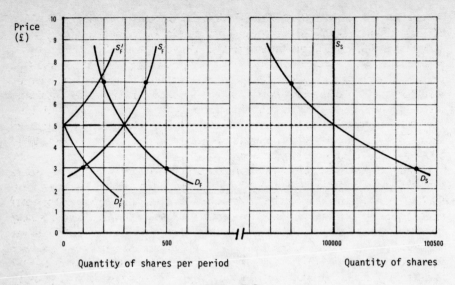

Price
(£)

Quantity of shares per period

Quantity of shares

Figure 5.3

lifetime. The flow curves are labelled S_F and D_F, and the stock ones S_S and D_S. The stock supply, S_S, shows the total number of shares in existence. The flow supply, S_F, shows how many of these shares would be made available for sale on a given day at each possible price; these shares are, of course, offered for sale by existing shareholders, and the upwards slope of S_F indicates that these citizens will be prepared to sell more shares at higher prices than at lower ones.

The flow demand, D_F, shows how many shares will be demanded in a given day at each possible price. Some of these would doubtless be wanted by existing shareholders seeking to own more shares; others would be wanted by people who had no shares in' this company but who wished to acquire some. The intersection of D_F and S_F gives the equilibrium price of the shares (£5.00 here) and the equilibrium quantity sold in a day (300), just as the equilibrium price and quantity of fresh trout sold in a week were determined by the curves shown in Figure 1.1.

In contrast to D_F, which shows how many shares in the company people want to *buy* in a given day at each possible price, the stock demand, D_S, shows the total amount of shares in it which people want to *own* at each possible price. This stock demand comprises not only the desires of people wishing to buy shares, as shown in D_F, but also the desires of any existing shareholders (usually the great majority) who wish to retain most or all of their shares. The construction of D_S can readily be explained.

Consider, first, what would happen if the price were £3.00. S_F shows that existing shareholders would offer 100 shares for sale; in other words, they want to retain all but 100 of their existing shares, that is 99,900. These 99,900 are not the only ones wanted, for D_F shows a demand for 500 from a mixture of existing shareholders wanting more shares and non-shareholders wanting some shares.

Altogether, a stock of 100,400 shares is demanded at this price (that is 99,900 + 500) as shown on D_S. Note that the gap between D_F and S_F at this price is 500 − 100, that is 400, and this also equals the gap between D_S and S_S.

Consider, next, what would happen if the price were £7.00. S_F shows that existing shareholders would offer 400 shares for sale; this means they would want to retain 99,600 of their existing shares. D_F shows that a further 200 shares are demanded by existing shareholders wanting more shares along with non-shareholders wanting some shares, so the total (stock) quantity demanded shown by D_S is 99,800. Again, the gap between D_F and S_F, which is here 300 − 500, or − 200, equals the gap between D_S and S_S.

Finally, consider the equilibrium price of £5.00 given by D_F and S_F. S_F shows that existing shareholders would offer 300 shares for sale and wish to keep 99,700. D_F shows that a further 300 would be demanded, making the total (stock) quantity demanded 100,000 as shown by D_S. This equals the total (stock) quantity available, so that D_S and S_S also imply an equilibrium price of £5.00. At this price, there is no gap between D_F and S_F and, in turn, no gap between D_S and S_S. In short, the equilibrium price and quantity can be found either from D_F and S_F or from D_S and S_S, though the former alone give also the equilibrium quantity sold in a period of time.

One final point about this market needs making. In the day for which S_F and D_F were relevant, some 300 shares would change hands. By the end of the day, no-one who had started the day owning shares in the company but who was prepared to sell for a price of £5.00 (or more) will have failed to do so. So S_F the next day could be as shown by S_F'. Likewise, no-one who had started the day wanting to buy some (or more) shares at a price of £5.00 (or less) will have failed to do so. So D_F the next day could be shown by D_F'. These moves in the flow supply and demand need not affect D_S since it is clear the stock demand at a price of £5.00 would stay at 100,000, for all the shares are now owned by people who wish to hold them if that is the price, and no-one else now wishes to buy them at that price. In practice, the flow supply and demand are likely to fluctuate from day to day as different investors form different and changing opinions on the merits of the shares concerned; in turn, the stock demand will also fluctuate. Accordingly, both the price and the quantity changing hands are liable to vary frequently.

Stock analysis and the housing market

Perhaps the second-hand market which most affects ordinary people is the one for houses. For simplicity, it will be supposed that all housing is owned. Figure 5.4 shows the possible flow curves (D_F and S_F) and stock curves (D_S and S_S) in a country's housing market where quantity is measured in square metres, and where, again for simplicity, it is assumed that a price of a square metre of housing is the same in all districts. S_S shows a total stock of 1,000m square metres, and it will be seen that the equilibrium price is £400 per square metre.

Now it is likely that the price elasticity of S_F will be very low, as shown in Figure 5.4. In general, higher prices will induce many existing owners to

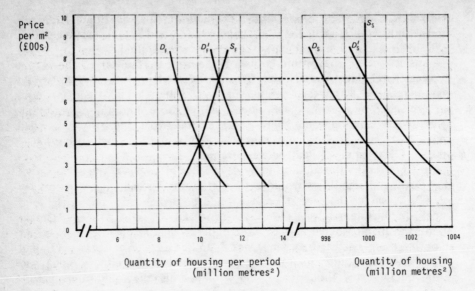

Figure 5.4

consider owning fewer square metres, but this could usually be done only by selling their present houses and buying smaller ones. People are reluctant to take action of this sort, partly because they feel 'attached' to their present houses, and partly because selling, buying and moving houses results in considerable bills from people such as solicitors, estate agents and removal firms.

Suppose that the flow demand for existing houses rose for some reason. Perhaps interest rates on mortgages, that is on loans made to people wishing to buy houses, have fallen a little, or perhaps building costs have risen a little so that the cost of building new houses (which are obviously a substitute for second-hand ones) has risen. Either way, more non-house owners will be seeking to purchase homes, and a few existing owners will be seeking to move into more spacious buildings. The new flow demand is shown by D'_F and the new stock demand by D'_S in Figure 5.4. It will be seen that at the previous equilibrium price of £400 per square metre, the flow quantity demanded rises by 2 million square metres, from 10 million to 12 million per period, and the stock quantity demanded rises by 2 million square metres from 1000 million to 1002 million. The new equilibrium price of £700 per square metre is shown where these two demand curves cut S_F and S_S respectively. It is worth adding that as time passes, so people wishing to buy and sell at the new price will make their purchases and sales, and so, in turn, both the flow demand and supply curves are likely to shift left.

Perhaps the most interesting implication of the figure is that what appears to be a trivial shift to the right in D_S by around 0.2 per cent can lead to an enormous rise in prices. This seems less surprising when one looks at D_F which has shifted to the right by some 20 per cent, and when one recalls the inelasticity of S_F. It is clear, though, that house prices can be very sensitive to factors which cause seemingly modest rises in the stock demand, and it is a point which anyone engaged in the market or thinking of joining it should bear in mind. House prices in the UK just about doubled in an 18-month period in the early 1970s.

There are two further points which deserve making. First, it may be wondered if a subsequent rise in mortgage interest rates would shift the flow demand to the left and send house prices crashing down. For instance in Figure 5.4, could the flow demand move back to D_F and take prices back to £400? This is most unlikely. S_F shows that people were previously prepared to sell 10m square metres a period at a price of £400; but if prices stayed at £700 for any length of time, then people might become less willing to sell at lower prices. Thus, S_F might shift a little to the left, and in turn D_S would shift a little to the right. These moves would make large price falls less likely.

Secondly, it will be realized by looking at the stock curves that there will be downwards pressure on prices if S_S shifts to the right as new houses are built (or at least built more rapidly than old ones are knocked down). But S_S can move only very slowly, so even if a rise in price from £400 to £700 encouraged a spate of new buildings, it would be some considerable time before this spate had a significant effect on house prices.

Part II

Household behaviour

6

The elements of the theory of household behaviour

Introduction to indifference analysis

It was explained in Part I how the forces of supply and demand fix the equilibrium price and quantity sold (per period of time) in any market where a homogeneous product is traded between many buyers and sellers. Much of the remaining parts of the book is concerned with exploring these forces of supply and demand in greater depth. This part is concerned with the theory of household behaviour; the present chapter gives a general introduction to this theory, and uses it to analyse the demands made by households (or consumers) for the goods and services which they buy, whilst the following chapter shows how the theory can be used to throw light on the supplies made by households, particularly of labour.

In developing any theory of behaviour, it is necessary to make some assumption about what the subject of the theory is trying to do. Generally, it is assumed the subject is trying to maximize something. For instance, a theory of behaviour by politicians (in a democracy) might assume they were trying to maximize votes, whilst a theory of behaviour by firms might assume (like the theories outlined later in this book) that they were trying to maximize profits. But what is a household trying to maximize when its members purchase goods and services? Economists generally assume their pattern of purchases is designed to maximize the satisfaction (or utility, as it is often called) they can get from their available income. Indeed, it is said that a rational household always seeks to maximize its utility. Notice that this does not mean households are all totally selfish; a rational household would prefer a large donation to famine relief in Ethiopia to a foreign holiday provided the donation gave it greater satisfaction. The following two sections look more closely at the concept of utility and at how levels of utility can be compared with the aid of graphs. Later sections relate the concept of utility to household demand.

Utility

One of the problems of a theory based on maximizing utility or satisfaction is that utility, unlike, say, votes or profits, cannot be quantified. However, in order to examine utility a little more closely, it is useful to pretend – just for this section – that it can, and that it is quantified in units termed utils. Column (1) of

Table 6.1 illustrates the total utility that one particular consumer might get each day from possible different levels of consumption of cups of coffee. It shows, for instance, that if his level of consumption of all other items remained unchanged, then one cup per day would give him 55 utils per day, whilst two would give 76 utils, and so on. It is not surprising to see that the total level of satisfaction changes with consumption, but it is interesting to look closely at how it so changes. This can be done with the help of the figures in column (2) which show what is termed *marginal utility*, that is the change in total utility (in a period of time) when the consumption of an item (in that period of time) changes by one unit. The figures in column (2) are placed between the lines of those in column (1) and show, for instance, that if daily consumption rose from one cup to two (or fell from two to one) then total daily utility from coffee would change by 21 units. In this example, it is supposed that successive one-unit increases in daily consumption would yield smaller and smaller increases in total utility. Although it cannot be proved, it is widely accepted that a similar result of decreasing marginal utility would apply to all commodities purchased by all consumers. In some cases, for instance grammes of toothpaste, marginal utility might rapidly fall to zero; in others, for instance cigarettes to chain smokers, marginal utility might fall very slowly indeed.

Diminishing marginal utility means, of course, that people appreciate unit *rises* in consumption less and less the more they consume. However, this should not be taken to mean that if the person concerned in Table 6.1 drank four cups of coffee each day then he would enjoy the first cup more than the last. This might be the case if he always took his entire daily consumption in a short period mid-morning, but is unlikely to apply if he spreads his cups out fairly evenly over the day. In this case, it is probable that each cup would give him about 23 utils a day (to bring the total up to 92). In contrast, if he drank just two cups a day, then each might give him about 38 utils (to bring the total to 76). In short, an individual cup is likely to bring more satisfaction the longer he has had to wait for it.

Table 6.1 Total and marginal utility

Cups of coffee (per day)	(1) Total utility (utils)	(2) Marginal utility (utils)
0	0	
		55
1	55	
		21
2	76	
		11
3	87	
		5
4	92	
		3
5	95	
		1
6	96	

Indifference curves

Individual households face a bewildering array of items on which they can spend their money, and the theory of household behaviour is concerned with their decisions about how much of each to buy. Ideally, this would mean considering all items simultaneously. For most purposes, however, the theory can be developed adequately by supposing consumers are confronted with two items alone. The theory of consumer preferences is based on what are termed indifference curves. An example of these is shown in Figure 6.1 where it is labelled IC. This curve relates to a particular consumer who is able to spend his money on beer and steak, and it shows various combinations of weekly purchases (and presumably consumption) of beer and steak between which he is indifferent. In other words, it shows various possible *combinations* of beer and steak consumption each of which would give him one particular level of total utility. Thus the consumer would be indifferent between consuming 1 litre of beer and 3kg of steak each week or 2 litres of beer and 2kg of steak. The curve indicates that if the consumer initially consumed 1 litre of beer and 3kg of steak, then he could forgo 1kg of steak and have his previous level of utility restored with an extra 1 litre of beer; but if he forwent a further 1kg of steak (and so consumed just 1kg of steak each week), then he would need a further 4 litres of beer (to bring his weekly beer consumption up to 6 litres) to maintain his initial level of utility. This is because each item is subject to diminishing marginal utility if consumption rises; thus each litre of beer forgone represents a bigger loss of utility, yet compensating for this gets harder and harder as each extra unit of steak adds a smaller amount to total utility.

One important feature of the curve is that its slope at any point is related to the relative marginal utility of beer and steak at the consumption levels represented by that point. Consider point P in Figure 6.1. The line XY is the tangent at P.

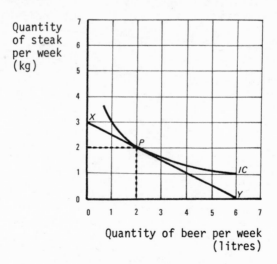

Quantity of steak per week (kg)

Quantity of beer per week (litres)

Figure 6.1

The slope of the tangent, and hence of the curve at P, is -0.5 (for the quantity of steak falls 3 units (kg) along XY whilst the quantity of beer rises 6 units (litres). Ignoring the minus sign, the slope would be 0.5, and this equals the marginal utility of beer (MU_B) divided by the marginal utility of steak (MU_S) at P. To see this, suppose the consumer was at P consuming 2kg of steak and 2 litres of beer. He could move a microscopic distance up the curve by sacrificing 1 millilitre (ml) of beer in return for some 0.5 milligrams (mg) of steak. In turn, this implies that, at P, his total utility would rise by equal amounts if he were given an extra 1 unit (ml) of beer or an extra 0.5 units (mg) of steak. This means that 1 unit (ml) of beer would have half the effect of 1 unit (mg) of steak, so that MU_B is half MU_S and $MU_B/MU_S = 0.5$.

The shape of the curve shown in Figure 6.1 has three properties which deserve mention. First, it slopes down from left to right. This occurs when the two items concerned are desirable as far as the consumer is concerned. Had the consumer been teetotal, then he would have had horizontal indifference curves between beer and steak like the one shown in Figure 6.2, for if he bought 3kg of steak then his total satisfaction would be the same no matter how much beer he bought (and presumably threw away). If one item is positively undesirable, then indifference curves slope upwards like the one shown in Figure 6.3. This would not arise with purchases of the sort under consideration since consumers would not buy and consume items they do not like. However this curve might apply to a household considering the purchase of different sorts of securities each with different forecast returns and different degrees of risk; the curve in Figure 6.3 could show a number of different return and risk combinations between which the household was indifferent.

Secondly, the curve is continuous. This suggests that the household can vary its consumption of the items under consideration by relatively small amounts.

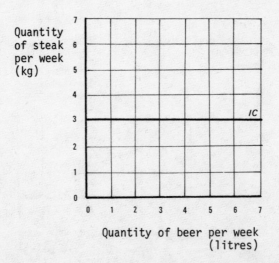

Figure 6.2

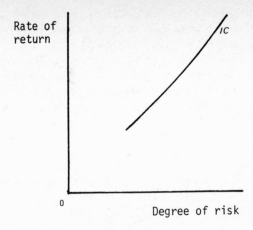

Figure 6.3

Suppose, though, steak were replaced by an item which could be adjusted only in relatively large amounts, such as rented television sets where a household might consider renting one, two or three, but would be unable to rent intermediate amounts such as 1.6. In this case, an indifference curve would give way to a series of dots, as in Figure 6.4, each representing points yielding similar total utility; but it would be meaningless to join these dots with a curve which passed through points where there was no whole number of televisions. If small variations were impossible for both items, as would apply with rented

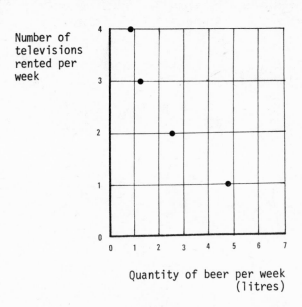

Figure 6.4

televisions and hired cars, then meaningful points would arise only at whole numbers of both items, and it is quite possible that no two such points would provide identical total utility.

Thirdly, the curve really is curved! This might not occur if the two items were related in certain ways. For instance, if they were perfect substitutes, as might apply to two brands of table salt, then the curve would give way to a straight line as in Figure 6.5; this shows that all combinations of salt brands amounting to 5g yield equal total utility. If, instead, the items were perfect complements, as would apply to left shoes and right shoes (at least for two-legged people), then

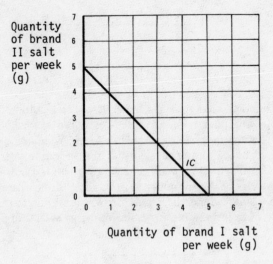

Figure 6.5

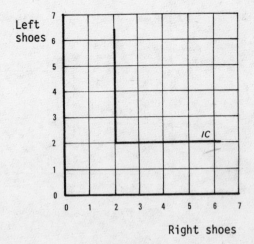

Figure 6.6

the curve would give way to two lines at right-angles as in Figure 6.6; this shows that there is no more utility to be gained from having 5 left shoes and 2 right ones (or vice versa) than from two of each.

For reasons of simplicity, this chapter will stick to an analysis of items which are regarded as desirable, where consumption levels can be varied by small amounts, and which are not related. Accordingly, it will use indifference curves like those in Figure 6.1. Readers may care to consider for themselves what would happen in other cases.

One final aspect of indifference curves needs to be discussed. A given curve passes through points which generate a particular level of satisfaction. For the consumer in Figure 6.1, there would in fact be an infinite number of indifference curves between beer and steak each representing one of the infinite number of different levels of satisfaction he could get from consuming varying amounts of these items. It is often useful to have figures showing a number of different curves, and this is done in Figure 6.7; such a diagram is called an indifference map. The furthest curve from the origin (IC_D) is the one representing the highest level of utility, for it passes through higher combinations of beer and steak than the others (and both items are assumed to be desirable). None of the curves in Figure 6.7 cross each other. It is possible to draw indifference curves which do, as in Figure 6.8, but they would then depict a nonsense situation. The points X and Y there each lie on IC_A, indicating that the consumer is indifferent between them. Likewise, he is apparently indifferent between Y and Z which each lie on IC_B. It follows that he should be indifferent between X and Z, but this cannot be so as he has more beer and more steak at Z than at X and (by assumption) he finds both desirable. To avoid nonsense situations, indifference curves in the rest of this book will not intersect.

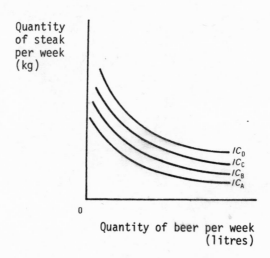

Figure 6.7

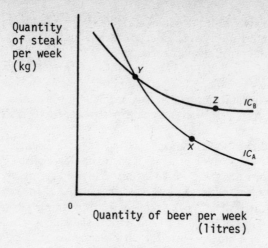

Figure 6.8

Maximizing utility

The last section has shown how an indifference map can be used to represent a consumer's tastes. However, when a consumer in a two-commodity world decides how much of each item to buy, his decision will be influenced by his income and by the items' prices as well as by his tastes. Information on income and prices can be shown on a diagram with the help of a budget line such as XY in Figure 6.9. Suppose the consumer has a weekly income of £9, and that beer has a price of £1.50 per litre whilst steak has a price of £3 per kg. In this case, the

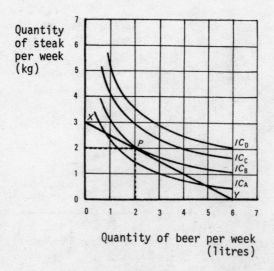

Figure 6.9

consumer could purchase 3kg of steak and no beer (as at X) or 6 litres of beer and no steak (as at Y) or any combination along XY. Of course, he could also go to any point inside the triangle X0Y if he chose not to spend all his money on beer and steak. Notice that the slope of XY is -0.5; ignoring the minus sign, this is 0.5 and equals the price of a unit of beer (P_B) divided by the price of a unit of steak (P_S), that is P_B/P_S.

What combination of beer and steak will the utility-maximizing consumer in this two-commodity world buy? The answer is the combination found at P where XY touches the curve IC_B, for P is on the highest indifference curve he can reach – given his budget line XY – and so P represents the highest level of utility he can attain. Notice that the slope of IC_B at P equals the slope of XY and is (ignoring the minus sign) 0.5. It was shown earlier that this equals MU_B/MU_S at P, and it was shown in the last paragraph that it also equals P_B/P_S. So, at P, the critical utility-maximizing point, it turns out that $MU_B/MU_S = P_B/P_S$. Put another way, $MU_B/P_B = MU_S/P_S$ at P. Three points should be made about this result.

First, it is, in fact, fairly obvious. Suppose, for instance, a consumer is faced with unit prices of £1.50 for beer and £3 for steak, but buys quantities which result in his having a MU_B of 6 and a MU_S of 6. In this case, MU_B/P_B is 4 and does not equal MU_S/P_S which is 2. It can readily be shown that this consumer is not maximizing utility. After all, he could give up one unit of steak, and so lose 6 utils, but spend the £3 saved on two units of beer, the first of which would produce 6 utils and the second a little less; his total utility would rise if he changed his consumption pattern in this way, and so he was clearly not maximizing satisfaction to begin with.

Secondly, the result must apply to any pair of commodities. So, in a many-commodity world, a rational consumer will adjust his purchases so that $MU_A/P_A = MU_B/P_B = MU_C/P_C$ and so on.

Thirdly, recall the formulation $MU_B/MU_S = P_B/P_S$. This applies to all rational consumers. Now all these consumers face the same prices for beer and steak, so each has the same P_B/P_S. It follows that each ends up with the same MU_B/MU_S. Of course, differing tastes mean that different people buy different quantities, but their differing purchase combinations result in each having the same relative marginal utilities.

Relating indifference analysis to demand curves

Indifference maps and demand curves

It is now possible to see how a consumer's demand curve can be derived from his indifference map. Consider a consumer whose income is devoted to purchases of asparagus and broccoli and whose indifference map is shown in Figure 6.10. This consumer has a weekly income of £6 and faces a fixed broccoli price of £1 per kg; thus she could buy 6 units of broccoli if her entire income were devoted to it, and any budget line for her starts at the point V on the vertical axis. The problem is to see how much asparagus she would buy at various possible

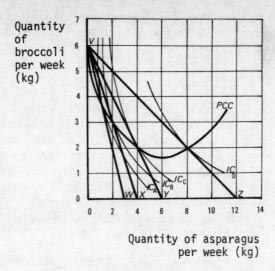

Figure 6.10

asparagus prices in order to construct her demand curve for asparagus. Figure 6.10 considers four different asparagus prices, each giving rise to a different budget line. These prices are £2, £1.50, £1 and £0.50 per kg. In turn, they would permit her to buy, 3, 4, 6 or 12 kg of asparagus if she devoted her entire income to it. Hence they generate the budget lines VW, VX, VY and VZ respectively. In fact, this consumer always buys a combination of both asparagus and broccoli, and these combinations can be found at the tangency points of her budget lines and the highest attainable indifference curves. With an asparagus price of £2, she is on VW and settles where this touches IC_A, and so buys 1kg of asparagus. With prices of £1.50, £1 and £0.50 she settles in turn where VX touches IC_B, VY touches IC_C and VZ touches IC_D and so in turn buys 2, 4 and 8kg of asparagus. This information is summed up in the demand curve shown in Figure 6.11 since it shows that at asparagus prices of £2, £1.50, £1 and £0.50 she would buy 1kg, 2kg, 4kg and 8kg respectively.

Returning to Figure 6.10, it is possible to plot a new curve through the tangency points of the budget lines and indifference curves. The new curve is called a price consumption curve (PCC) as it shows the consumption position for different asparagus prices. To begin with it slopes down; this indicates that less money is devoted to broccoli – and hence more is devoted to asparagus – as asparagus prices fall, a situation revealing an elastic demand for asparagus. The converse holds after PCC starts to rise.

Shifts in demand curves

It is easy to see from Figures 6.10 what factors could cause the asparagus demand curve in Figure 6.11 to shift. For example, a change in tastes would alter

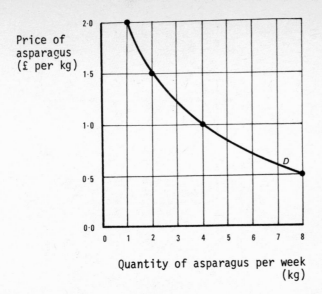

Figure 6.11

the consumer's indifference map and so result in different tangency points on each budget line; thus the quantity of asparagus demanded at each price could change. A change in the price of another item (the only other item here is broccoli) would cause point V to move; hence all the budget lines would shift and so the quantity of asparagus demanded at each asparagus price would change. Again, a change in income will affect the budget lines and the quantities of asparagus demanded at each possible price.

The possible effects of a change in income merit closer attention. Suppose the consumer starts with her income at £6 and faces asparagus and broccoli prices of £1 and £0.50. In this case she starts at the point where VZ in Figure 6.10 touches IC_D. This information is reproduced in Figures 6.12 and 13, though the indifference curves there have slightly different shapes. Now a rise in income to, say, £7 per week means the consumer would have the new budget line V' Z' (which is parallel to VZ) and would settle where this just touched a new indifference curve. If the consumer had the indifference curves shown in Figure 6.12, then she would end up buying more asparagus which she would thus regard as a normal good. If she had the indifference curves shown in Figure 6.13, then she would buy less asparagus which she would regard as an inferior good. It is possible to draw a new curve through the tangency points in each case. This is called an income consumption curve (ICC) as it shows the consumption position for different income levels. The ICC has a positive slope so long as both items are normal goods, as is assumed at all income levels in Figure 6.12 and at low income levels in Figure 6.13; but it slopes backwards when one item is inferior, as happens with asparagus at income levels in Figure 6.13 higher than the one shown by the line VZ.

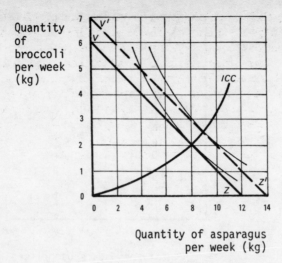

Figure 6.12

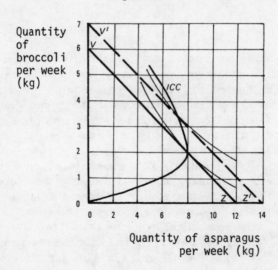

Figure 6.13

Income and substitution effects

Demand curves generally slope downwards indicating that purchases rise when price falls. There are two reasons why this is likely to be true. Suppose, for example, that the price of gin falls. One effect, known as the substitution effect, is that gin is now relatively cheaper compared with other items than it was before, and this will necessarily tempt consumers to buy more gin and less of other items. Another effect, known as the income effect, is that consumers' real incomes (that is their purchasing powers) have risen, and this will lead them to buy more normal goods and fewer inferior goods. If gin is a normal good, then both the income effect and the substitution effect will be working towards increased purchases when its price falls so that purchases should rise substantially. If it is an inferior good, then the substitution effect will still be encouraging increased purchases but the income effect will be encouraging fewer purchases, and the result is likely to be that purchases rise by little. In principle, the income effect with a highly inferior good could swamp the substitution effect and cause purchases to fall when price falls! However, there is no firm evidence that there has ever been such an item.

7

Labour supply

Income–leisure choice

In the analysis of indifference curves given in the last chapter the individual was regarded as choosing the commodity bundle which maximized his utility. In other words, the individual was assumed to derive utility from the consumption of commodities; furthermore, the budget line related income to total expenditure. But the same analytical technique can be used to consider an individual's choice of how many hours to work. Of course, in supposing that the individual can choose how many hours to work, the discussion is limited to those individuals who are paid at an hourly rate and have freedom, within limits, to choose the hours they work; the discussion is not relevant to many salaried people who have little or no choice about how many hours they work. Even so, the approach is very fruitful and allows us to consider issues of the effects of changes in taxes on hours worked and possible effects of reducing the standard working week (i.e., where the standard hours are reduced say, from 40 hours per week to 35 hours per week).

In order to consider the supply of hours worked, it is necessary to be clear about what it is that gives an individual satisfaction or utility and also what constrains an individual in choosing how many hours to work. It is assumed that the individual can vary the hours which he works. If he works, the individual earns income which allows him to purchase goods and services. On the other hand, if he does not work he does not earn income, but can use his 'leisure' hours doing other things. Thus 'leisure' is a term which is used to refer to the hours that an individual is not working, and does not necessarily mean sitting around doing nothing. A fundamental assumption of the analysis is that individuals want leisure and that they can only be enticed to work if they are paid a wage in order to forgo their leisure. This means that a rise in leisure leads to a rise in utility for the individual. In addition, a rise in income also leads to a rise in utility because a rise in income gives the individual a greater command over goods and services.

From what has been said about income and leisure it is clear that the individual will derive utility from both of these, and so we construct a set of indifference curves, shown in Figure 7.1, which have the same form as those in Figure 6.7. Notice, in particular, that *leisure* is measured on the horizontal axis, and that for a given level of income, total utility rises if the amount of leisure rises.

Now consider the budget constraint. In constructing this assume that the time

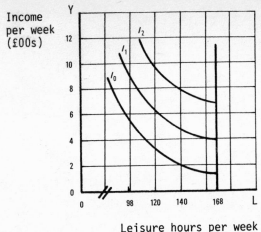

Leisure hours per week

Figure 7.1

over which the choice is to be made is one week. There are a total of 168 hours available in the week. Suppose that 14 hours per day is put to one side for eating and sleeping, leaving a possible 10 hours per day – that is, 70 hours per week – for working or non-work pursuits. For the present assume that the individual can work any number of hours he chooses up to the 70 hours. If the individual chooses to work, it is assumed that he is paid at the same rate for each hour worked (overtime will be considered in a later section). Suppose the individual is paid £10 per hour. Depending on how many hours the individual works, he will have a particular level of income.

To establish the level of income it is necessary to know whether the individual has any unearned income, say in the form of child benefits. Suppose he has, and let this unearned income be denoted by Y_u, and for the moment assume it is equal to £100. Hence, no matter how many hours the individual actually works, he will have a weekly income of at least £100. The situation is shown in Figure 7.2. Since in Figure 7.2 the individual has leisure on the horizontal axis, then hours worked is measured from point M (the maximum hours of leisure in the week, namely 168), and moving to the left. For each hour the individual works he earns £10. Thus, at point P, for example, he works 28 hours (his leisure now being 98 + 42) and his earned income is £280, which would raise his total income to £380 (that is, £100 + £280). If he spent his available 70 hours actually working then he would earn £700, which would raise his total income to £800 (as shown by point S in Figure 7.2). The line segment ST in Figure 7.2 simply shows the hours for eating and sleeping and for which the individual earns no income. His budget constraint is, therefore, given by the line segment MRST. (Notice that the angle of RS from the horizontal is the wage rate, here W = £10.)

Given the indifference map shown in Figure 7.1 and the constraint in terms of Figure 7.2, how many hours would the individual choose to work? The situation is shown in Figure 7.3. The individual is assumed to maximize his utility.

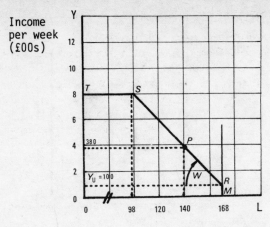

Figure 7.2

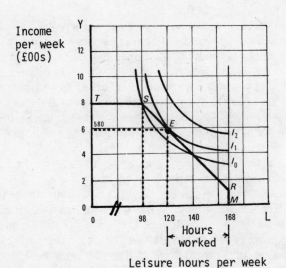

Figure 7.3

Therefore, he will wish to settle down at the highest possible indifference curve, subject to the solution lying on the constraint MRST. This will be the indifference curve I_1 in Figure 7.3. The optimal choice for this individual between income and leisure is given by point E. At point E the individual will choose to take 120 hours of leisure (or 22 out of his possible 70). The mirror-image of this is that he will choose to work 48 hours (i.e., 168 − 120). For each hour he works he earns £10, and so his earned income is equal to £480, which in addition to his £100 of unearned income, gives him a total income of £580.

Income and substitution effects

Just as in consumer choice where a distinction can be made between income and substitution effects, so the same can be done in the present application. The discussion however, will be fairly brief so that the analysis can be put to immediate use. Figure 7.4 shows what happens to an individual's choice between income and leisure (income and work) when his *unearned* income rises. From the diagram it can be seen that his unearned income rises from £100 to £150 and finally to £200. The individual's optimal choice between income and leisure moves from point E to point F and finally to point G. The result is to *increase* his total leisure hours from 120 and 122 and finally to 125 (i.e., his work hours reduce from 48 to 46 and finally to 43). This is an important result. A rise in unearned income, with the wage rate remaining constant, leads to a rise in the hours of leisure – a fall in the hours worked. The line through all possible optimal solutions (the line through points E, F and G) is called the *income expansion path*, and is denoted IEP.

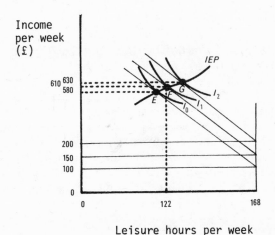

Figure 7.4

Consider now a rise in the wage rate with unearned income remaining constant at £100, as shown in Figure 7.5. Suppose the wage rises from £10 to £12 and then to £15 per hour. At a wage rate of £10 the individual will maximize his utility by working 40 hours (168 − 128 = 40), receiving a total income of £500. At a wage rate of £12 the individual will maximize his utility by moving to point F, taking 125 hours of leisure and working 43 hours. At the wage rate of £12 per hour, therefore, the individual will have an income level of £616 (£516 plus £100). Finally, at a wage rate of £15 per hour the individual chooses to work 48 hours (168 − 120) and his total income is £820 (£720 plus £100). The curve joining all possible equilibrium points of a change in the wage rate, all else remaining constant, is shown by the curve PEP in Figure 7.5 (not drawn to scale), and is called the *price expansion path*.

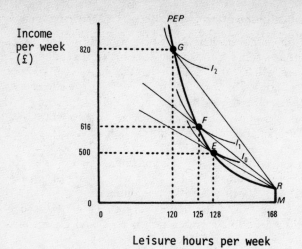

Figure 7.5

It is to be noted that the effect of the rise in the wage rate illustrated in Figure . 7.5 is to raise the hours worked. But this may not be the situation in all cases. To see why, it is useful to consider the price effect in terms of two component parts: the income effect and the substitution effect. This is done in Figure 7.6. In Figure 7.6 the wage is initially £10 per hour and the individual is at equilibrium at point E on indifference curve I_0. At point E, therefore, the individual works 40 hours (168 − 128) and has an income of £500 (£400 plus £100). Now suppose the wage rate rises to £15 per hour, so that the individual moves to point F on indifference curve I_1. He reduces his leisure hours to 125, and so works 43 hours at a wage rate of £15 per hour, giving him a total income of £745 (£645 + £100).

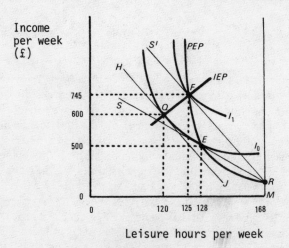

Figure 7.6

But the rise in the wage rate has two effects. First, it means that every hour the individual chooses not to work he must now forgo £15 rather than £10. Second, the fact that his income has now risen means that he will wish to spend some of that increased income in terms of leisure. These two effects can be separated as follows. Suppose the individual's income is reduced so that he is on the same indifference curve that he was to begin with, namely I_0 in Figure 7.6. Thus, we find a line parallel to RS' which is just tangential to indifference curve I_0, as shown by HJ in Figure 7.6. This gives us point Q. (It must be remembered at all times that point Q is purely hypothetical.) The movement from point E to point Q, therefore, denotes the effect of the individual substituting more hours because of the higher opportunity cost of forgoing leisure (£15 rather than £10). Thus, the movement from E to Q denotes the substitution effect. Notice that at point Q the individual chooses to take 120 hours in non-work activities, and so he chooses to work 48 hours. This means that the substitution effect *raises* the hours worked by 8 hours.

The income effect of the wage rise is given by the movement from point Q to point F. Since the income expansion path is upward sloping (as shown earlier) then the effect of this is to *reduce* the hours worked – in this example by 5 hours.

It is clear, then, that the substitution effect of a rise in the wage rate is to raise the hours worked while the income effect is to reduce the hours worked. The hours worked will rise over-all if the substitution effect is in excess of the income effect. Hence, the result in Figure 7.5 assumes that the substitution effect outweighs the income effect. Had the income effect outweighed the substitution effect then the price expansion path would begin to bend to the right.

The supply curve of labour

Just as the demand curve for a commodity can be derived from the price consumption curve, so it is possible to derive the demand curve for leisure from the price expansion path. Of course, the demand curve for leisure is closely related to the supply curve of hours worked. The derivation is shown in Figure 7.7. The rise in wages from £10 to £15 moves the individual from point E to point F. He therefore reduces his hours of leisure from 128 to 125; thus he reduces the quantity of leisure demanded. Equivalently, he raises the quantity of work supplied from 40 hours to 43 hours.

If the income effect exactly offsets the substitution effect, then the price expansion path is vertical. This means that there is no change in leisure hours as a result of the rise in the wage rate. It follows, then, that the demand curve for leisure is vertical and the supply curve of hours worked is also vertical. Finally, if the income effect swamps the substitution effect, then there is an increase in the demand for leisure hours as a result of the wage rise; or, equivalently, the supply curve of labour bends back on itself. The bending backward supply curve of labour is illustrated in Figure 7.8.

Notice in Figure 7.8 that it is only at 'high' wages that the supply curve of labour begins to bend back on itself. The reason is that, for such an individual, as the wage rate rises his income rises sufficiently for him to consider leisure a

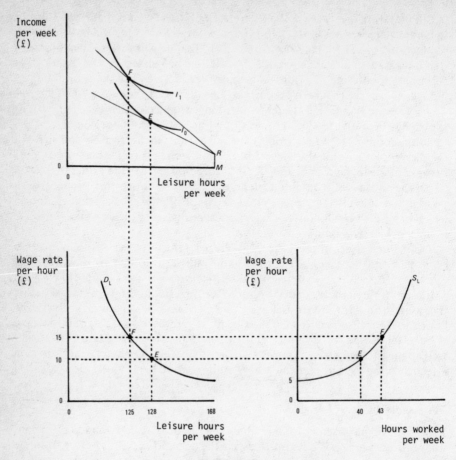

Figure 7.7

much more worthwhile prospect – he can now do things in his leisure time because he has sufficient income to do them with.

The effect of a shorter working week

In a number of occupations there exists a fixed minimum set of hours which must be worked in any one week, referred to as the *standard working week*, for example 40 hours or in some occupations 38 hours. Of course, it may be possible for an individual to work in excess of this minimum. The most important difference between the standard hours and overtime hours is that they are paid at different rates. It is generally the case that overtime hours are paid as a multiple of standard hours, for example at 'time-and-a-half' or 'double time'. In other words, overtime is paid at one-and-a-half the rate of standard hours or twice the rate that standard hours are paid. The multiplication factor ($1\frac{1}{2}$ or 2 in the examples just given) is referred to as the *overtime premium*.

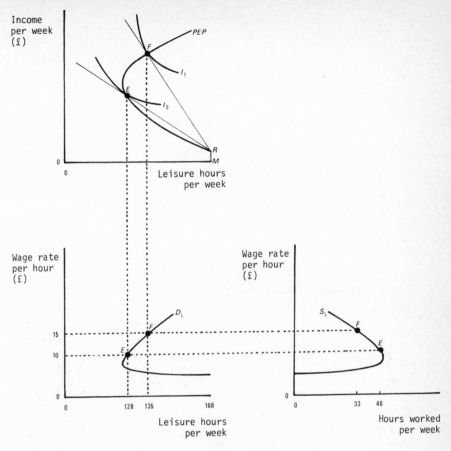

Figure 7.8

With the high levels of unemployment that many Western economies have been experiencing, there has been a proposal to reduce the standard working week. Even the Organization for Economic Cooperation and Development (OECD) has proposed that the working week within Europe should be reduced from 40 to 35 hours. There is a great deal of controversy surrounding this policy proposal, but we can use our present analysis to shed some light on the effects it might have on the hours worked of an individual.

Before considering the effects of a shorter working week, it is necessary to introduce into the analysis the standard working week and the overtime premium. Both of these are illustrated in Figure 7.9.

The individual receives £100 unearned income, his wage is £10 per hour for standard hours and he is required to work at least a standard working week of 40 hours. Notice that at the standard working week of 40 hours the individual's total income would be £500 (£400 plus £100) if he worked just these hours. This is shown by point U in Figure 7.9. But suppose the individual can also work

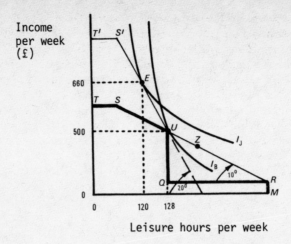

Income per week (£)

Leisure hours per week

Figure 7.9

overtime if he so chooses. Let us further suppose that the overtime premium is 2; in other words, overtime hours are paid at twice the hourly rate of standard hours. Thus for every hour worked beyond the 40 hour week, the rate is £20 per hour. This means that for hours beyond the standard hours the individual would be choosing some point on the line segment US' rather than US. Notice that it is being assumed that he has a maximum of 30 hours which he can work overtime (leaving him 98 hours per week for eating and sleeping) which gives him a possible maximum income of £1,100 (£100 + £400 + £600).

What then is the budget constraint? If the individual must either work the standard working week or not work at all, then segment UR is not available to the individual. Hence, the budget constraint is MRQUS' T'. Given the aim of the individual is to maximize his utility, how many hours of leisure (how many hours of work) will the individual choose? This depends not only on his budget constraint but also on his preference structure. Indifference curves for different individuals, John and Bill, are drawn in Figure 7.9, denoted I_J and I_B respectively. Given I_J, John would move to point E on the line segment US', choosing 120 hours of leisure, and hence have a total of 48 hours spent working – of which 40 would be paid at the standard rate and 8 at the overtime rate. John's total income would be £660 (£100 + £400 + £160). Bill, on the other hand, would reach his highest possible indifference curve I_B by moving to point U and working just the standard working week. He would have a total income of £500 (£100 + £400). (Notice in passing that if Bill could work for less than the standard working week, then he would move to some point such as point Z on the line segment UR. This, to some extent, explains absenteeism.)

Consider now reducing the standard working week from 40 hours to 35 hours. What is the result of this for John and Bill? The result is illustrated in Figure 7.10. The constraint line now becomes MRKVS" T". First consider John. John will move from point E to point E', and as far as John is concerned this is a pure income effect. He *reduces* the hours which he works from 48 to 46. On the other hand, his income now rises from £660 to £670 (£100 + £350 + £220). The effect on Bill is less straightforward. However, the most likely result is that shown in Figure 7.10, with Bill moving from the 'corner' solution at U to point U' on the segment VS''. Bill will now work 38 hours (35 standard and 3 overtime hours). In the case illustrated, Bill's total income rises to £510 (£100 + £350 + £60), although it could well have fallen even with Bill doing overtime. It would also have been possible, if Bill had a strong preference for leisure, to have a solution at point V, where Bill would again work just the standard working week and now earn only £350 (with a total income of £450).

What comes across in terms of Figure 7.10 is the worry that shortening the working week will simply lead to a leakage into overtime. John although working less hours in total is now working 11 hours overtime (rather than his former 8 hours) and Bill is now working 3 hours overtime (rather than working no overtime hours). Associated with this leakage into overtime is a further worry. Employers now have to pay John and Bill more wage-income even though they are working less hours! In the example above, John is now paid £670 rather than £660, while Bill is paid £510 rather than £500. This, then, has the tendency to be inflationary.

Of course, much of the debate over shortening the standard working week is

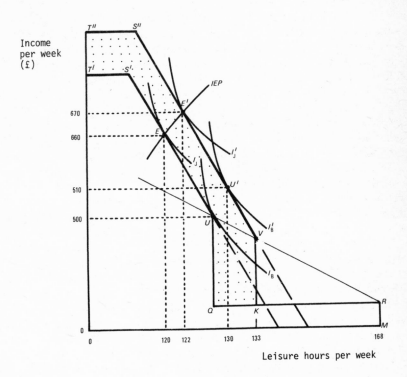

Figure 7.10

to do with its impact on the level of employment, and hence on the level of unemployment. It must be realized that the present analysis is in terms of *hours* worked. However, if the hours worked falls but the wage-bill rises, then there is not necessarily much likelihood of employers raising the *number* of workers employed. What this analysis indicates, then, is that any discussion about reducing unemployment by reducing the standard working week must look very closely at the leakage into overtime work. It may be that the unions will have to accept some compromise deal concerning the amount of overtime work that *existing* workers can undertake. But this takes us beyond the scope of the present analysis.

8

Subsidies versus cash handouts

This short chapter shows how the theory of household behaviour outlined in Chapter 6 can be used in the context of the welfare state to compare the effects of helping people with subsidies and helping them with cash handouts or transfer payments.

Suppose, for example, it is desired to help poor families rent more spacious housing accommodation. This policy might be pursued by giving them cash handouts to spend as they please (but hoping some of the cash will be devoted to housing) or by arranging to meet part of their rent payments for them with a rent subsidy.

Subsidies

Consider the family in Figure 8.1 which has an initial income of £90 per week and finds landlords wanting rents of £1 per square metre (m²) per week. Its initial budget line is VW showing, for example, that it could in principle devote all its income to renting 90m² of housing and have no money for other items, or that it could be homeless and spend £90 on other items. It maximizes utility where VW touches IC_A, the highest attainable indifference curve, and hence rents 40m² with £50 left for other items. Now suppose the government sought to help this family by introducing a subsidy which met one half of its rent. The family would be on the new budget line VX. This starts at V, showing that if it opts for homelessness then it gets no money from the government and is no better off than before; it ends at X, showing that if all income were devoted to housing, then 180m² could be rented (for £180), the government paying one half and the family the other. The family here would end up where VX touches IC_B and so rent 60m². It has to find only half the £60 rent for this space, and so it pays £30 rent and has £60 of its original income of £90 left for other items.

Cash handouts

Now the family would be able to rent 60m² and still have £60 left over for other items if, instead of the government using £30 to subsidize its rent, the government gave it £30 in cash; for this would raise its income from £90 to the £120 it would need. But suppose the government did give it £30 in cash, what would the family do? It would move on to the budget line YZ which passes through the

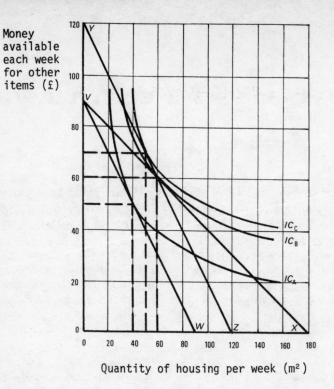

Quantity of housing per week (m²)

Figure 8.1

point chosen with the rent subsidy to show that this point could indeed be afforded. However, with the budget line YZ the family opts for the point where it touches the highest attainable indifference curve, IC_C, and so it rents just 50m² and has £70 left for other items.

Notice that the family reaches a higher utility level (IC_C) with the cash than with the rent subsidy (when it reaches IC_B), though it rents less space (50m² instead of 60m²). The point is that the family has greater flexibility with the cash, and it chooses to spend less of its aid on housing and more on other items than it would do if government help was available only for housing. This argument applies to all aspects of welfare spending: in general, people could reach higher utility levels with cash than with aid tied to specific items. Why, then, is aid often so tied? Partly, perhaps, because taxpayers are more willing to pay taxes to finance help for the poor if the poor are encouraged to use most of that help for (say) housing than if they are likely to use much of it for (say) beer and bingo. In the case of housing, though, it is perhaps also because – in some families at least – the choice between housing and other items is largely made by one member whose preferences might lead to less housing being rented than the other members would like. It is, however, in the interests of the other members for the government to choose a policy which forces the decision-maker on to a budget line like VX instead of one like YZ.

9

Criminal behaviour

Introduction to the theory of uncertainty

Economic theory is designed to explain some of the things observed around us which are economic in nature. One such behaviour is crime. Most crimes possess a significant economic element – offences against property account for about 90 per cent of all indictable offences (burglary alone accounts for about 25 per cent). Crimes of violence and sexual crimes, serious as they are, account for only about 5 per cent of all indictable offences. One major concern of the policy-makers is whether to try to reduce the amount of crime by increasing expenditure on the police force or by imposing greater fines. The decision to some extent depends on which is the more effective in reducing the rate of crime. In an age of local and central government cut-backs, this is a very vital issue.

Such criminal behaviour and the possible effects of raising fines or increasing expenditure on the police force can be analysed in economic terms. In later sections an economic model of criminal behaviour will be considered. But as will be seen in a moment, a thief may or may not get caught. What this amounts to is that his income is uncertain since it will depend on whether or not he gets caught. At the same time, the individual will have some idea of the likelihood that he may get caught. In this sense we assume that the individual has a *subjective* assessment of the probability of getting caught. In such an uncertain world what, then, is the criterion of choice? How is it possible to analyse decision-making in a world of uncertainty? These are more difficult questions to answer than decision-making under certainty. In the first few sections, therefore, an arithmetical example will be developed which will be used to derive all the important results of decision-making under uncertainty that will be required in our discussion of criminal behaviour.

It is worth adding that the same analysis is the basis of most models of choice under uncertainty – such as an individual's decision whether to gamble or whether to insure. In this chapter, however, our sole concern is with a model of criminal behaviour.

Expected utility and state preferences

Consider a typical individual who derives utility from income. If the individual was in a world of certainty, then he would simply wish to maximize his utility subject to some budget constraint. But suppose the world is not certain, suppose that two states of the world are possible – referred to as state S_0 and state S_1 – although only one of these states will occur. If state S_0 materializes, then the individual would have a certain level of income, denoted Y_0; while if state S_1 materializes, then his income would be Y_1. The problem is, of course, that the individual does not know which state of the world will materialize, and hence he does not know which level of income will be actualized. On what basis, then, does this individual make a choice?

It is not unreasonable to suppose that the individual could replace the objective of maximizing utility with the alternative assumption of maximizing his *expected utility*. But in saying this, it is necessary to define more rigorously what we mean by 'expected utility'. In order to do this, and to lay the foundations for later discussions, Table 9.1 sets out computations derived for a given individual. Column (1) gives some different possible levels of income for the individual. Column (2) presents a series of numbers denoting the total utility the individual would have at each income level. Of course, it would also be possible to show the total utility for intermediate incomes such as 1.70, and this is done for two income levels for reasons which will become apparent later; in fact, all the figures shown are based on an arbitrary formula which, it was supposed, relates utility to income. (More specifically, in deriving all the figures in this table the functional form $U(Y) = 100 - 90EXP(-0.15Y)$ has been used for the utility function. It is not necessary for the reader to be familiar with such a complex function, but it is presented here so that anyone who wishes can check the computations). The third column denotes the marginal utility. The figures in Table 9.1 for the marginal utility are *not* measured by taking the difference between total utility for each level of income, as the procedure undertaken in

Table 9.1 Utility of risk-averse individual

| Y | Risk-Averse and p = 0.5 | | | |
	U(Y)	MU(Y)	E = 60	E = 70
1	23	11.6	97	117
2	33	10.0	87	107
3	43	8.6	77	97
4	51	7.4	69	89
5	57	6.4	63	83
5.45	60	6.0	60	80
6	63	5.5	57	77
7	69	4.7	51	71
7.25	70	4.6	50	70
8	73	4.1	47	67
9	77	3.5	43	63
10	80	3.0	40	60
11	83	2.6	37	57
12	85	2.2	35	55
13	87	1.9	33	53
14	89	1.7	31	51
15	91	1.4	29	49

Table 6.1 might suggest; instead they are marked out at each income level shown on the basis of the formula used in producing the figures in column (2). (More specifically, the marginal utility is given by $U'(Y) = 13.5EXP(-0.15Y)$, which gives *point* values for the marginal utility for any given level of income.)

In a world where two states are possible, which give rise to two possible levels of income – Y_0 and Y_1 – then there are two possible levels of utility, $U(Y_0)$ and $U(Y_1)$. Suppose that state S_0 has a probability p of occurring. Hence, state S_1 has a probability of $(1 - p)$ of occurring. It is important to bear in mind that these are *subjective* probabilities – in the sense that they are an assessment by the individual. Then the *expected utility*, denoted $E[U(Y)]$, is a weighted average of the two possible utilities, where the weights are their respective probabilities. In other words,

$$E[U(Y)] = pU(Y_0) + (1 - p)U(Y_1)$$

Now assume that the individual wishes to maximize this expected utility. It is perhaps helpful to realize that the choice criterion in a world of certainty is just a special case of this. To see why, suppose that income level Y_0 was going to occur with certainty. Then the probability of this occurring is unity, so that $p = 1$. Hence,

$$E[U(Y)] = U(Y_0)$$

and so maximizing the expected utility is the same as maximizing utility when the outcome is certain.

Now suppose the individual reckons that the probability that state S_0 will occur (p) is equal to one-half (so that the probability that state S_1 will occur is also one-half). The intention now is to derive a series of indifference curves each denoting points of equal *expected* utility. Once this has been done, then maximizing expected utility is the same as choosing the point on the highest possible indifference curve. The similarity with consumer choice under certainty should be quite obvious. Under certainty a series of indifference curves is derived which denote equal levels of utility (here actual utility not expected utility), so that, once again, maximizing utility is the same as moving to the highest possible indifference curve.

Suppose, for example, that a level of expected utility is set equal to 60. The first thing to notice is that, in Table 9.1, this is the level of utility when income is equal to $Y = 5.45$. It is possible to think of income $Y = 5.45$ as denoting the level of income that would give a level of utility of 60, no matter whether state S_0 occurred or state S_1 occurred. This would be like a situation of certainty where income was 5.45 and the level of utility was 60. All such points lie on a 45° line, as shown in Figure 9.1, and are referred to as *certainty points*. If, however, income in state S_0 were equal to $Y_0 = 2$, then the utility of this level of income is 33. The question is, then what would the level of income in state S_1 have to be for the expected utility to be equal to 60. We can derive this with the help of column (4). Column (4) denotes each level of utility such that the weighted average of this with column (2), weighted by their respective probabilities, is equal to 60. Thus, with $p = 0.5$ it is readily calculated that taking a half of each figure in column (2) and adding this to a half of each figure in column (4) gives a value of

60. (E.g., $(0.5) \times (23) + (0.5) \times (97) = 60$, $(0.5) \times (33) + (0.5) \times (87) = 60$, etc.)
If, therefore, income in state S_0 is equal to $Y_0 = 2$, then the level of income in
state S_1 which would leave the individual with an expected utility of 60 is
$Y_1 = 13$.

With the help of columns (2) and (4), therefore, it is possible to derive a series
of points which belong to the same indifference curve for expected utility of 60.
Thus, income levels $Y_0 = 4$ and $Y_1 = 7$ also give rise to an expected utility of 60
(since $U(Y_0) = 51$ and $U(Y_1) = 69$, and $(0.5) \times (51) + (0.5) \times (69) = 60$). Using
these figures it is possible to construct an indifference curve as shown in Figure
9.1, and denoted $E = 60$. In the same way, it is possible to construct an
indifference curve denoting a higher level of expected utility. Let this higher
level be equal to 70. Then with the help of columns (2) and (5) another
indifference curve can similarly be constructed. Take first the certainty point on
the main diagonal in Figure 9.1. At income level $Y = 7.25$, which occurs in both
state S_0 and state S_1, expected utility is equal to 70. One point on the same
indifference curve is the one with income in state S_0 equal to $Y_0 = 4$ and income
in state S_1 equal to $Y_1 = 14$, since $(0.5) \times (51) + (0.5) \times (89) = 70$. The curve
denoted $E = 70$ is constructed from all such points.

It is clear from Figure 9.1 that the indifference curves denoting levels of equal
expected utility have the same properties as the more traditional indifference
curves, which were outlined in Chapter 6. They are (a) downward sloping, (b)
convex to the origin, and (c) do not intersect. However, they are different from
the more traditional indifference curves to the extent that they are constructed
for a given level of probability p. This is quite clear when it is recalled that
columns (4) and (5) are constructed using a particular level of probability,
namely $p = 0.5$ in Figure 9.1. In addition, the indifference curves in Figure 9.1
are symmetrical about the certainty line OC. This can be seen by noting that for

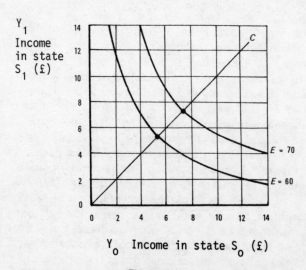

Figure 9.1

a level of expected utility of 60, the income combination ($Y_0 = 2$, $Y_1 = 13$) and ($Y_0 = 13$, $Y_1 = 2$) both belong to the same indifference curve. This is true for all symmetric points about the certainty line OC.

Risk-averse individuals

The previous section derived a series of indifference curves each denoting a particular level of expected utility, which are drawn under the assumption that the probability of state S_0 occurring is p (so that the probability that state S_1 will occur is $(1 - p)$). It has also been shown that situations of certainty can be represented by points lying along the main diagonal, such as OC in Figure 9.1. Suppose an individual's income level were 7.5. Since he has this income then it will be known with certainty. However, suppose the same individual is given the chance of raising his income to 13 (winning additional income of 5.5) or reducing it to 2 (losing income of 5.5) with a probability of 0.5. Why these particular numbers? Since the individual will either have income level 13 or income level 2, but does not know which, he can calculate his *expected* income. This is simply a weighted average of his two possible incomes, each weighted by their probability of occurring. Hence,

$$E(Y) = pY_0 + (1-p)Y_1$$
$$= (0.5) \times (2) + (0.5) \times (13)$$
$$= 7.5$$

It follows, therefore, that his expected income is the same as his actual income. Given that his expected income is equal to his actual income, will he keep with the certainty of income level 7.5 or take a gamble in the hope of gaining the income level of 13? Given the present utility function, the answer is that he will not!

The reason can be seen in terms of Figure 9.2. Point E represents the

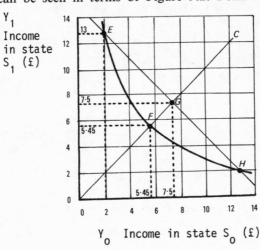

Figure 9.2

uncertainty income combination on the indifference curve denoted $E = 60$ (i.e., this indifference curve denotes an expected utility of 60). The line OC denotes the certainty line, where $Y_0 = Y_1$. The line EG denotes the line for which expected *income* is always equal to 7.5. The equation of this line is simply

$$7.5 = 0.5Y_0 + 0.5Y_1$$

The equation is satisfied where $(Y_0, Y_1) = (2, 13)$ and where $(Y_0, Y_1) = (7.5, 7.5)$. In other words, anywhere along this line expected income is equal to the level of 7.5, which is the individual's actual income. Would he choose the uncertainty, represented by point E, or the certainty represented by point G? Clearly, point G must represent a higher indifference curve than point E. (For the given utility function, income level 7.5 has a utility of 71, which is greater than 60). Therefore, the individual will choose point G over point E: he will choose the certainty over the uncertainty. We refer to such an individual as a *risk-averter*: that given the same expected utility, he will choose the certainty over the uncertainty.

Before leaving the certainty equivalent it is worth noting that the *slope* of the line EG in this example is equal to -1 (i.e., the slope of EG $= -(13 - 7.5)/(7.5 - 2) = -5.5/5.5 = -1$). In general, however, the slope is equal to, $-p/(1 - p)$

Marginal rate of substitution

The *marginal rate of substitution* MRS, is the slope of an indifference curve at a point. Furthermore, the marginal rate of substitution is equal to minus the ratio of marginal utilities, as indicated in Chapter 6. Is this true in situations of uncertainty? The answer is that it is similar.

Since two states of the world are being considered which are uncertain, then we must attach to each marginal utility the probability that it will occur. Again, take the two income levels as Y_0 and Y_1, then the marginal utility of these income levels is given by $MU(Y_0)$ and $MU(Y_1)$ respectively. Typical marginal utilities are shown in Column (3) of Table 9.1. Hence, the marginal rate of substitution *at a point* is given by,

$$MRS(Y_0, Y_1) = -pMU(Y_0)/(1 - p)MU(Y_1)$$

To illustrate this, consider again point E in Figure 9.2. The marginal rate of substitution can be calculated as follows:

$$MRS(E) = -(0.5)(10)/(0.5)(1.9) = -5.3$$

Notice also, that in absolute terms the marginal rate of substitution at point E is greater than the absolute slope of the line EG, i.e. $5.3 > 1$.

If we move down the indifference curve denoted $E = 60$ in Figure 9.2 we can readily establish that the marginal rate of substitution declines in absolute value. Thus, at the certainty point where the indifference curve cuts the certainty line (point F), the marginal rate of substitution is given by

$$MRS(F) = -(0.5)(6)/(0.5)(6) = -1$$

while at point H it is,

$$MRS(H) = -(0.5)(1.9)/(0.5)(10) = -0.19$$

Table 9.2 Utility of risk-averse individual

| Y | Risk-Averse and p = 0.575 | | | |
	U(Y)	MU(Y)	E = 60	E = 70
1	23	11.6	111	134
2	33	10.0	96	120
3	43	8.6	84	107
4	51	7.4	73	96
5	57	6.4	63	87
5.45	60	6.0	60	83
6	63	5.5	55	79
7	69	4.7	48	72
7.25	70	4.6	47	70
8	73	4.1	43	66
9	77	3.5	37	61
10	80	3.0	33	57
11	83	2.6	29	53
12	85	2.2	26	50
13	87	1.9	23	47
14	89	1.7	21	44
15	91	1.4	19	42

Change in the probability

In the discussion of crime, presented later in this chapter, particular attention will be paid to the effect of changing the probability of getting caught. In terms of the analysis so far presented, this simply amounts to a change in the probability p.

It has already been established that the indifference map is constructed for a given probability p. Figure 9.1, for instance was constructed under the assumption that p = 0.5. It is highly likely, therefore, that if there is a change in the probability then a *different* indifference map will occur. This is, in fact, the case. To show this, and to illustrate in exactly what way the indifference map alters, Table 9.2 presents similar calculations as those in Table 9.1, with the exception that now the probability of state S_0 occurring is p = 0.575 and the probability of state S_1 occurring is (1 − p) = 0.425.

The situation is drawn in Figure 9.3, where the original indifference curves are E = 60 and E = 70 and the new set are E' = 60 and E' = 70. It is readily seen that the *increase* in the probability raises the absolute slope of any particular indifference curve and that this can be established for all points along the certainty line. Since income levels are the same in both states of the world along the certainty line, then $MU(Y_0) = MU(Y_1)$, hence along the certainty line we have,

$$MRS = -pMU(Y_0)/(1-p)MU(Y_1) = -p/(1-p)$$

Consequently, with p = 0.575,

$$MRS = -0.575/0.425 = -1.35$$

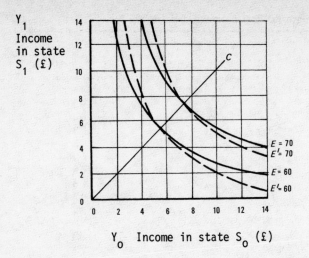

Figure 9.3

which in absolute terms is greater than unity. Furthermore, the new indifference curve for E' = 60 must cut the certainty line at exactly the same point as E = 60. The reason for this is because whether the probability rises or falls, if income is known with certainty then it will be unaffected by any change in the probability. It is only the uncertain points away from the main diagonal that will be affected by any change in the probability.

Two observations are worth making with regard to the new indifference map. First, it is still the case that the situation of certainty will be chosen over the one of uncertainty. Second, the new set of indifference curves are no longer symmetrical about the certainty line. This can be seen in terms of Table 9.2. For the indifference curve E' = 60 two points giving rise to this same level of expected utility are:

$$(Y_0, Y_1) = (4, 8) \text{ and } (Y_0, Y_1) = (8, 3)$$

which are not symmetrical points. Symmetrical indifference curves, for this utility function, are typical only where the probability of each state occurring is the same.

Risk-neutral and risk-taker

So far the analysis has dealt in detail with the individual who is risk-averse. There is not the space to develop in any detail the situation for a risk-neutral individual or a risk-taker. Suffice it to say that a risk-neutral individual has a *linear* utility function while a risk-taker has a convex utility function. The implications for indifference curves are that a risk-neutral individual has linear indifference curves while the risk-taker has indifference curves which are concave to the origin.

Table 9.3 Utility of Risk-taker

			p = 0.5		p = 0.575	
Y	U(Y)	MU(Y)	E = 60	E = 70	E = 60	E = 70
1	31	2.4	89	109	100	123
2	33	2.7	87	107	96	120
3	36	3.2	84	104	92	116
4	40	3.7	80	100	88	111
5	44	4.3	76	96	82	106
6	48	5.0	72	92	76	99
7	54	5.8	66	86	69	92
8	60	6.7	60	80	60	84
9	67	7.8	53	73	50	74
10	76	9.1	44	64	39	63
11	85	10.5	35	55	26	49
12	97	12.3	23	43	10	34

Note: $U(Y) = 15 + 13.5 EXP(0.15Y)$

The risk-neutral individual is not hard to see. If the utility function is linear then marginal utility is constant. So regardless of the level of income $MU(Y)$ is the same. Hence,

$$MRS = -pMU(Y_0)/(1-p)MU(Y_1) = -p/(1-p)$$

Thus, for a given probability the marginal rate of substitution is constant. Hence, the indifferences curves for the risk-neutral individual are straight lines.

For the risk-taker this is more difficult to establish. What is provided is a set of calculations in Table 9.3 similar to those in Table 9.1. From these calculations the reader can draw the utility function and construct indifference curves for the individual in exactly the same manner as in this section.

Having presented all the formal analysis, it is now possible to use it to discuss some economic aspects of criminal behaviour.

An economic model of crime

The general economic approach to crime adopted in this chapter is a model first put forward by Isaac Ehrlich in the United States. This model uses an analysis similar to that employed in analysing household behaviour. In consumer behaviour, outlined in Chapter 6, the consumer had a set of stable preferences. The individual's optimal choice of commodities is obtained by moving to the highest indifference curve subject to the budget constraint. In Chapter 6, it was shown how the individual's equilibrium changed as a result of a change in income or a change in relative prices.

In the remainder of this chapter a similar model to explain some aspects of criminal behaviour is developed. In particular, it is possible to show how an individual decides on:

1 how much time to devote to crime;
2 how the individual's decision is altered when there is an increase in the possibility of getting caught; and,
3 how the individual's decision is altered as a result of an increase in the fines imposed if he is caught.

Our first task, then, is to determine the optimal time spent in criminal behaviour.

Optimal time spent in criminal behaviour

The model depends on a number of assumptions which set limits on its applicability in analysing criminal behaviour. These assumptions will be noted as they occur. The first assumption is that the individual sets aside a fixed amount of time for the purposes of sleep, consumption and leisure and hence devotes a fixed amount of time to obtaining an income. This income may be obtained from legal activities, or from illegal activities, or from a mixture of the two. Legitimate income-obtaining activities include an individual's job, while illegitimate activities include burglary. When a person is engaged in robbing a house he cannot simultaneously be at (legitimate) work, and vice versa. In this sense, the two activities are independent of one another. The analysis, therefore, excludes illegitimate activity undertaken at one's place of employment, but does include many forms of criminal behaviour in which the police are more directly involved.

The second assumption that is made is that there is a fixed total amount of time available over which the decision is made: a day, a week or a month. In the example now to be developed it is a week. Of the 168 hours available, it is further supposed that the individual puts 118 hours to one side for sleep, consumption and leisure, leaving a total of 50 hours for obtaining an income either from legitimate activity, or illegitimate activity or a mixture of the two. One main concern is with how much a person in fact divides his time between these two activities.

A third assumption is that the individual is concerned about the level of income that he could obtain with different allocations of his time. This aspect of the theory is clarified by the example described in Table 9.4. We assume that this individual receives £10 per hour for any period he spends in legitimate employment, while obtaining a 'booty' of £18 per hour for any period he spends in illegitimate activity. However, it is also assumed that if he is caught then he is fined to the extent of eight-ninths of his booty. (It is assumed that the booty itself is not appropriated by the police even if he is caught.)

If this person spends all 50 hours in legitimate activity then he earns a weekly income of £500. If he engages solely in illegitimate activity then he receives an income of £900 if he is not caught, but only £100 if he is caught and fined. This information can be illustrated by means of Figure 9.4. If the individual is engaged solely in legal activity then his position would be represented by point A, which can be thought of as denoting the income of £500 obtained even if he is (erroneously!) caught and given the appropriate (zero) fine – obviously, he gets

Table 9.4 Monetary amounts for different situations

	Legitimate Activity		Illegitimate Activity			Income	
	No. of hours	Total wages	No. of hours	Total 'booty'	Fines if caught	if not caught	if caught and fined
Situation A	50	£500	0	0	0	£500	£500
Situation B	0	0	50	£900	£800	£900	£100
Situation P	12[	£125	37[	£675	£600	£800	£200

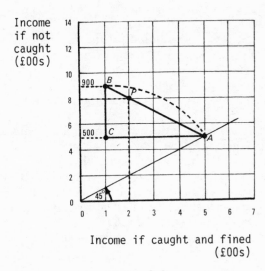

Income if caught and fined
(£00s)

Figure 9.4

no more than £500 if he is not caught. Another way to view point A is that it denotes the individual's income with certainty, since the only uncertainty arises when he engages in illegal activity. Thus, point A lies on a 45° line OA. If the individual is engaged solely in illegitimate activity, then his position would be represented by point B.

Points between A and B in Figure 9.4 show income combinations obtained if the individual divides his time between legal and illegal activities. For instance, at point P an individual spends one-quarter of his time in legal activity and three-quarters in illegal activity. The value on the X-axis is obtained by adding to his legal income of £125, one-ninth of his illegal income of £765 (i.e. £75), since this axis represents the situation where the individual is caught and fined, giving him a total of £200. The level of income if he engages in some illegal activity and is not caught is composed of £125 from legal activity plus £675 from illegal activity, giving a total of £800.

A fifth assumption is that the transformation curve AB in Figure 9.4 is linear. This is a most extreme assumption and could be dropped without altering the predictions of the model (but would complicate the discussion). Ehrlich in fact assumes a transformation curve that is concave to the origin, as shown by the dotted curve in Figure 9.4. However, in the present analysis the assumption of the straight line transformation curve will be retained. Thus, in Figure 9.4, point P gives AP/AB = 3/4, and consequently the ration AP/AB denotes the proportion of *time* spent in illegal activity (which is *only* true if the transformation curve is a straight line). As an individual changes the *time* he spends in either one of the activities he moves along the line AB. Beginning at point A he spends no time in illegal activity. As he moves closer to point B he spends more time in illegal activity. At point B he spends all of his time in illegal activities. The line AB is a constraint, just like the budget line in consumer demand is a constraint, and the solution must be on the line itself.

To obtain the best (optimal) solution for the individual his tastes must be introduced by means of a set of indifference curves. In earlier sections it was demonstrated that indifference curves denote constant expected utility. Two possible indifference curves are shown in Figure 9.5. Furthermore, the indifference curves in Figure 9.5 are convex to the origin. This means that the individual is risk-averse.

It is now possible to combine the transformation line and the indifference curve, as shown in Figure 9.6. The individual will maximize his expected utility by moving to position P on AB so reaching the highest indifference curve possible – subject to the fact that he must lie on the line AB. At this point, he spends three-quarters of his time in illegal activity. His income per week if he were caught and fined would be £200 while if he were not caught his total income from legal and illegal activity would be £800.

In this model it is quite possible to have 'corner solutions'. Two situations are illustrated in Figure 9.7. In Figure 9.7a the individual will maximize his expected

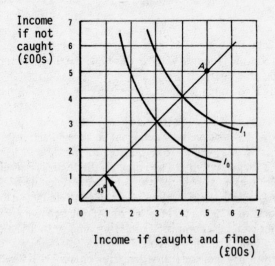

Income if not caught (£00s)

Income if caught and fined (£00s)

Figure 9.5

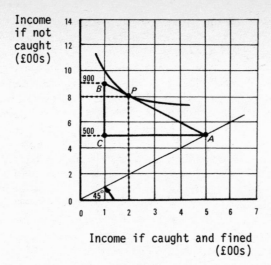

Income if not caught (£00s)

Income if caught and fined (£00s)

Figure 9.6

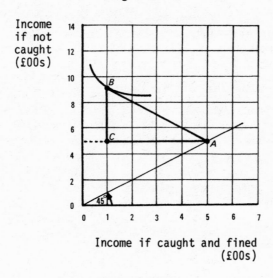

Income if not caught (£00s)

Income if caught and fined (£00s)

Figure 9.7(a)

utility if he positions himself at point B. In other words, this individual, although still risk-averse, will spend all of his time in illegal activity. The reason for this is because the individual is not very risk-averse and the rate at which income can be acquired from illegal activity for each unit of time he gives up doing legal activity is relatively greater. (In other words, the absolute slope of the transformation curve is greater than the absolute slope of the indifference curve at point B.) In Figure 9.7b, on the other hand, the individual is quite risk-averse and spends all of his time doing legal activity. In this instance it is because

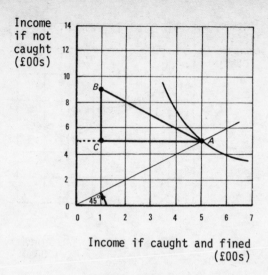

Figure 9.7(b)

the absolute slope of the indifference curve is greater than the absolute slope of the transformation curve at point A.

Increase in the probability of being caught

What is the outcome if there is an increase in the probability of being caught? This may arise either because the police intensify their efforts, or because of an increase in expenditure on the police, so allowing more resources to be used in detection. This in no way affects the transformation line AB, since this line is determined by the income levels in the various situations (see Table 9.4). The probability of being caught, as we explained earlier, is embodied in the indifference curves. Hence a change in the probability of being caught changes the indifference map. In an earlier section it was demonstrated that a rise in the probability of getting caught produces a series of steeper indifference curves, each intersecting the certainty line at the same point as the original set of indifference curves. The result of this is illustrated in Figure 9.8. Consequently, increasing the probability of being caught results in the individual moving from point P to point Q on AB. As the new indifference curves are steeper, the new equilibrium must be to the right of point P along AB. In other words, in general the individual will spend *less* time in illegal activity. In terms of Figure 9.8 the individual will spend half of his time in illegal activity rather than three-quarters of his time.

It is possible for a change in the probability to have no effect. How is this possible? If an individual is at point B, as shown in Figure 9.7a, then the change in the probability of being caught, although making the indifference curves steeper, is not a sufficiently large change to move him away from position B. (In other words, it is still the case that the absolute slope of the transformation curve

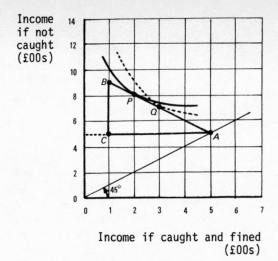

Figure 9.8

is greater than the absolute slope of the new indifference curve at point B.) If, on the other hand, the individual had an optimal solution at point A to begin with, as shown in Figure 9.7b, then a rise in the probability of being caught will simply reinforce his decision to remain at that point and engage in no illegal activity.

Increase in fines

In Britain, fines are imposed by the courts and are set independently of the police. An increase in fines alters the transformation line, as illustrated in Figure 9.9. Before the change in fine the transformation curve is denoted by AB, with

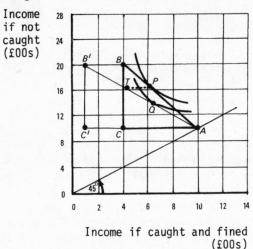

Figure 9.9

point A denoting an income level of £1000 on the 45° line OA and point B representing income levels £400 and £2000 respectively. If the individual engages solely in legal activities then the new penalties will in no way affect him, he will remain at point A. If he engages in full-time crime and goes undetected, then he still stands to gain income £2000; but if he is caught and fined then his income level falls to £100. In this situation the full-time criminal is now typified by point B' and the new transformation line is AB' rather than AB. Since fines in no way affect the preference map, the new equilibrium is at point Q on the line AB'.

The question now arises: Is the time spent in crime at the new situation (AQ/AB') greater, the same as, or less than in the old situation (AP/AB)? So long as point Q is to the right of point T along AB', then less time is spent in crime. (This arises from the fact that AB'B and ATP are similar triangles, hence AP/AB = AT/AB'). It is possible to show this with the help of figures in Table 9.1. Suppose the initial equilibrium is at combination $Y_0 = 5$ and $Y_1 = 11$, which is on the indifference curve for $E = 70$. The marginal rate of substitution at this income combination is $-(6.4)/(2.6) = -2.5$. Now move horizontally across holding income at 11 in state S_1, then the corresponding point for $Y_0 = 2.4$ and $Y_1 = 11$ gives a marginal rate of substitution of $-(9.4)/(2.6) = -3.6$, which is greater in absolute amount. However, the absolute slope of AB' is less than the absolute slope of AB (in fact slope AB $= -1.7$ while that of AB' $= -1.1$), and since the equilibrium is characterized by the marginal rate of substitution equalling the slope of AB', then it follows that the slope of the indifference curve at the equilibrium point Q is less than -3.6. Since indifference curves are convex then a smaller marginal rate of substitution must be tangential at a point to the right of point T. The conclusion is, therefore, for the risk-averse individual then less time is spent in crime as a result of the increase in fines.

The risk-taker

Throughout the discussion so far only the risk-averse individual has been considered. How different are the predictions when the individual is a risk-taker? In terms of our present analysis, a risk-taker is depicted by indifference curves which are concave to the origin rather than convex. In general, a tangential solution along AB for the risk-taker minimizes his expected utility. In all likelihood, he will maximize his expected utility at point B where he engages solely in crime, as shown in Figure 9.10a. In this instance, a rise in the probability of being caught will make the individual even more likely to opt for point B. Similarly, an increase in the fine will reinforce the individual to remain at point B. As indicated by Figure 9.10b, even if the individual is a risk-taker, it is still possible that he will engage in no criminal activity. As shown in Figure 9.10b, the individual will maximize his utility by being at point A. In this case a rise in the probability of being caught could move the individual away from point A; while an increase in the fine will simply leave the individual at point A. What can be noted from Figure 9.10, however, is that for a risk-taker he will, in

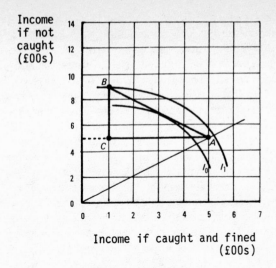

Figure 9.10(a)

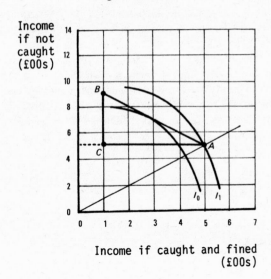

Income if caught and fined
(£00s)

Figure 9.10(b)

this model, either engage in no criminal activity, or will spend all of his time in criminal activity!

Conclusion

What conclusions can be drawn from the above analysis? As already pointed out, the analysis cannot deal with crime undertaken whilst at work, and so does not deal with crime of the 'black' economy type. The distinction is adequately brought out by a shop's loss of articles. 'Shrinkage' is a term denoting employees' acquisitions of goods within the work-place – either in the form of tools, or the goods actually produced or sold. The present model cannot deal with this form of crime. What it can deal with, however, is shop-lifting. The model is more suitable for dealing with crimes involving property which are undertaken outwith a person's employment and this is when the police are more involved.

The separate consideration of the probability of being caught and of increased fines is useful because the former involves the police whilst the latter involves the judiciary, which in the UK are quite separate. However, the analysis shows that an increase in the probability of being caught and an increase in the level of fines both lead to less time being spent in crime for the risk-averse individual. The analysis is purely *qualitative*: it cannot indicate which is more effective in combating crime. This is important. *A priori* reasoning alone about the effects of these two changes cannot come down in favour of one over the other in revealing the deterrent effect. What it suggests, therefore, is that empirical work must be undertaken.

As presented here the model is discussed in terms of income (a flow); but it could be presented in terms of wealth (a stock), as Ehrlich did. This is not important at the elementary level, but it could be important in distinguishing different types of crime, e.g., petty theft as distinct from the 'Great Train Robbery' or the theft of Monet's *Impressionism: Sunrise* in 1985.

A potentially tricky assumption is that the transformation curve AB is linear. However, this assumption was chosen for ease of exposition. Ehrlich does not require this condition, but to include it means that the mathematics become more complex without any real change in the *qualitative* results.

Part III

Firms and their outputs

10

The elements of the theory of the firm

Introduction to the theory of the firm

The scope of the theory of the firm

Part I of this book explained how the equilibrium price and quantity are determined in any market where there are many buyers and sellers of a particular item. In some cases – such as cabbages or raspberries – the buyers are usually households, and in others – such as the services of van drivers or paper boys and girls – the sellers are usually households; accordingly, Part II examined the factors which determine the demands and supplies of households. However, in some cases – such as the services of van drivers – the buyers are producers, and in others – such as cabbages – the suppliers are producers. Part IV is concerned with demands by producers, and the present Part III with the supplies of producers.

The material covered in this introduction is often termed 'the theory of the firm'. In some respects this is a helpful term, for it emphasizes that it is concerned only with producers which are firms, that is to say businesses which produce goods and services for sale. It should be appreciated that there are three main groups of producers which are not firms, and the following pages say little of relevance for them. These three groups are government departments, which provide (but do not sell) services such as state schools and defence, charities, which provide (but do not sell) services such as accommodation in children's homes and life-boat rescues, and households which provide (but do not sell) goods and services for themselves, such as home-grown beans and housework. However, the term 'the theory of the firm' is perhaps a little misleading in that it does not emphasize that it is concerned only with what firms supply and not with what they demand.

Much of this chapter will be concerned with analysing the behaviour of those firms which operate in the sort of markets considered in Part I, that is markets or industries where there are many sellers (and buyers) of an identical or homogeneous product. It will be shown how it is possible to derive an individual supply curve for each of these producers, and also how the market supply curve can be derived from these individual supply curves; in turn, this market supply curve interacts with the market demand curve to fix the equilibrium market price actually faced by each supplier, and the individual firms' supply curves show how much each supplier will supply at that particular price. However, the chapter will also look at firms operating in industries where there are many suppliers each producing slightly different products, and at firms which are the sole producers of particular products, that is monopolists. It will be shown that it is not possible to derive supply curves for these producers or for the markets in which they operate, and for this reason it is not appropriate to use the analysis of Part I to show how the prices of these producers' products are determined; however, the theory outlined in the present chapter does show how the equilibrium price of each of these producers' products is determined along with the equilibrium quantity each will produce.

It is clear that the theory of the firm is concerned with how firms will behave in terms of deciding matters such as their output levels and prices. In order to develop a theory of behaviour, it is always necessary to make some assumptions about what the person or institution whose behaviour is concerned is seeking to achieve. For instance, the theory of household behaviour in Part II assumed that households seek to achieve maximum possible utility or satisfaction. The theory of the firm outlined here makes the assumption that individual firms seek to achieve the maximum possible level of profits. Two points need to be made about this assumption.

First, profit maximization may not be the goal of all firms. In discussing this point, economists often divide firms into three groups as follows: (1) those which are owned by central or local governments and are known respectively as public corporations (that is, broadly speaking, the nationalized industries) and municipal corporations; (2). incorporated or limited liability companies, which are owned by shareholders and run by directors appointed by the shareholders, and which put 'Ltd' or 'plc' after their names; and (3) unincorporated businesses owned and run either by one person in the case of sole proprietors or up to a legal limit of 20 in the case of partnerships. Broadly speaking, it is felt that profit maximization is likely to be pursued more assiduously by firms in group (3) – where the owners who will receive the profits also run the firm – than by firms in group (2) – where there is some separation of ownership and control, though this separation is blurred a little by the fact that company directors usually own some shares in their companies and so have some incentive to seek high profits in order to secure high dividends. However, it is arguable that the theories presented here give useful insights to firms in both groups (2) and (3); on the other hand, they offer less help in explaining the behaviour of firms in group (1) since governments seldom if ever ask firms owned by them to seek to maximize their profits; accordingly, the theories presented here are not really applicable to this group.

Secondly, it is perfectly possible to develop theories of firms' behaviour which assume they have different goals from profit maximization, though such theories are not examined in this book.

Profits and costs

The central proposition of the theory of the firm presented here is that firms will set the level of output which enables them to maximize their profits; in other words, they will set the level of output where the difference between their total revenue and their total cost is the maximum possible. It should be noted that where a firm is unable to make a profit at any level of output, then it will set that level of output where its loss is the minimum possible. In order to understand these goals a little more deeply, it is necessary to explain precisely what economists mean by profits and costs. The situation is slightly different for unincorporated and incorporated businesses, and can be described for these two cases with the help of Table 10.1, which refers to ZIP (the Zinc Ingot Partnership), and Table 10.2, which refers to UGH (the United Gum Holdings plc). These, of course, are hypothetical concerns, and it is supposed that ZIP supplies zinc ingots whilst UGH supplies chewing gum. The tables relate to a particular week in which, for simplicity, it is supposed each firm produced and sold six tonnes of output at a price of £440 per tonne to produce a total revenue of £2,640. The question is how much of this £2,640 had to be spent on costs and how much was left over as profits.

The tables give one answer to this question in column (A), an answer often suggested on business accounts (though the accounts shown here are simplified by ignoring matters such as stocks of finished goods and raw materials, taxes – such as value added tax – which may be levied on ZIP's and UGH's products, and any subsidies which they may attract). Broadly speaking, costs here are reckoned to cover the expenditure incurred by ZIP and UGH in the week concerned in producing their output that week; this covers their labour costs – wages and salaries plus other items such as national insurance contributions and contributions to pension funds on behalf of employees – plus their purchases of intermediate goods and services – that is items purchased from other producers and rapidly 'used up' in production, a heading which includes money spent on items such as raw materials, energy, transport, advertising and rent. These costs amount to £460 and £1,000 respectively for both firms, and so £1,460 in all, and this leaves each firm with what are known as *gross trading profits* of £1,180. In each case, some of these profits (£80) are used to pay interest on borrowed money, and some (£100) – under the heading depreciation – are regarded as being set aside to replace items of capital as and when they wear out and need to be replaced, the amounts shown being the amount by which existing capital falls in value (in the period concerned in the account) as a result of wear and tear and obsolescence. In the case of ZIP (and all unincorporated businesses), all remaining trading profits (here £1,000) are held to be paid to the owners; but in the case of UGH, some (£500) is paid in corporation tax, some (£300) is paid as dividends to the shareholders who own it and the rest (£200) is retained, probably to enable the firm to buy more capital in an effort to expand. (At present most incorporated UK businesses are liable to pay corporation tax at a rate around 50 per cent of their gross trading profits after allowing for interest and depreciation, and in UGH's case the tax is taken to be 50 per cent of £1,180 less £80 and £100, which is 50 per cent of £1,000.)

As it happens, economists do not use in their theories the conventional view of profits shown by the gross trading profits in column (A). In their view, it is more

Table 10.1 Account for Zinc Ingot Partnership (for a particular week)

£

Income £	(A) Conventional view of costs and profits		(B) Economists' view of costs and profits		(C) Fixed costs	(D) Variable costs
	Costs		*Costs²*			
Sales of goods & services produced 2640	Labour	460	Labour	400 1860	0	460
	Intermediate goods & services	1000 1460	Intermediate goods & services	1000	20	980
			Interest	80	80	0
			Depreciation	100	100	0
			(Some) Payments to owners	220	220	0
	Profits¹		*Profits³*			
	Interest	80	(Remaining) Payments to owners	780		
	Depreciation	100				
	Payments to owners	1000 1180		780		
Total 2640		2640		2640	420⁴	1440⁴

Notes:
1 This is known as the gross trading profit.
2 This covers the costs shown in column A plus part of the profits shown in column A; profits included here are termed normal profits.
3 This covers part of the profits shown in column A; profits shown here may be termed excess profits, pure profits or supernormal profits.
4 Total fixed costs plus total variable costs equal total costs shown in column B.

Table 10.2 Account for United Gum Holdings plc (for a particular week)

£

Income £	(A) Conventional view of costs and profits		(B) Economists' view of costs and profits		(C) Fixed costs	(D) Variable costs
	Costs		*Costs*[2]			
Sales of goods & services produced 2640	Labour	460	Labour	460	0	460
	Intermediate goods & services	1000	Intermediate goods & services	1000	20	980
		1400	Interest	80	80	0
			Depreciation	100	100	0
	Profits[1]		(Some) Dividends	200	200	0
	Interest	80	(Some) Corporation tax	200	200	0
	Depreciation	100		2040		
	Corporation tax	500	*Profits*[3]			
	Dividends	300	(Remaining) Dividends	100		
	Retained earnings	200	(Remaining) Corporation tax	300		
		1180	Retained earnings	200		
				600		
Total 2640	**2640**		**2640**		**600**[4]	**1440**[4]

Notes:
1. This is known as the gross trading profit.
2. This covers the costs shown in column A plus part of the profits shown in column A; profits included here are termed normal profits.
3. This covers part of the profits shown in column A; profits shown here may be termed excess profits, pure profits or supernormal profits.
4. Total fixed costs plus total variable costs equal total costs shown in column B.

helpful to regard a firm as making a profit only if its total revenue exceeds the amount which would be necessary to persuade the owners to set up the firm if they were starting all over again. It is reasonable to suppose that no-one would be tempted to set up a firm if its total revenue failed to cover the interest on the money borrowed to help set it up or the depreciation sums needed to replace capital when it wears out. Accordingly, these two items are shown as costs in the economists' definition of costs in column (B). In the case of ZIP, some of the owners' earnings are also considered to be costs. The point is that these owners will doubtless have used some of their private savings to set the firm up, and they may well work for the firm, so they would not want to set the firm up unless their earnings from it at least equalled the interest (or dividends) they would have got by doing something else with their savings together with the salaries (or wages) they would have got by working in other jobs; it seems ZIP's owners reckon they would have got a total of £220 by putting their savings elsewhere and working in other jobs and this is regarded as a cost which leaves the remaining £780 of the payments to them as a profit. (Note that the figure of £220 must be estimated by seeing how much of their savings ZIP's owners had put into it, and by working out how much they could earn in other jobs; this information could not be found by looking at conventional accounts, no matter how detailed they were). In the case of UGH, some (£200) of the dividends are regarded as a cost. The amount concerned is the minimum amount of dividends the initial shareholders would have hoped for in order to tempt them to use their savings to buy shares in UGH and so enable it to raise the money needed to get it going; obviously this amount depends on the return these people could have got by investing their money elsewhere. (Note that this amount could be estimated by talking to the original shareholders but not by looking at conventional sets of accounts for UGH). The remaining dividends (£100) are regarded as profits in column (B). Some of UGH's corporation tax (£200) is also held to be a cost; the point is that in order to pay the £200 of dividends regarded as a cost, UGH has to earn a gross trading profit of £580, for £80 must be paid in interest, £100 must be set aside for depreciation and 50 per cent of the £400 left must be paid in corporation tax; in other words, UGH cannot pay the necessary £200 in dividends unless it is doing sufficiently well that it also has to pay £200 in tax. The remaining corporation tax (£300), plus all retained earnings, are regarded as profits in column (B).

The division of total revenue in column (B) is different from that in column (A). In essence, part of the column (A) accounting profits – a part termed *normal profits* – are treated in column (B) as a cost. The remaining column (A) profits, the part which is regarded as profits by economists and shows up as profits in column (B), may be termed *pure profits, supernormal profits,* or *excess profits.*

Fixed costs and variable costs

All the costs shown in column (B) in Tables 10.1 and 10.2 relate in some way to the acquisition of inputs. This is clear enough in the case of labour costs (such as wages) and intermediate goods and services (such as raw materials). As for interest and depreciation, these are costs incurred respectively in connection with borrowing to buy extra capital and with money saved ready to replace worn-out capital. As for the cost part of ZIP's owner's earnings, this covers the costs involved in encouraging those owners to work for ZIP and to use some of their savings to help buy its capital; and the cost part of UGH's dividends (and corporation tax) covers the cost of persuading shareholders to buy shares and so help the company to buy its capital.

Now it is possible to vary the amounts of some inputs used much more quickly than the amounts of others. Economists use the word long-run to refer to whatever period of time is necessary for a firm to be able to vary the amount of all inputs used and hence to be able to vary the amount spent under each category of cost. The term short-run refers to a period of time in which some but not all inputs are variable. In the case of ZIP and UGH, the short-run might be a period of up to one year and the long-run a period greater than that. Column (C) in each table shows how much of the column (B) costs are fixed costs – that is, how much of the column (B) figures is devoted to spending on inputs whose amounts cannot be varied within one year – and column (D) shows how much of the column (B) costs are variable costs – that is, how much of the column (B) figures is devoted to spending on inputs whose amounts can be varied within one year.

The division of the column (B) costs between columns (C) and (D) reflects some arbitrary but plausible decisions. All labour costs here are taken to be variable, but in principle some – perhaps relating to workers on long-term contracts – might have been fixed. Most spending on intermediate products is taken to relate to variable costs – for the amounts of raw materials, transport and so on, can usually be varied quickly – but some is taken to relate to fixed costs – for instance, the firms may have contracts with companies from whom they rent property which makes it hard to vary quickly the amount of space they rent, and they may not be able readily to vary the amount of machinery and buildings which have to be insured. Interest and depreciation are regarded as fixed costs here, for it may not be easy to pay off loans quickly and so reduce the amount of interest which has to be paid, and it may not be easy quickly to sell off plant, buildings or machinery and so reduce the amount by which these fall in value over time. Likewise, ZIP's owners' earnings and UGH's dividends are held to be fixed costs. In each case, this is partly because it may not be easy quickly to sell off plant, buildings and machinery and give the proceeds to the firm's owners, thereby reducing in turn the amount of earnings or dividends they would regard as equivalent to what they could get by putting (the now smaller amount of) their savings in these firms elsewhere. In ZIP's case, it is also because its owners might not be able quickly to stop working for ZIP and start working for another concern.

One important point about fixed costs should be noted. They are fixed in that they relate to inputs whose amounts cannot readily be altered, and thus the firms themselves cannot readily alter their spending under these headings. However, the amounts shown under those headings can alter rapidly as a result of factors beyond the firms' control. For instance, a rise in insurance premiums, rents or interest rates can instantly raise the sums devoted to the relevant items. Again, a rise in the general level of wages and salaries would raise the payments ZIP's owners would have wanted to be persuaded to work for it, and a rise in the general level of interest and dividends could raise the returns they and UGH's shareholders regard as the amount they would want to be persuaded to put their money in these concerns if they were starting again.

Short-run analysis

Short-run costs and output

 If a firm wishes to maximize its profits, then it will seek that level of output where the gap between its total revenue and its total costs is greatest. Accordingly, it will be anxious to know what its total revenue and its total costs would be at each possible level of output. The present section will consider how its costs might vary with output in the short-run, that is, over the period of time in which some inputs are fixed whilst others are variable. The following sections will consider how revenue might vary with output, and then take variations in costs and revenue together to predict how firms will behave. These sections are followed by others which consider how costs might vary with output in the long-run and predict how firms will behave in the long-run. In general, the analysis will consider how a firm might set its weekly output level; a weekly period is taken only for convenience, and identical conditions would apply to firms where it was usual to fix (say) hourly, daily or monthly output levels.

In the short-run, a firm has some fixed costs (taken throughout the rest of this chapter to include normal profits) and some variable ones, since (as explained earlier) some inputs will be fixed and others variable. Columns (1) and (2) of Table 10.3 show the total fixed costs (TFC) and the total variable costs (TVC) of a hypothetical firm for various weekly output levels; column (3) shows the sum of these which represent its total costs (TC). It will be seen that at an output of, for example, six tonnes a week, this firm has a fixed cost of £420, a variable cost of £1,440 and a total cost of £1,860. As it happens, similar figures applied to ZIP in Table 10.1 in the week concerned there. By referring to columns (C) and (D) of Table 10.1, it is possible to see just what sort of items are covered in columns (1) and (2) of Table 10.3.

For reasons which are explained later, the theory of the firm makes little direct use of figures for TFC, TVC and TC; instead, it concentrates chiefly on what are termed average and marginal costs, and these will be considered in turn. Figures for average costs are given in columns (4), (5) and (6), which relate respectively to *average fixed costs* (AFC), *average variable costs* (AVC) and *average total costs* (AC). At any given output level (Q), say six tonnes per week, the average costs show how much of the total costs can be attributed to each unit of output. The TFC for an output of six tonnes is £420, so £70 (that is TFC/Q) can be attributed to each unit of output; hence the AFC at this output level is £70. The TVC for an output of six is £1,440, so £240 (that is TVC/Q) can be

£

Table 10.3 Costs for a hypothetical firm

Output per week-tonnes (Q)	(1) Total fixed costs (TFC)	(2) Total variable costs (TVC)	(3) Total costs (TC)	(4) Average fixed costs (AFC)	(5) Average variable costs (AVC)	(6) Average costs (AC)	(7) Marginal fixed cost (MFC)	(8) Marginal variable cost (MVC)	(9) Marginal cost (MC)
0	420	0	420	–	–	–			
1	420	320	740	420	320	740	0	320	320
2	420	520	940	210	260	470	0	200	200
3	420	660	1080	140	220	360	0	140	140
4	420	840	1260	105	210	315	0	180	180
5	420	1080	1500	84	216	300	0	240	240
6	420	1440	1860	70	240	310	0	360	360
7	420	1960	2380	60	280	340	0	520	520

attributed to each unit of output; hence the AVC at this output level is £240. The TC for an output of six is £1,860; so £310 (that is TC/Q) can be attributed to each unit of output, hence the AC at this output level is £310. Note, though, that AC at any output can be found instead by adding the AFC and AVC at that output level. An important point to grasp is that if only the AFC, AVC and AC figures are known for a given output level, then it is possible to work out the TFC, TVC and TC; given the AFC of £70, the AVC of £240, and the AC of £310 at an output level of six tonnes, it is possible to work out the TFC of £420 (as AFC.Q), the TVC of £1,440 (as AVC.Q) and the TC of £1,860 (as AC.Q).

Columns (4), (5) and (6) show the AFC, AVC and AC for each possible output level. The numbers recorded there are plotted in the appropriately labelled curves shown in Figure 10.1. The AFC curve slopes down from left to right all the way; this simply reflects the fact that as Q rises, so the TFC can be regarded as being spread over more units of output.

The AVC curve in Figure 10.1 has a U-shape which is most readily explained by considering a simple firm such as an apple orchard which uses just four inputs; for the present example, three of these (trees, ladders and baskets) will be held to be fixed and the fourth (labour) will be held to be variable. Suppose each picker costs the firm £100 for a week's work. It is possible that employing just one picker would result in 5 tonnes being picked per week, at a TVC of £100 and an AVC of £20 per tonne. Now, employing three pickers might result in more

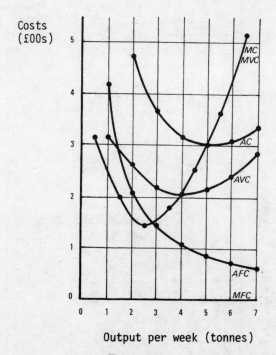

Output per week (tonnes)

Figure 10.1

than 15 tonnes being picked, as these pickers might be able to work more effectively as a team than by working separately, so that perhaps 20 tonnes would be picked at a TVC of £300 and an AVC of £15 per tonne. However, employing five men might not raise total output very much as there might be relatively few apples left, and it would be necessary for the pickers to spend much time picking small hard-to-reach ones, so maybe only 25 tonnes would be picked at a TVC of £500 and an AVC of £20 per tonne. In short, the AVC curve will fall for a while if employing more variable input(s) facilitates teamwork but rise when employing more of these inputs results in small additions to output owing to there being limits to what can be achieved with constant amounts of the fixed inputs. ⟶ Diminishing marginal returns.

The AC curve in Figure 10.1 is also U-shaped. This curve effectively shows AFC plus AVC, and AC must be high at low outputs when both AFC and AVC are high, and AC must be high at high outputs when the high AVC starts to off-set the low AFC. If AC is high at both ends, then it is likely to be U-shaped! ✓

Marginal costs refer to how much costs *change* when output *changes by one unit*. Columns (7), (8) and (9) of Table 10.3 refer to *marginal fixed cost* (MFC), *marginal variable cost* (MVC) and *marginal total cost* (MC) respectively; the numbers are put between the lines of the other columns since, for example, the numbers in the row between a quantity of 5 and 6 show what happens to costs when output is changed by one unit from 5 tonnes to 6 or 6 tonnes to 5. The MFC column shows what happens to TFC when Q changes by one unit, and it has a lot of zeros since TFC (as shown in column (1)) does not alter when Q alters; for instance, TFC stays put at £420 when output changes from 5 to 6 or 6 to 5. The MVC column shows what happens to TVC when Q changes by one unit and is more interesting than column (3); the £360 between outputs of 5 and 6 shows that TVC would alter by £360 if Q changed from 5 to 6 or from 6 to 5 (£360 being the difference between the TVC of £1,080 if Q is 5 and £1,440 if it is 6). The numbers in the MC column show what happens to TC when Q changes by one unit, and it turns out that its numbers must be the same as those shown in the MVC column; this is because it is only variable costs which alter when Q alters, so, for instance, the change in TC when Q changes from 5 to 6 or 6 to 5 is £360 (the difference between £1,500 and £1,860) which is the same as the change in TVC. The lines for MFC, MVC and MC are plotted on Figure 10.1. The MFC line follows the horizontal axis, since MFC is always zero, whilst the MVC and MC lines coincide with one another because the MVC and MC numbers in the tables are the same at any particular output level.

The MC or MVC curve in Figure 10.1 is U-shaped for reasons which can best be explained with reference to the apple orchard mentioned earlier. At low out-puts, the firm has few pickers. In these circumstances, taking on extra manhours of pickers' labour progressively increases the scope for teamwork so that, for a while at least, each extra tonne picked may require fewer extra hours labour than the last and so add less to total costs; in short, marginal costs may fall as output rises when output is low. At high outputs, the firm has many pickers and so the possibilities for teamwork may have been fully exploited. In these circum-stances, each rise in output by one tonne may mean picking even smaller and more awkwardly placed apples, so that each extra tonne needs more exta man-hours work than the last and so adds more to total costs; in short, marginal costs are likely to increase as output rises when output is high.

An important point to note about the MVC (or MC) curve is that it goes through the lowest points of both the AVC and AC curves. This can be explained by regarding the MVC (or MC) curve as showing (at each output level) how much TVC (or TC) changes when Q is raised by one unit. So long as the addition to TVC (or TC) is less than the AVC (or AC), then the production of the extra unit will reduce the firm's AVC (or AC) when it is produced; in other words, so long as the MVC (or MC) curve is below the AVC (or AC) curve, so the AVC (or AC) curve must be sloping downwards. Conversely, if the addition to TVC (or TC) is more than the AVC (or AC), then the production of the extra unit will raise the firm's AVC (or AC) when it is produced; in other words, so long as the MVC (or MC) curve is above the AVC (or AC) curve, so the AVC (or AC) curve must be sloping upwards. Put together, these facts mean the MVC and MC curve must pass through the bottom points of the AVC and AC curves.

In general, economists regard all firms as facing short-run fixed and variable costs which give rise to curves with the shapes shown in Figure 10.1, though it is usual to omit the AFC curve and to estimate AFC at any Q (if this is necessary) as the gap between AC and AVC at that point. These AC, AVC and MC curves are plotted again in Figures 10.2 and 10.3. which can be used respectively to

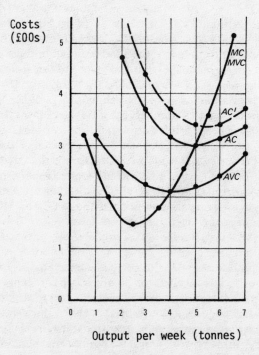

Output per week (tonnes)

Figure 10.2

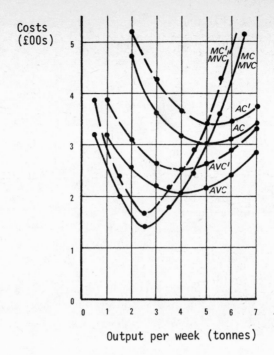

Output per week (tonnes)

Figure 10.3

show what would happen (a) if a firm's fixed costs (at each output level) changed – perhaps as a result of an increase in rents – and (b) if a firm's variable costs (at each output level) changed – perhaps as a result of increased in raw material prices and wage rates. To explore these two possibilities, the reader might care to produce (a) a revised Table 10.3 in which all the numbers in column (1) rose by 50 per cent from £420 to £630, and (b) a revised Table 10.3 in which all the numbers in column (2) rose by 20 per cent.

In case (a), there would, of course, be no change to the TVC or MVC numbers, but clearly the TC and hence AC numbers would rise. The MFC numbers would continue to be zero (as TFC would now stay put at £630 for each Q) and MC would be unaltered because both MVC and MFC are unaltered. Accordingly, the result is as shown in Figure 10.2 in that only that the AC curve moves, the new one being labelled AC′. Like AC, this will be intersected at its lowest point by the MC curve. Of course, a fall in fixed costs would cause AC to move down.

In case (b), there would, of course, be no change in the AFC or MFC numbers; but both the AVC and MVC numbers would rise, as in turn would both AC and MC (which equals MVC). Accordingly, the result is as shown in Figure 10.3 in that the AVC, AC and MC (or MVC) curves all move upwards. The new MC′ must intersect the new AVC′ and AC′ curves at their lowest points. Naturally, a fall in variable costs would cause the AVC, AC and MC curves all to shift down.

Revenue and output

In order to predict the output which a given profit-maximizing firm will set, it is necessary to know not only how its total costs will vary with its output, but also how its total revenue will so vary. The revenue position depends a little on the relationship between the firm and its industry. Many relationships are possible, but economists tend to focus on four: arguably, most firms have a relationship which approximates to one of these. The main features of these four types of firm are outlined below.

First, there is the perfect competitor which is a firm that is one of many relatively small firms producing an identical or homogeneous product. This sort of firm operates in a market where the price is fixed by the forces of supply and demand considered in Part I. A critical feature of this firm's situation is that it will sell its output only at the price fixed in the market; in effect, it faces a horizontal demand curve like the one shown in Figure 10.4 which applies to a firm that faces a market price of £440 for each unit of output. It must be stressed that this curve shows the individual demand curve for the output of one particular firm, and does not show the total market demand curve for that product. To see why the firm's individual demand curve is horizontal, suppose that the firm in Figure 10.4 is one of many zinc ingot producers operating in the market for zinc ingots where the forces of market supply and market demand outlined in Chapter 1 have established a price of £440 per tonne. Now, if this particular firm tries to set a price above that amount, then it will sell no ingots at all, for its customers can go to one of the many other firms in the industry; hence the demand curve in Figure 10.4 shows that sales would be zero at any higher price. Of course, the firm could, in principle, sell its ingots for a price below £440 per tonne, but, as it forms but a small part of the market, it is regarded as being able to sell as much as it wants at £440 per tonne (without significantly altering the

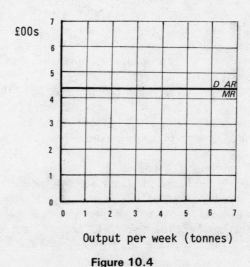

Output per week (tonnes)

Figure 10.4

market supply curve for ingots and so not cutting their market price) so in practice there is no point in ever setting a lower price. This point is reflected in the horizontal demand curve which indicates a willingness by buyers to buy from this one (relatively insignificant) firm as much at £440 per tonne as it chooses to sell at that price. An implication of a horizontal demand curve is that if the firm did choose to set a price even slightly below the market price, then it would be deluged with orders from customers who previously made purchases from its rivals. There is much debate among economists about whether, in fact, any firms do face a horizontal demand curve as assumed in perfect competition. For instance, one zinc ingot producer might find that it could put its price up a little way above £440 without losing all its customers; for some customers might still prefer it on grounds of finding its location geographically convenient, and others might be unaware that ingots were available at a slightly lower price else-where. However, it is arguable that many firms especially in the markets for fresh foods and primary materials (such as iron ore or timber), operate in condi-tions very close to perfect competition.

Secondly, there is the monopolistic competitor which is a firm that is one of many relatively small firms producing slightly different products. The differen-tiation may occur because of some clear differences in type and quality, as might arise between restaurants in a large town, or for other reasons such as location where this is important to consumers, as might arise between filling stations in rural areas. The critical point here is that when each producer's product is slightly different then, unlike the perfect competitor, it will find that there are a number of different prices it could set without either selling nothing or being deluged with orders; in other words, it faces a downward sloping demand curve like the one shown in Figure 10.5 (though the one shown there is a straight line purely as a matter of convenience). The key points here are that a rise in price will not generally drive all customers away, as some will prefer the product of the firm concerned, and that a fall in price will result in a modest increase in

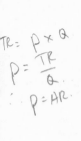

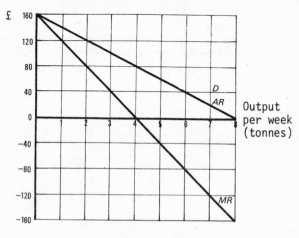

Figure 10.5

customers rather than in a deluge since many of its rivals' customers will prefer to stick with their slightly different products.

Thirdly, there is the oligopolist, which is one of a few firms in an industry. In some industries, such a those for national daily newspapers or luxury cars, there may be substantial product differentiation between oligopolists' products, whilst in others, such as sugar or frozen peas, there may be little; even so, differentiation in the minds of consumers is likely in the latter cases because people will become familiar with brand names, and may stick loyally to one brand even if it sells at a slightly higher price than another. The critical feature in an oligopoly situation is that as there are few firms in the industry, so some firms (if not all) will be relatively large. It follows that a cut in price by one firm could have an appreciable affect on the demand for the products of the others, and they might feel obliged to react by cutting their own prices; in turn, the original firm might react to these reactions. This makes analysis a little tricky, and oligopoly is not considered in this book.

Fourthly, there is a monopoly which is the sole producer of its product. It is tempting to imagine a monopoly as some giant firm of perhaps multinational proportions. In fact, multinationals generally produce a wide range of products. To economists, such enterprises should be regarded as a conglomeration of many firms each with its own product and each, perhaps, operating in a highly competitive situation. Of course, there are some large firms which are monopolists (or near-monopolists) though some of the most obvious large monopolists in the UK are those concerned with the supply of electricity, and coal which are nationalized businesses and not generally profit-maximizing. There are a few large non-nationalized monopolists, such as British Telecom, but most privately owned monopolists are small unglamorous local monopolies, such as ferries. It is clear that a monopolist is likely to find that it could raise its price without losing all its customers, and cut it without being swamped by new orders, so, like a monopolistic competitor, it too will have a downward sloping demand curve of the sort shown in Figure 10.5. Note, though, that the downward slope for the monopolist arises simply because a fall in price encourages people to buy more of the product concerned (as with any downward sloping market demand curve) and not, as was the case with the monopolistic competitor, because customers are lured away from other firms in the industry; there are no other firms in the monopolist's industry!

Revenue curves

The preceding paragraphs have explained that this chapter is concerned with perfect competitors, which face horizontal demand curves, and with monopolistic competitors and monopolists which face downward sloping ones. The revenue situation in these two different cases can be explored further with the help of Tables 10.4 and 10.5. Table 10.4 refers to the perfect competitor of Figure 10.4 which finds it can obtain a price of £440 per tonne for any quantity of ingots it wishes to sell, a situation reflected by the numbers shown for output per week (Q) and – in column (1) – price (P). Column (2) shows the total

Table 10.4 Revenue for a perfect competitor

£

Output per week-tonnes (Q)	(1) Price per tonne (P)	(2) Total revenue (TR)	(3) Average revenue (AR)	(4) Marginal revenue (MR)
0	440	0	–	
				440
1	440	440	440	
				440
2	440	880	440	
				440
3	440	1320	440	
				440
4	440	1760	440	
				440
5	440	2200	440	
				440
6	440	2640	440	
				440
7	440	3080	440	

revenue (TR) it would receive for each level of output (found as P.Q). As will become clear shortly, economists are more interested in the concepts of *average revenue* and *marginal revenue*. Column (3) shows the average revenue (AR) it would get for each level of output. This shows how much of the total revenue can be attributed to each unit of output and is simply TR/Q which equals P; notice that at any output (say 6) the TR (of £2,640) can readily be found by multiplying that output Q (here 6) by the AR (£440). Column (4) shows the marginal revenue (MR) which is the amount by which TR would *change* if output *changed* by one unit. The numbers here are put between the lines; they indicate that if output changed by one unit from, say, 3 tonnes to 4 or 4 tonnes to 3, then TR would alter by £440, which is the price of the unit of output concerned. The AR and MR numbers for this firm are plotted on Figure 10.4; they coincide with the demand curve shown there.

Table 10.5 refers to the firm shown in Figure 10.5 which could in principle be a monopolistic competitor or a monopolist. The output and price columns show that this firm would sell nothing at a price of £160 (or more) per tonne and that it would be able to sell more the lower its price is below £160 per tonne. Column (2) shows the total revenue (TR) from each level of sales (found as P.Q) and column (3) shows the average revenue (AR) from each unit sold; as before, AR is simply TR/Q and equals P. Column (4) shows the marginal revenue (MR) and reveals, for instance, that TR would change by £60 if Q changed from 2 tonnes to 3 or 3 tonnes to 2. Some MR figures are preceded by a minus sign. These occur along the range of prices where a fall in price leads to a fall in TR (though not, of course, to a fall in Q) and where a rise in prices leads to a rise in TR; in short, MR is negative when demand is price-inelastic. The AR and MR curves are plotted in Figure 10.5. As in Figure 10.4, the AR curve coincides with the demand curve, but in contrast to that figure, the MR curve here is below the AR curve; in cases like this, where AR is a straight line, MR is also a straight line, and starts at the

Table 10.5 Revenue for a monopolistic competitor or monopolist

£

Output per week-tonnes (Q)	(1) Price per tonne (P)	(2) Total revenue (TR)	(3) Average revenue (AR)	(4) Marginal revenue (MR)
0	160	0	–	
				140
1	140	140	140	
				100
2	120	240	120	
				60
3	100	300	100	
				20
4	80	320	80	
				−20
5	60	300	60	
				−60
6	40	240	40	
				−100
7	20	140	20	
				−140
8	0	0	0	

same point as AR on the vertical axis, but cuts the horizontal axis at a quantity half the one found where AR cuts this axis.

It is worth considering why the MR curve in Figure 10.5 is below the AR curve. Suppose the firm wishes to raise its weekly output (Q) from 2 to 3. To sell 3 tonnes a week instead of 2, it must cut the price of its product from £120 to £100. It is clear that the third unit sold each week will bring in £100. However, the total weekly revenue will not rise by that £100 because the first two tonnes sold each week are now sold for £100 each instead of £120 and so bring in £200 instead of £240. In short, the increase in weekly revenue is less than the amount brought in by the third unit sold each week, and in turn MR (here £60) is less than the new price (or AR) now being set (£100). This is a different situation from that of the perfect competitor, for it can sell one extra unit each week without cutting its price at all, and so its weekly TR would rise by the price of the extra unit sold, and in turn its MR would equal that price (or AR).

The perfect competitor in the short run

The most straightforward way of setting out to find which level of output would secure the most profit for a perfect competitor would be to plot curves showing the total revenue and the total cost for each possible level of output. Figure 10.6 does just this for a perfect competitor whose total cost figures are taken to equal those shown by the figures in column (3) of Table 10.3, and whose total revenue figures are taken to equal those shown by the figures in column (2) of Table 10.4. The problem with this diagram is that it is hard to see at a glance precisely where the gap between the TR and TC curves is largest. It seems to be at an output level of about 6 tonnes per week; supposing it were exactly 6 per week, then the TR at

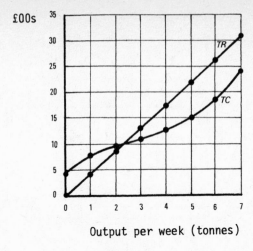

£00s

Output per week (tonnes)

Figure 10.6

this output of £2,640 can be estimated from the figure, as can the TC of £1,860, and hence the total excess profit is £780. (These figures correspond to those for ZIP in Table 10.1, and the reader can refer to that table and the adjacent text for fuller details of what the costs and excess profit figures mean.)

However, it is much more convenient to have a figure where two lines cross at the profit-maximizing output. As it happens, a figure with this feature can be constructed by using MC and MR curves; indeed, this is why previous sections have explained the concepts of marginal revenue and marginal cost. Figure 10.7 shows such a figure for the firm considered in Figure 10.6, the MC curve being based on column (9) of Table 10.3 and the MR curve being based on column (4) of Table 10.4. It can be shown that maximum profits (or lowest losses) are generally earned at the right hand intersection of the MC and MR curves, so in this case the best level of output (Q) is indeed 6 tonnes per week. The explanation of this result is that at any higher Q, say 7, the firm would be in a position where MC exceeds MR, which means a change in Q by one unit would alter TC more than TR, so that a fall in Q would cut TC more than it would cut TR and hence it would lead to a bigger profit; conversely, at a lower Q, say 5, MR would exceed MC, which means a change in Q by one unit would alter TR more than it would raise TC, so that a rise in Q would raise TR more than it would raise TC and so it would raise profits. Incidentally, the left-hand intersection of MC and MR is the minimum profit (or maximum loss) position, for a rise in Q from this point would raise TR more than TC and so raise profits, and a fall in Q would cut TR less than TC and so also raise profits.

Now while the MC and MR curves enable the profit maximizing Q to be found, they do not enable either the TR and TC obtained at that point, or the total profit, to be estimated. This difficulty can quickly be remedied by adding in the AR and AC curves based on column (3) of Table 10.4 and column (8) of

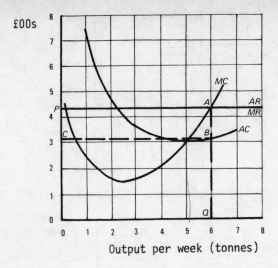

Figure 10.7

Table 10.3, the former of course coinciding with the MR curve. Indeed, this is why previous sections have explained the concepts of average revenue and average costs. At an output of 6, it can be seen that the AR is £440, and the TR is this multiplied by Q (£2,640) which is represented by the area OQAP. The AC of this output is £310 so the TC is this multiplied by Q (£1,860) which is represented by the area OQBC. The total excess profit is the difference between TR and TC and is represented by the area ABCP.

It was noted earlier that it is possible to derive a supply curve for a perfect competitor, and this can be done by considering how much such a firm would produce at each possible price. Figures 10.8a to f show how much output (Q) one perfect competitor might produce at six possible prices shown respectively as P_6, P_5, P_4, P_3, P_2, and P_1. At each of these prices the firm would have a horizontal demand curve at that price, and this would represent its AR and MR curves at that price. The relevant AR and MR curves are shown on each figure. To work out its output, it is necessary to show also some information about its costs, and so its AC, MC and AVC curves are shown in each figure; these cost curves are the same in each case since the only thing being changed here is the price at which the firm is able to sell its product.

In general, the output to consider is the one at the intersection of MR and MC. This occurs at Q_6 in Figure 10.8a and at Q_5 in Figure 10.8b. It follows that each of the points marked with large dots on these figures will be on the firm's supply curve, for they show Q_6 would be produced at a price P_6 and Q_5 at a price P_5. These figures show situations broadly similar to that in Figure 10.7; however, the price (or AR) is closer to AC at Q_5 in Figure 10.8b than it is at Q_6 in Figure 10.8a, and Q_5 is less than Q_6, so less excess profit is earned in Figure 10.8b where the price is lower. In Figure 10.8c, the relevant intersection of MR and MC is at

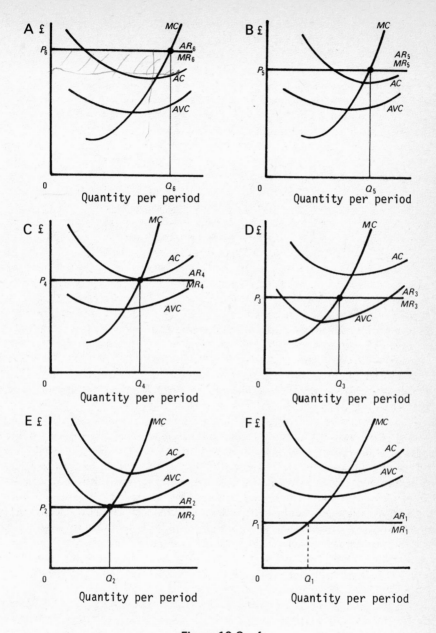

Figure 10.8a–f

Q_4. Here P (or AR) just equals AC so no excess profit is earned; instead the firm breaks even, and the point marked with the dot is said to be the *break-even point*; the firm will be happy to break even and produce Q_4 at a price P_4 so this point is also on the supply curve.

The situation is more interesting at the price P_3 shown in Figure 10.8d, for the AR curve here is below AC at every output level indicating that there is no output level at which the firm can break even. The firm would clearly be unhappy and would doubtless consider selling its assets of plant, buildings and machinery and hence ceasing to exist; it would refrain from this course of action only if it thought the market demand for its product might rise before long, and so raise the price for its product to P_4 or more, or if it thought it could in time achieve lower cost curves, perhaps by installing more or better machinery. However, the present section of this chapter is concerned with the short run in which some inputs are fixed; thus it is concerned with the period of time in which existing assets cannot be sold and new capital cannot be acquired, so the question arises of what output will be set each week in this period which could last several months or more. The output Q_3 needs considering as this is at the relevant intersection of MR and MC; but might it be better to produce nothing at all? In fact, it is better to produce Q_3 and the dot in the figure shows that Q_3 would be produced at the price P_3. The point is that if the firm had a zero output, and hence a zero TR, then it would – in the short run – have a loss equal to its unalterable TFC; but with an output of Q_3, the AVC is below the price (or AR) so that TVC (that is Q.AVC) is less than TR (that is Q.AR). This means that its variable costs are more than covered by its revenue so that some revenue can be put towards paying the fixed costs; in turn, the loss would be less than TFC and so less than the loss made with a zero output.

Similar considerations come into play at the lower price P_2 in Figure 10.8e, and the even lower price P_1 in Figure 10.8f, for in each case a loss is again inevitable. The outputs to consider are Q_2 and Q_1. At Q_2 in Figure 10.8e, price (or AR) just equals AVC so TR would just equal TVC; with this output, there would be a loss equal to TFC, just as there would (always) be with a zero output. The firm could toss up between a zero output and Q_2, though the dot on Figure 10.8e suggests it would produce Q_2. However, this dot is at what is termed the *shut-down point*, for at any lower price a zero output would be produced, and the firm would not only be up for sale (unless it expected things to improve) but would shut down whilst waiting for someone to buy its assets (or whilst waiting for things to improve); that is to say it would lay off its staff and buy no intermediate products (except where it had long-term contracts) so that its TVC equalled zero and it produced nothing. Such a situation can be seen in Figure 10.8f. The most promising positive output here is Q_1 where MR equals MC, but at Q_1 the AVC exceeds the price (or AR) so that TVC would be above TR; in other words, producing at Q_1 would mean not even covering variable costs and so having a loss larger than the loss of TFC which arises with a zero output. Thus there is no dot at Q_1 in Figure 10.8f.

Looking at the dots in Figures 10.8a–e, it can be seen that they show that the firm's supply curve is the upward sloping part of its MC curve above the point where it cuts the AVC curve.' In principle, there is a supply curve for each per-fectly competitive firm and the relationship between these curves and the market supply curve is shown for a hypothetical case in Figure 10.9. The left-hand dia-gram here relates to a typical firm whose supply curve (S_F) shows how much it would produce at each possible price; at a price of, say, £100 it will supply 30 tonnes per week. The central figure presents the market supply curve (S_M) and shows how much would be supplied by the industry at each possible price; for instance, at a price of £100 all the firms in the industry would between them supply 1,000 tonnes per week. (This information could be readily derived from the supply curves of all individual firms, if these were available, since it would be possible to work out from them how much all the firms would supply between them at each possible price.) The market supply curve intersects with the market demand curve (D_M) to give the equilibrium price of, as it happens, £100 per tonne, so the typical firm faces a horizontal demand curve (D_F) – which is also its AR and MR curve – at this price and it will produce 30 tonnes per week. In the interests of symmetry, the right hand diagram shows the situation for a typical consumer in this market. The demand curve there (D_c) show how much this particular consumer would demand at each possible price; at a price of £100 per tonne this consumer wants 5 kg per week. The market demand curve shows how much all buyers between them want at each possible price, the total at £100, for instance, being 1,000 tonnes per week. Note that the individual consumer effectively faces a horizontal supply curve (S_c) at the level of the equilibrium price, for no producer will sell her anything for a lower price (after all, all firms can sell as much as they wish at the equilibrium price and so will not sell anything for less) whilst the consumer can buy as much as she wishes at the equilibrium price (for her purchases will always be too small to move the market demand curve significantly and so too small to raise the equilibrium price, no matter how much she is likely to buy).

This discussion of perfect competitors in the short run will be concluded by considering three types of event which will alter the profit-maximizing output of a typical firm. These are all illustrated in Figure 10.9. First, the number of firms in the industry could change. It takes time for individual firms to start up or run down, a point which might suggest that the number of firms in the industry could change only in the long-run; however, it is clear on reflection that the typical firm could in principle find the number of rivals in its industry changing on a weekly or even daily basis. A fall in the number of firms will shift the market supply curve to S_M' which raises the equilibrium price (to £150 per tonne in this case) and hence shifts the firm's demand curve to D_F' and causes it to produce more (40 tonnes per week); incidentally, the consumer faces the new supply curve S_c' and buys less (4 kg per week). Of course, a rise in the number of firms would reduce the price and cause the firm shown to supply less and the buyer to buy more.

Secondly, the market demand curve might shift, perhaps as a result of a change in tastes. Assume the market started at its initial equilibrium, and that now tastes change in favour of the product concerned so that the demand curves for the typical consumer and the market shift right to D_C' and D_M'. This raises

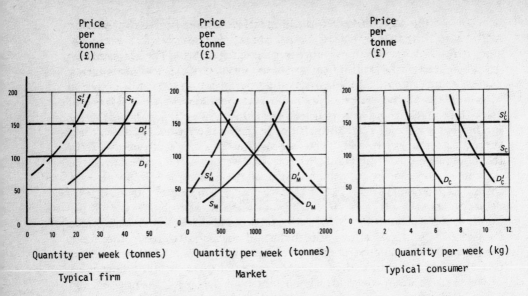

Figure 10.9

the equilibrium price (to £150 per tonne in this case) which means the firm's demand curve moves up to D_F' and it supplies more (40 tonnes per week); incidentally, the consumer faces the new supply curve S_C' (and ends up buying 6 kg a week, shown where S_C' cuts D_C'). Of course, a fall in demand would have the opposite results.

A third way in which the situation can be affected is if the firm's variable costs alter. Suppose they rise. It was shown in Figure 10.3 that this would raise the firm's MC curve, its AVC curve and its AC curve; it follows that it also raises its supply curve as this coincides with the MC curve above its intersection with the AVC. Once again, suppose the market starts at its initial equilibrium, and suppose to begin with that only the firm concerned faces a rise in variable costs; in this case its supply curve becomes S_F' and it produces less at 10 tonnes per week. In practice, any event which raises its variable costs (perhaps a rise in wage rates or input costs) is likely to affect all other firms in the industry too; thus it will shift all their individual supply curves and hence shift the market supply curve to, say, S_M'. This will raise the price (to £150 per tonne in this case) and means the firm will face the new demand curve D_F' and so will supply 20 tonnes per week; this is still below its initial output. Of course, a fall in variable costs in the industry has the opposite results.

An important point to note is that neither the firm's short-run position nor the market is affected by a change in fixed costs. It was shown on Figure 10.2 that a change in fixed costs will not alter a firm's MC or AVC curves and so it will not alter its supply curve; in turn, it would not affect anything shown in Figure 10.9. Of course, it would reduce the profits (or raise the losses) that individual firms get (at their unchanged output levels).

It is possible to say a little more about the effects of these events. Suppose the firm was initially making excess profits, so that at an output of 30 tonnes per week its AC was less than the price (or AR). Clearly a fall in the price caused by a fall in demand or by new firms entering the industry could result in the firm making a loss and considering closure in the long-run; so, too, could a rise in total costs (and hence in the AC curve) as a result of a rise in either variable or fixed costs. In the short-run, the firm would shut down if it found its price (or AR) was below its AVC, that is if the price results in the firm's demand curve passing below the lowest point on its supply curve; this could come about if the price it faced fell or its variable costs rose, but not if its fixed costs rose alone.

Monopolistic competition and monopoly in the short-run

As with perfect competition, it would be possible to explore the short-run equilibrium or profit-maximizing outputs of monopolistic competitors and monopolists with diagrams showing TR and TC curves; but the problems discussed in connection with Figure 10.6 – that no curves cross at the optimum output – mean that the analysis usually centres on diagrams based on MR and MC curves. Figure 10.10a shows such a diagram which could apply to a monopolistic competitor or to a monopolist; this diagram has the AR (or demand) curve and AC curve as well as the MR and MC curves. For the reasons explained earlier (in the context of the perfect competitor) the right-hand intersection of MR and MC generally shows the profit-maximizing output which here is 2 tonnes per week. Once the firm has decided on this output, it will naturally sell it for the highest price it can obtain, and this can readily be found from the point on the demand curve vertically above its output level, and is the price £60 per tonne; the point is that the demand curve shows that the output of 2 can be sold for the price £60 whilst any higher price will result in lower sales. This price also shows the AR at this output level, so the total revenue of £120 is represented by the area of the rectangle with two sides of dashed lines. Total costs are given by output times the average cost (which at the output 2 is £45 per tonne) or £90. Thus the total excess profit here is £30.

The firm in Figure 10.10a produces the output 2 at a price £60. It might be thought that a supply curve could be found by seeing how much it would supply at each possible price. Unfortunately, it is not possible to construct a neat supply curve because the firm would not always supply one particular quantity at any given price. To see this, consider what the firm shown in Figure 10.10a would do if it faced in turn the demand (or AR) curves shown in Figures 10.10b, 10.10c and 10.10d; in the interests of simplicity, these curves are shown as straight lines and the AC curve is omitted in each case. Note that the cost curves are in the same place each time and that each MR curve is drawn correctly so that it starts at the same point on the vertical axis as the relevant AR curve and intersects the horizontal axis midway between the origin and the intersection of AR with that axis. In the Figure 10.10b case, the firm sets a lower output (1 tonne per week) than in Figure 10.10a but happens to have the same price (£60 per tonne) as in Figure 10.10a. Taken together, Figures 10.10a and 10.10b might suggest the

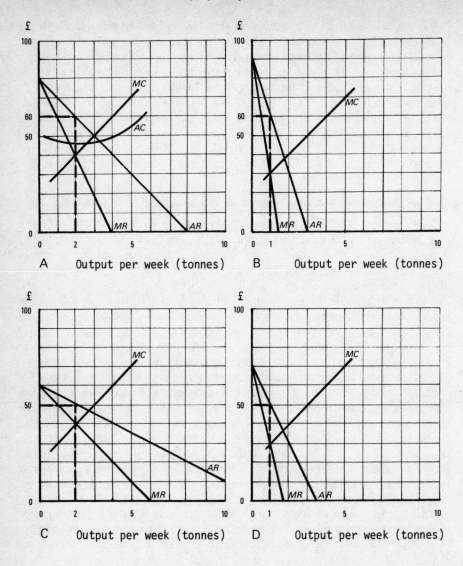

Figure 10.10a–d

firm has a horizontal supply curve, and always sets a price of £60 per tonne; but Figures 10.10c and 10.10d show it could set the lower price of £50 and yet have either the quantity 2 tonnes or 1 tonne per week as the case may be. In fact, a whole range of different outputs could be set at each of a whole range of prices and so it is not possible to draw a supply curve; supply curves for firms can be found only for perfect competitors where, at any one possible price, there is just one output level which would ever be set. It follows that a supply curve for a

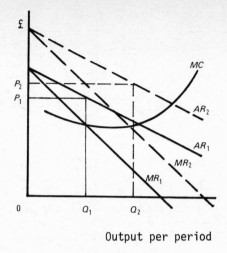

Figure 10.11

monopolistically competitive industry cannot be derived, since there are no individual firms' supply curves to base it on; also, there is no supply curve for a monopolist to use to represent the supply curve for its industry.

The output of the firms under consideration here can vary for similar reasons to those applying to perfect competitors. Consider the firm shown in Figure 10.11 which at present faces the revenue curves labelled AR_1 and MR_2 and sets the output Q_1 (where MR_1 cuts MC), which it sells at a price P_1. A rise in demand would shift the (demand or) average revenue curve to AR_2, and hence shift the marginal revenue curve to MR_2 and result in a higher quantity Q_2 (where MR_2 cuts MC) with the higher price P_2. Conversely, a fall in demand would shift the (demand or) average revenue curve from AR_2 to AR_1 and so result in a shift in the marginal revenue curve from MR_2 to MR_1 and cut output (from Q_2 to Q_1) and price (from P_2 to P_1). The demand curve could shift as a result of changes in the general level of demand for the products of the industry in which the firm operates, for this would affect most – if not all – firms in a monopolistically competitive industry, and would obviously affect the monopolist in a monopolistic industry. The demand curve for a typical monopolistic competitor would also tend to rise if other firms left the industry (as their customers would switch to the remaining firms) and fall if new entrants joined (as some customers of the typical firm would switch to the new entrants).

The output of a monopolistic competitor or a monopolist would also react to changes in its variable costs, such as rises in wage rates or raw material prices. Suppose the firm in Figure 10.12 initially has the marginal cost curve MC_1, and sets the output Q_1 (where MR cuts MC_1) which it sells at a price of P_1. A rise in the firm's variable costs shifts the marginal cost curve upwards (as shown in Figure 10.3) to MC_2, so the firm now sets the lower output Q_2 (where MC_2 cuts MR) which it sells for the higher price P_2. In practice, any event such as a rise in

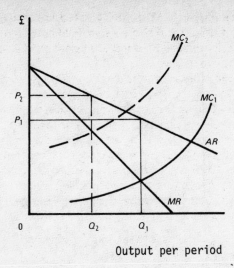

Figure 10.12

raw material prices which raised one monopolistic competitor's variable costs would also be likely to raise the variable costs and, in turn, the prices of its rivals. As just noted, rises in their prices would actually tend to raise the demand curve for its own products, thus putting further upwards pressure on its price but reducing the tendency for it to cut its output. Of course, a fall in variable costs would have the opposite effects to a rise.

Note that a rise in fixed costs, which might result from higher interest rates or insurance premiums, does not alter the MC curve (as shown in Figure 10.2).

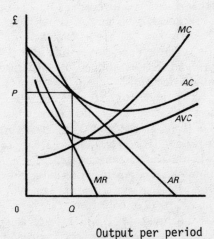

Figure 10.13

Thus if the firm in Figure 10.12 started with the curve MC_1 and an output of Q_1 sold at a price P_1, then a rise in fixed costs would not affect the MC curve and so would not affect its output or price, though it would, of course, reduce its profits or raise its losses.

Of course, a monopolistic competitor or a monopolist might find that falls in demand or rises in costs resulted in it ceasing to make an excess profit. Figure 10.13 shows such a firm in the break-even position where the output, fixed at Q by the intersection of MR and MC, leads to a price (or AR) of P (at the point on the demand curve above Q) which just equals the average cost of this output; thus total revenue (of AR.Q) just equals the total cost (of AC.Q). Any further rise in variable or fixed costs would raise AC, and any further fall in demand would reduce AR, so that losses would be made. The firm would then consider selling all its capital unless it thought things would improve. If a fall in demand shifted AR down till it touched AVC, or a rise in variable costs shifted AVC up till it touched AR – a position shown in Figure 10.14 – then the firm would be at the shut-down point. The output level Q where the AR and AVC curves touch is the best positive output level, for here AR equals AVC so that TR equals TVC and losses equal TFC, just as they would with a zero output. At any positive output level other than Q, AR would be less than AVC so TR would be less than TVC. Since Q is the best positive output level, MR and MC must cut at that level as shown. The firm could toss up between a short-run output level of Q per week or shutting down and producing nothing each week. Either way, the firm would seek to sell its assets as soon as possible unless it expected things to improve. Even if the firm decided not to shut down in the Figure 10.14 position, it would subsequently do so if there was the slightest rise in AVC or fall in AR.

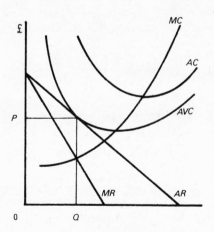

Output per period

Figure 10.14

Long-run analysis

Long-run costs

The previous sections of this chapter have shown how profit-maximizing firms will set their output levels in the short-run, that is, for the period of time in which some inputs are variable so that the amounts used can readily be adjusted to the levels desired, whilst others are fixed and cannot be so varied. In the case of the firms shown in Figures 10.7 and 10.10, for example, the short-run profit-maximizing outputs might be maintained each week for a year, or even several years, if some inputs (such as plant) were fixed for that long. In essence, the rest of this chapter considers what weekly output would be set in the long-run when the firm has had time to adjust its use of *all* inputs to the desired levels. As before, weekly outputs are used for convenience; the analysis could equally well be expressed in terms of hourly, daily or monthly output (or any other period) for firms where this would be appropriate.

The key assumption so far has been that firms will set whatever short-run output secures the maximum profit, that is, the biggest gap between total revenue and total cost. Likewise, the key assumption in what follows is that firms will seek in the long-run whatever output level secures the maximum profit. This output level can easily differ from the best short-run level for one simple reason, namely that the greater flexibility in the long-run over input levels means that the total cost of each output level is generally lower in the long-run than in the short-run; in turn, the profit generated by each output level is also different. The rest of this section will consider how costs may be related to output in the long-run. The following sections will build on this to see how firms will fix their output levels in the long-run.

As with the analysis of short-run costs, it is usual to use figures showing

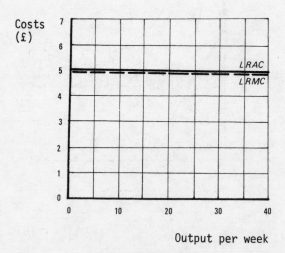

Output per week

Figure 10.15

average and marginal costs rather than total costs. For the moment, the discussion will focus on average costs. Figure 10.15 shows a possible long-run average cost (LRAC) curve for a firm. This indicates, for example, that, given time to adjust all its inputs to the appropriate levels, it could produce 10 units a week for an average cost of £5 or a total cost of £50, that it could produce 20 units a week for an average cost of £5 or a total cost of £100, and that it could produce 40 units a week for an average cost of £5, or a total of £200. This horizontal LRAC seems very plausible. After all, it seems possible that if a firm could produce 20 units a week for £100, then, by eventually halving its use of all inputs, it could produce 10 units a week for £50, and by eventually doubling its use of all inputs it could produce 40 units a week for £200.

However, economists seldom consider LRAC curves like the one in Figure 10.15. More frequently, they use a U-shaped one rather like that shown in Figure 10.16. This one suggests that the firm could produce 10 units a week at an average cost of £7, or £70 in all, whilst 20 units could be produced at £5 each or £100 in all, and 40 units at £6 each or £240 in all. One implication is that if the firm expanded from a small weekly output, then it would initially find its average cost falling, so that its total costs rose proportionately less than output. This situation is termed *internal economies of scale*; this term arises because the firm is enjoying economies (or falls in average costs) as a result of an event internal to (or inside) the firm, namely a change in its scale (or size) of operations. These economies occur often, sometimes because an increase in the scale of output enables a firm to purchase specialist machinery or labour, and sometimes because an increase in scale has inherent advantages; the classic example relates to container ships where a doubling of length, breadth and height could mean using just four times as much steel for a ship which has eight

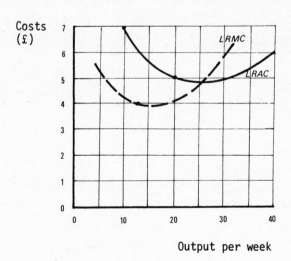

Figure 10.16

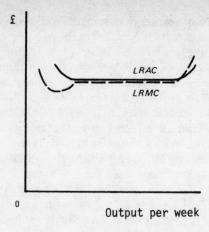

Figure 10.17

times the carrying capacity. (There is a more extensive discussion of economies of scale in Chapter 12.)

Another implication of the U-shaped LRAC is that if scale is expanded beyond the level of the lowest point of LRAC, then average costs rise so that total costs rise proportionately more than output. This situation is termed *internal diseconomies of scale*. There is limited evidence for these; but it is certainly possible that management costs could rise proportionately more than output, in which case these diseconomies might well occur. Consider, for example, a firm operating one plant (with 100 employees) which wished to double its output; it might find it needed not only a new plant (with 100 more

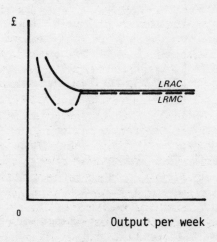

Figure 10.18

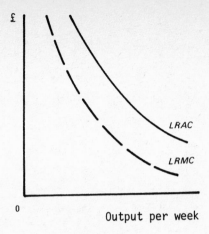

£

LRAC

LRMC

0

Output per week

Figure 10.19

employees to run it) identical to the first, but also new extra staff to co-ordinate the two plants. In practice, LRAC curves could take either of the shapes shown in Figure 10.15 or 16, or even the 'saucer' shape of Figure 10.17, the 'L shape' of Figure 10.18 or the 'backwards-J' shape of Figure 10.19, but the U-shape will be used in the examples which follow.

There is a long-run marginal cost (LRMC) curve associated with each LRAC, and such LRMC curves are shown (dashed) on Figures 10.15 to 19. These curves show the long-run marginal cost at each output level; that is to say, they show at each output level how much total weekly costs would change if weekly output changed by one unit from that level and if the firm was given sufficient time to alter the amounts used of all inputs. This is rather different from the concept underlying the MC curves in earlier figures which related to short-run marginal costs; these showed how much total weekly costs would change at each output level if weekly output changed by one unit from that level and if the firm was given time to alter the amounts used of only some inputs. The LRAC and LRMC curves are related in the same way as AC and MC ones, in that the LRMC lies below LRAC when LRAC slopes down to the right and lies above it when it slopes upwards to the right (and so the LRMC passes through the minimum point of a U-shaped LRAC curve). When the LRAC has no slope, as occurs throughout in Figure 10.15 and for parts of Figures 10.17 and 10.18, then the LRMC is neither above the LRAC nor below it, but coincides with it.

It is useful to understand the relationship between a firm's long-run and short-run cost curves. This is best explained with the help of an example such as a lead ingot producer. Suppose lead ingot producers use four main inputs, namely lead ore, labour, electricity and furnaces. The first three inputs may be taken to be variable in the short-run, whilst the number of furnaces is fixed. Of course, all inputs can be varied in the long-run. The firm's LRAC may be supposed to have a U-shape like the one in Figure 10.20; the LRMC is omitted

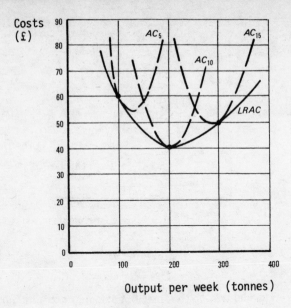

Figure 10.20

for simplicity. This LRAC curve shows the lowest average cost attainable by the firm for all levels of output given time to alter all its inputs including furnaces. Thus 100 tonnes a week could be produced at an average cost of £60 provided the firm can have, say, 5 furnaces; 200 tonnes a week can be produced for £40 each with, say, 10 furnaces; and 300 tonnes a week can be produced for £50 each with, say, 15 furnaces.

It is interesting to consider what the cost of each output level would be in the short-run when the number of furnaces is fixed. Not surprisingly, this depends on how many furnaces the firm has. Suppose it has 10. Clearly it could produce 200 tonnes a week at £40 each, but it would not be able to produce 300 tonnes for as little as £50 each, for to do so requires 15 furnaces; instead, it must try to run its 10 furnaces for many hours a day, perhaps involving payments to its employees of high overtime or night-time shift wage rates, and perhaps it must have a number of maintenance engineers permanently on standby so that break-downs can be readily remedied. Nor could it produce 100 tonnes a week for as little as £60 each, for to do so requires 5 furnaces; it might actually find it best to use only 5 of its 10 furnaces, but the other 5 would still need to be insured, and interest on any loans taken out to purchase them would still have to be paid. The short-run average cost curve AC_{10} shows the cost of each level of output when the firm has 10 furnaces. This touches LRAC at the one output (200 tonnes a week) where 10 is the ideal number of furnaces, but it is otherwise above LRAC. Likewise AC_5 and AC_{15} show respectively the costs of each output level when there are 5 and 15 furnaces; again, these touch LRAC at the output levels where 5 and 15 are the ideal furnace numbers, but are otherwise above LRAC. These

AC curves indicate, for example, that an output of 100 tonnes, which can be secured most cheaply with 5 furnaces, would be cheaper with 10 furnaces than with 15 since there would be even more costs relating to idle furnaces with 15 than with 10. Also, an output of 300 tonnes, which can be secured most cheaply with 15 furnaces, would be cheaper with 10 furnaces than with 5 since there would be even more need for overtime and so on with 5 than with 10. Of course, it would be possible to add in further short-run AC curves for all possible furnace numbers. Like the three shown in Figure 10.20 each would touch LRAC at just one point and be above the LRAC as all other points.

It follows that any firm has a single LRAC with an associated family of (short-run) AC curves. The whole family of curves will move if the cost of any input changes. Suppose LRAC in Figure 10.21 represents the initial LRAC for a lead ingot producer; the short-run ACs are omitted for simplicity. Now a rise in the price of any input (say ore) would make each output level more expensive to produce, and LRAC would move up, perhaps to LRAC' (and of course all the short-run ACs would also move up with it since the costs of each output level with, say, 10 furnaces would be higher than before). Conversely, a fall in the price of any input would shift LRAC down, perhaps to LRAC" (and, of course, all the ACs would move down with it). Incidentally, it would be possible for the lowest points of LRAC", LRAC and LRAC' to occur at rather different output levels.

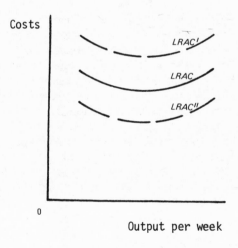

Figure 10.21

When input prices rise and LRAC shifts up, a firm is said to suffer *external diseconomies* since factors beyond its control (input prices) have made production more costly. Conversely, when input prices fall and LRAC shifts down, it is said to enjoy *external economies*. Now some input prices will be sensitive to the scale of the firm's industry. For instance, lead ore prices might well rise if new firms entered the industry and raised the demand for ore, and if this occurred then the existing firms would be said to suffer *external diseconomies of scale*; on the other hand, if new firms enabled lead ore shippers to purchase giant container ships and hence deliver ore to users at lower prices, then existing firms would be said to enjoy *external economies of scale*. Of course, many input prices such as wage rates, interest rates, electricity prices and so on, could well change frequently without any change in the scale of the firm's industry.

These economies and diseconomies relating to changes in input prices are often termed *pecuniary economies* and *pecuniary diseconomies*. However, LRAC could fall even if all input prices stayed put. This could happen if there was some technological progress. For instance, a chemical might be found which could be added to lead ore to speed up the refining process thereby reducing the cost at all output levels. This would cause LRAC to shift down, but here the firm would be enjoying a *technological economy* rather than a pecuniary one.

Perfect competitors in the long-run

It is now possible to consider what weekly output a typical perfect competitor will aim to produce in the long-run. Consider the firm in the left-hand part of Figure 10.22. It faces the LRAC shown, with the associated LRMC, and at present it has a given number of fixed inputs which put it on the short-run AC shown with the associated short-run MC. Its short-run individual supply curve could be derived from its MC, and along with the individual supply curves of its competitors could be used to derive the industry (short-run) market supply curve, S, shown in the right hand figure. This intersects with the market demand curve, D, to give the current equilibrium price, P, which results in the firm facing the horizontal AR and MR curve shown in the left-hand figure. In the short-run, the firm will produce Q_1 per week, where MR cuts MC; at higher outputs, MC is greater than MR indicating that a fall in output would cut costs more than revenue and so raise profits, whilst at lower outputs MR exceeds MC indicating that a rise in output would raise revenue more than costs and also

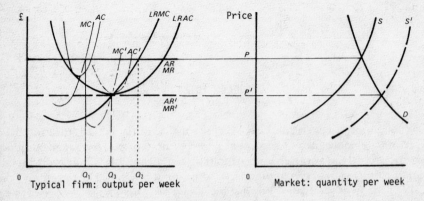

Figure 10.22

raise profits. However, looking at MR and LRMC it can be seen that in the long-run (when all inputs can be varied) successive rises in weekly output could be secured from Q_1 which would raise total revenue more than total costs (since LRMC is below MR until the output level Q_2) and hence raise total profits.

On this reasoning, it is arguable that the firm would seek the output Q_2 in the long-run. However, the firm will not actually set this output in the long-run for the simple reason that the price will not stay at P in the long-run. In its short-run position at Q_1, the (typical) firm shown is earning excess profits, for at Q_1 it is clear that AR exceeds AC so that TR (equal to AR.Q_1) will exceed TC (equal to AC.Q_1). When the typical firm in an industry earns excess profits, new firms are likely to wish to enter the industry; to understand why, recall that when a firm earns excess profits then it is earning more profits than would be necessary to persuade its owners to set it up if they were starting again, and hence it will be earning more than is necessary to tempt other similar people to set up similar firms. It is assumed in perfect competition that new firms can readily enter the industry, and so, in turn, that the industry size will indeed rise if typical firms are making excess profits. This will shift the (short-run) market supply curve, S, to the right thus forcing the price down.

How far will the price fall? It will fall to the level shown by P′ when the typical firm has a new AR′ and MR′ curve which just touches the lowest point of its LRAC. Why does the market supply curve move to the position shown by S′ which secures the price P′? The reason is straightforward. If fewer firms had entered, then S would have moved less far and the new price would be above P′, indicating that the new AR and MR curve would be above some points on LRAC and showing in turn that for a range of output levels the typical firm could still earn excess profits; the industry will not settle down in such a position in the long-run, for with excess profits still possible new firms would continue to enter. On the other hand, had so many new firms entered that the new supply curve was to the right of S′, then the price would be below P′ and the firm's new AR and MR curve would be below LRAC at all points, showing in turn that a loss would be made at all output levels; the industry will not settle in such a position in the long-run, for with losses being made some firms would leave the industry so that the market supply curve would shift left and the price would rise.

It follows that in the long-run the industry size must be such that the price will be P′ and the firm will face the revenue curve labelled AR′ and MR′. Given this marginal revenue curve, it will fix its weekly output in the long-run at Q_3 where LRMC cuts MR′. Moreover, it will adjust those inputs which can be altered only in the long-run so that it is on the new short-run cost curves AC′ and MC′; note that its new short-run equilibrium is also at Q_3 where MC′ cuts MR′. Note, too, that the firm will be just breaking even, for at Q_3 it finds AR′ just touching (and so just equal to) both AC′ and LRAC. This is an inevitable long-run result in a competitive industry where any (necessarily temporary) excess profits lure new firms in.

The effects of a change in the price of one of the industry's inputs can be readily seen. Suppose, for instance, that wage rates rose. In this case, each firm's LRAC would rise and so each would make a loss instead of breaking even. Some firms would leave the industry, causing the (short-run) market supply curve to shift left and the price to rise. This would continue until the price rose to the level of the bottom point of the remaining firms' (new) LRACs so that, once again, they were just able to break even.

A perfectly competitive firm does not have a long-run supply curve, for in the long-run the firm can face only one price, (P' in Figure 10.22) and it will set the one output (Q₃ in Figure 10.22) where it can just break even. However, there *is* a long-run supply curve for the *industry*, and this can be derived by seeing what happens to the long-run equilibrium of a typical firm and its industry if there is a change in demand. This is done in Figure 10.23. Initially, the market has settled at a long-run equilibrium with the price P (given where the present short-run market supply curve S cuts the market demand curve D) and industry output A. The typical firm finds the price P gives it the AR (and MR) curve shown so that its long-run equilibrium is output Q. Suppose it has indeed adjusted the inputs which can be adjusted only in the long-run so that its present short-run cost curves are those shown by AC and MC. It will produce the output Q and will be just breaking even. If market demand rises, say to D', then the price in the short-run will rise to P'. This will give the firm a new average and marginal revenue curve shown by AR' (and MR') and, in the short-run, it will produce at the higher output level Q' where MR' cuts MC. It will be making excess profits, since AR' exceeds AC at Q'. Consequently, new firms will join the industry, shifting the (short-run) supply curve to the right. This could well continue until the supply curve settled at S' restoring the original price P, so that as far as the firm is concerned, the final output will be at Q once again. As for the industry, the price in the long-run has returned to the original level whilst output has risen from A to B. Subsequent rises in demand could, in the long-run, result in further rises in the industry's output whilst leaving prices, in the long-run, at P; this possibility is shown by the industry's long-run supply curve labelled LRS.

However, the long-run industry supply curve might not be horizontal, and

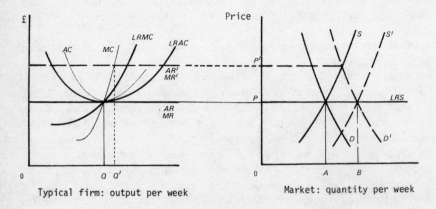

Figure 10.23

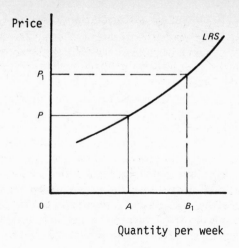

Figure 10.24

Figures 10.24 and 10.25 show two alternatives. In each case the industry is initially in a long-run equilibrium and producing output A at a price of P when demand rises. This rise inevitably causes the price to rise (as in Figure 10.23) and stimulates new entrants. But in Figure 10.24 it is supposed that these new entrants force up the price of some inputs causing external diseconomies of scale for existing firms. This pushes up all their LRAC curves and means that entries will stop when the price is at the bottom of these new curves; this will be at a higher price than P, say P_1. Maybe industry output will settle at B_1. The LRS curve shows that this industry could have long-run equilibrium outputs of A and B_1 at prices of P and P_1 respectively. Conversely, it is supposed in Figure 10.25,

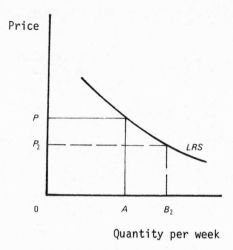

Figure 10.25

that new entrants somehow create external economies of scale for existing firms so pushing their LRACs down. Entries continue until price is at the bottom of these new curves, that is, at a lower price than P, say P_2, when industry output is perhaps B_2. The LRS here shows this industry could have long-run equilibrium positions with outputs of A at price P or B_2 at P_2.

The long-run in monopolistic competition and monopoly

It will be recalled that the short-run analyses for monopolistic competitors and monopolists are effectively the same. In the long-run, though, the analyses are slightly different. To see this, consider Figure 10.26, which could in principle relate to either sort of firm. It shows the firm's present short-run cost curves, AC and MC, along with its downward sloping revenue curves, AR and MR, and from these it is possible to see the weekly output which is set in the short-run (Q_1) and the price at which it is sold (P_1). Note that AR exceeds AC at Q_1 so that excess profits are being earned in this example. In the short-run, there is no point raising output above Q_1 as MC exceeds MR to the right indicating that output rises would raise costs more than profits. However, the LRMC suggests output rises could be secured more cheaply in the long-run (when all inputs can be varied), and the firm would certainly be tempted to raise output to Q_2 in the long-run, this being the point where LRMC cuts MR; to sell this higher weekly output, price would have to be cut from P_1 to P_2. Since the rise in output in the long-run raises profits, it follows that even more excess profits would be earned at Q_2 than at Q_1.

As it happens, Q_2 *is* the weekly output a monopolist will set in the long-run. The long-run position for a monopolist is shown in more detail in Figure 10.27 which reproduces most of 10.26. Figure 10.27 emphasizes that the monopolist will adjust those inputs which can be altered only in the long-run to be at the

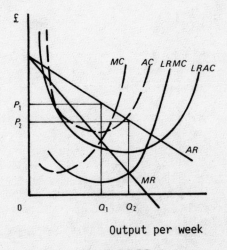

Output per week

Figure 10.26

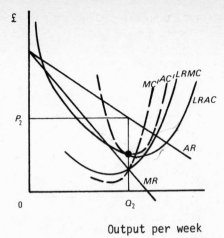

Output per week

Figure 10.27

most suitable level for the output level Q_2, so it will end up with a new short-run AC' which touches LRAC at this output level, and it will have a new short-run MC' associated with it. It can be shown that both LRMC and MC' cut MR at Q_2, the optimum output level as shown; so when the firm eventually settles down at Q_2 it will be in a new short-run equilibrium position as well as in the long-run one, and it will set the price P_2. As shown, the firm will have excess profits in the long-run since LRAC (and AC') are below AR at Q_2. In principle, of course, a monopolist might have high or low excess profits or, by chance, just break even in the long-run. It would not make a loss in the long-run, for if the firm reckoned that it would make a loss at the best possible output level when it had time to adjust the amount of all inputs used, then it would not in the long-run produce that output level and earn a loss; instead, it would sell off its assets and disappear.

Returning now to Figure 10.26, it must be emphasized that Q_2 *does not* represent the long-run equilibrium for a monopolistic competitor. The firm here was earning excess profits to begin with at output Q_1. If it is a typical firm in a monopolistically competitive industry, then it may be supposed that the widespread occurrence of excess profits will lure in new firms. It is assumed in monopolistic competition that new firms can readily enter the industry, and these will take away some of the customers of existing firms. This means that the demand or AR curve of the typical firm will shift left, and the MR curve will shift left with it. How far will the AR curve move? As with perfect competition, it will move until it just touches the LRAC at one point, with AR in a position like that shown by AR' in Figure 10.28 (where the long-run curves are reproduced from 10.26). If the AR ended up to the right of AR', then there would be a range of output levels where it was above LRAC, and so where excess profits could be made, thus enticing more new entrants; if it were to the left of AR', then it would be below LRAC at all output levels indicating that the typical

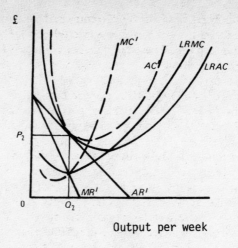

Output per week

Figure 10.28

firm would make a loss whatever output it set, a situation which would drive some firms out of the industry.

It follows that in the long-run the monopolistic competitor faces the demand curve AR′ with its associated MR′. A loss would be made at any output other than Q_2 where the firm finds AR′ touching LRAC so that it can break even. This is clearly the best output, and so MR′ must cut LRMC at this level. The output Q_2 will be sold for the price P_2. The firm will adjust its usage of those inputs whose amounts can be varied only in the long-run to be the most suitable amount for an output Q_2 and so it will end up on the short-run curve AC′ with the associated MC′. When the appropriate amounts of these inputs have been secured, and output settles down at Q_2, then Q_2 will also become the best short-run output level, that is the one where MC′ cuts MR′, as illustrated in the figure.

Figures 10.27 and 10.28 have shown how the long-run equilibrium price and output of a monopolist and a monopolistic competitor can be determined once the demand for their products (which fixes AR and MR) and their costs (given by LRAC and the associated LRMC and short-run cost curves) are known. Of course, changes in demand could lead to different long-run price and output combinations. However, the various combinations could be almost anywhere; as they need not all fall on one (curved or straight) line, so there is no long-run supply curve for individual firms of this sort. Indeed, unlike perfect competition, it is not even possible to derive a long-run supply curve for a monopolistically competitive industry; the reason is that all firms have slightly different products and slightly different prices, so it is not possible to indicate a single price at which the industry will settle in the long-run.

The critical difference between monopolists on the one hand and perfect and monopolistic competitors on the other is clearly that monopolists are held able to earn excess profits without new rivals entering their industry. Why is this? It is because there are usually felt to be barriers to entry in the monopolist's industry. Indeed, without such barriers the industry would probably not have been monopolistic in the first place. These barriers could include (1) the possibility that the monopolist is well-known, which means new rivals would have to undertake substantial advertising with its associated costs to secure a reasonable market share, (2) the possibility that there are substantial internal economies of scale for any firm in the industry, which means that it could take a new firm many years to reach a size when its costs were low enough to enable it to set a price comparable with the existing firm, and (3) the possibility that the existing firm has patents, technical knowledge, or close ties with suppliers and distributors, all of which could give it a cost advantage over new entrants. In contrast, the presence of many firms in both perfectly and monopolistically competitive industries suggests that barriers to entry are negligible; instead, there is assumed to be what economists term freedom of entry.

These differences mean the effects of a change in demand are also different for a monopolist and a monopolistic competitor. If the demand curve or AR (and so MR) moved to the right for the monopolist in Figure 10.27, then it would initially move to a higher output where the new MR cut MC', though it would settle in the long-run where the new MR cut LRMC; and it could permanently enjoy higher excess profits. If the AR (and so MR) moved to the right for the monopolistic competitor in Figure 10.28, then it would initially raise output to where the new MR cut MC and earn some excess profits; but these excess profits would lure new entrants in, taking away customers and driving AR (and MR) to the left again, so that in the long-run the firm would very likely end up with an output near to Q_2 once again.

A change in costs also affects the two types of firm differently. If, say, wage rates rose for the monopolist in Figure 10.27, then all its cost curves would shift upwards. The higher LRMC would cut MR at a lower output than Q_2 so that output would fall as, of course, would excess profits. If costs rose so much that the firm made a loss, then it would close down (unless it thought demand would shortly rise). If wage rates rose in the industry of the monopolistic competitor in Figure 10.28, then all its cost curves would rise. Instead of breaking even, it would inevitably make a loss and so might close down. However, it might prefer to hold on in the hope that some of its rivals would close down instead, for then some of their customers would switch to it, shifting its demand curve or AR (and MR) to the right. In this case, it could end up where the new (further to the right) AR just touched the new (higher) LRAC; this might be at an output close to Q_2, but this output would be sold at a higher price than P_2.

11

Taxes, subsidies and firms

Firms are liable to pay a number of different types of taxes, and may receive a number of different types of subsidy. This chapter seeks to build on the theory of the firm outlined in Chapter 10 to see what effect different taxes and subsidies may have on (i) perfectly competitive firms and industries and (ii) monopolistic competitors and monopolists. As in Chapter 10, it is assumed that each firm's behaviour is determined by a desire to maximize profits.

Taxes and subsidies on costs

Some taxes and subsidies directly affect particular elements of firms' costs. In some cases, they affect costs which are variable in the short-run. For example, labour costs, which are for the most part regarded as variable, will effectively be raised by taxes on labour and cut by subsidies on labour. As far as UK employers are concerned, the national insurance contributions they pay on behalf of employees are equivalent to a tax on labour, as also were the selective employment tax (in use from 1966 to 1973) and the national insurance surcharge (in use from 1977 to 1984); there are a number of employment subsidies in use at the present time, and these are discussed in more detail in Chapter 18. A change in any of these taxes or subsidies alters firms' variable costs. The results of such changes were explored in Chapter 10; generally, they lead to price changes in both the short-run and the long-run.

There are some taxes and subsidies which affect costs that are fixed in the short-run. For example, rates on the buildings owned and used by a firm increase the cost of using these buildings. As it happens, firms also pay rates in respect of any buildings they rent and use as well as ones they own and use; however, there is much debate about how far they really shoulder the burden of rates on the property they rent, for a general rise in such rates might be largely offset by falls in rents if landlords feared they would otherwise end up owning many vacant buildings. Insofar as increased rates on businesses do raise their fixed costs, the effects will be as described in Chapter 10; in essence, there will be no effect on prices in the short-run, but there are likely to be price rises in the long-run. Converse effects would be produced by rises in any subsidies which reduced firms' fixed costs. Perhaps the most important of these are investment grants which have often been made to help firms purchase plant or machinery (and sometimes even buildings) for these grants generally reduce the sums they would otherwise have to borrow and so in turn reduce the interest payments they have to make.

Taxes on profits

In apparent contrast to taxes on costs are taxes on profits. The most important of these in the UK is the corporation tax on companies. One interesting feature of taxes on profits is that if such a tax were levied entirely on a firm's excess profits, then it would have no effect on its price or output if it was a profit maximizing firm. This can be readily shown with the aid of Figure 11.1 where the curve E shows the excess profit one firm would earn at a variety of possible output levels. For convenience, the firm is the one considered in Figure 10.6 whose total cost and total revenue figures for various output levels were given in Table 10.3 and 10.4; at any output level, its excess profit in the difference between its total revenue and its total cost (taken to include normal profits). Assuming this firm seeks to maximize its (excess) profit, it will set an output level of 6 units per week and have an excess profit of £780 per week, for this is the highest point on E.

Suppose, now, that each firm had to pay a percentage of its excess profits – say 50 per cent – in tax. In that case, any output level would leave it with half the excess profit previously generated. The curve E' in Figure 11.1 shows the new excess profit for the firm from each output level. Each point on E' is half way up to the corresponding point on E. The firm will set its output at the highest point on E'. This is, of course, at the same output level (6) where E had its highest point, though the firm will now end up enjoying half as much excess profits as before (£390 instead of £780). In general, then, such a tax will

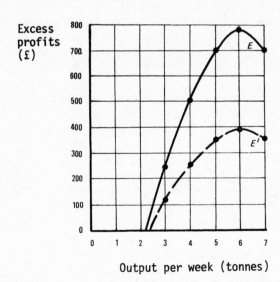

Output per week (tonnes)

Figure 11.1

not cause firms to change their output levels. Accordingly, firms such as mono-polistic competitors and monopolists which can choose their own prices will not alter their prices either, for any change in their prices would obviously change their sales and so their output levels, yet they want these levels to be unchanged.

The prediction that a tax on the excess profits of a profit-maximizing firm will not affect its output can be explained in another way. It will be recalled from Chapter 10 that each such firm sets its output at the point where marginal cost equals marginal revenue. Now a tax on excess profits does not affect its costs; nor does it affect the demand for its products or its AR and MR curves. So if the MC and MR curves stay put, then so will the profit-maximizing output level.

In practice, however, corporation tax is not confined to companies' excess profits. The rules for deciding how much tax any particular firm should pay are complex, but the starting point is its total profit (as conventionally defined) less interest and depreciation. In the absence of other adjustments, the firm con-sidered in Table 10.2, for example, would pay tax on its total (conventional) profit of £1,180 less interest of £80 and depreciation of £100, so its taxable profit would be £1,000. However, it was explained in Chapter 10 that this firm's excess profits might be just £600 (as shown in column B of Table 10.1) which is well below its taxable profit. It follows that corporation tax may be levied not only on a firm's excess profits but also on at least part of its normal profits which economists regard as part of its fixed costs. To the extent that this is the case, a firm will find its fixed costs rising, just as a tax on any other component of its fixed costs would raise them. As recalled in the last section, there would be no effect on output price in the short-run if fixed costs rose, but there could well be a rise in price in the long-run.

This result can be explained intuitively. The shareholders in a company can be regarded as setting it up in order to obtain dividends. They will want a certain level of expected dividends to persuade them to put their money into the company, and this level forms part of its normal profits. A rise in corporation tax raises the total profit the firm must earn to pay out that level of dividend. If the firm was previously earning more than enough profits to pay this dividend level, then its owners may have been enjoying larger dividends than they initially wanted, and the rise in corporation tax may merely reduce this bonus and cause no change in the (presumed to be profit-maximizing) output. On the other hand, the firm may previously have been just managing to pay the dividends the share-holders wanted; this is especially likely in a competitive industry where excess profits may be modest or even nil. In this case, a rise in corporation tax could lead to the typical firm in the industry now being unable to pay the minimum dividend sought by shareholders. Some firms will leave the industry, thereby reducing the industry's output, whilst those which remain may then be able to raise their prices just enough to raise their profits back to normal levels.

Taxes and subsidies on products

Some taxes and subsidies may be directed at the sales of a firm's products (rather than at its costs or its profits) and these have already been met in Chapter 2

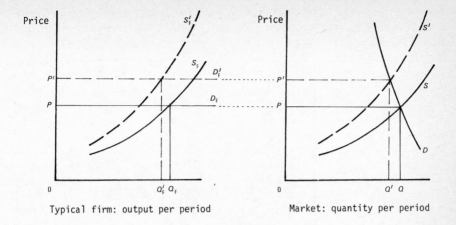

Figure 11.2

which was concerned with markets with many buyers and sellers of homogeneous products, that is, in effect, with the markets supplied by perfectly competitive industries. Given these, it is possible to extend the analysis a little by showing the effects of such taxes and subsidies on a typical firm as well as on the market, and this is done in the case of an ad valorem tax in Figure 11.2. The right-hand diagram here relates to the market. The initial market supply curve (S) intersects the market demand curve (D) to fix the equilibrium price (P) and quantity (Q). The left-hand diagram shows the situation of a typical firm facing the equilibrium price (P) and hence facing the horizontal demand curve (D_F) shown. This cuts the firm's individual supply curve (S_F) at the output level Q_F which is what the firm will decide to produce. The firm's supply curve is, as shown in Chapter 10, part of its marginal cost curve.

Suppose, now, that a 50 per cent ad valorem tax is imposed on producers of this product. For the reasons outlined in relation to Figure 2.5, this will create a new supply curve for the market, shown by S', on which each point is half as high again above the horizontal axis as the point on S immediately below. The firm also acquires a new supply curve (S_F') related in a similar fashion to its original one. The new market equilibrium is where S' cuts D and this produces a new quantity (Q') and price (P'), and a new demand curve for the firm (D_F'). In turn, this cuts S_F' at Q_F' to show the new output level for the firm. It will be seen that output falls for both the typical firm and the market in reaction to the rise in price.

The effects of a specific tax would be similar, except that the new market and firm supply curves would be parallel to the original ones. The effects of subsidies could be shown by introducing new supply curves below the original ones rather than above them.

A slightly different analysis is needed for taxes and subsidies placed on the products of monopolistic competitors and monopolists. Essentially, this is because such firms do not have supply curves (for the reasons explained in

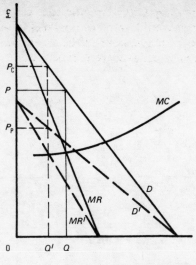

Output per period

Figure 11.3

relation to Figures 10a to d). Instead, it is usual to assume that any taxes paid by these producers on their products, or subsidies paid to them in respect of their products, are actually paid directly by their consumers or paid directly to them. It was argued in Chapter 2 (in the discussion of Figures 2.5 and 2.6) that the effects of taxes or subsidies are in fact the same irrespective of whether payments are made between producers and governments or between consumers and governments, so this assumption, though generally incorrect, does not lead to false conclusions!

The effects of an ad valorem tax on such a firm are shown in Figure 11.3. The firm has the marginal cost curve labelled MC, and initially faces the demand (or average revenue) curve labelled D and its associated marginal revenue curve MR. Output is set at Q where MR cuts MC, and is sold for the price P. Suppose the government introduces a 50 per cent ad valorem tax payable by producers. The results would be the same as with a 50 per cent tax on consumers and the diagram shows the effects of such a tax. As explained in connection with Figure 2.6 such a tax produces a new demand curve, shown here by the new demand curve D′, on which each point is two-thirds the height above the horizontal axis as the point on D immediately above. Associated with this new demand or average revenue curve is a new marginal revenue curve MR′. Output will now be set at Q′ where MR′ cuts MC. This output is sold by producers at the price P_p. In the assumed circumstances, consumers would pay P_p plus the tax and so would face the final price P_c. Thus the tax raises the price paid by consumers (from P to P_c) and cuts the price received by producers (from P to P_p). Also, it cuts output (from Q to Q′).

Had the government imposed a specific tax, then the new demand and marginal revenue curves would have been parallel to the old ones and would have been below them by the amount of the tax. Subsidies, of course, would shift the demand and marginal revenue curves upwards.

12

Economies of scale and learning curves

In Chapter 10 features of costs in relation to the firm was considered. In this chapter consideration will be given to how these concepts are used to discuss the question of economies of scale and also what have become known as 'learning curves' or 'experience curves'.

It is important from the very outset to distinguish clearly *returns* to scale from *economies* of scale. In order to make this distinction it is useful to clarify what economists mean by a *production function*. A production function is a physical relationship between input and output (assuming only a single output is produced). It denotes the maximum output that can be produced from a given set of inputs, such as land, labour and capital; or, alternatively, for a given output it represents the minimum combination of inputs necessary to produce that output level. It therefore refers to efficient production in a technical sense; that is to say, *technical efficiency*. When all inputs can be varied then the analysis is dealing with the long-run; while if at least one input is fixed then the analysis is dealing with the short-run. It is important to note that the long-run is not long enough for a change in technology to take place. In other words, the production function is for a given technology. A change in technology means a change in the whole relationship that exists between inputs and output. Both returns to scale and economies of scale refer to the long-run; however, returns to scale refers to a feature of the production function (to be explained below) while economies of scale refers to a feature of long-run average costs.

Returns to scale

In the long-run all factor inputs are variable. This means that capital can be varied as well as labour, build more plants, and increase the size of management. By *scale* is meant increasing all factor inputs in the same proportion, for instance doubling all factor inputs. It is clear, then, that when consideration is given to scale reference is to the long-run because only then can *all* factors be changed.

But what is so particular about scale? To see this, first consider a very simple example. Consider a box with sides 1cm. The surface area is $6 \times 1 = 6\text{cm}^2$ (since a box, including the lid, has six sides each of $1 \times 1 = 1\text{cm}^2$ in area). The volume of the box, however, is 1cm^3 (i.e., $1 \times 1 \times 1 \times 1 = 1\text{cm}^3$). Now double the dimensions of the box to 2cm. The surface area increases to $6 \times 4 = 24\text{cm}^2$ while the volume increases to $2 \times 2 \times 2 = 8cm^3$. Hence, the surface area increases by a factor of four while the volume increases by a factor of eight. Consider, then, an oil tanker or a ship carrying grain; its carrying capacity increases substantially for a small increase in the ship's size. This, in turn, will lower the average cost of carrying oil or grain. Although average costs are likely to fall, the point being made at the moment is that the substantial increase in volume is purely a technical result and has nothing to do with prices or how the firm operates in factor or product markets.

The same principle holds with firms. A firm can double in size, that is to say it can double its scale of operation by doubling all factor inputs. If it did this then three logical possibilities can occur with respect to output. (1) Output can more than double; (2) output can just double; and, (3) output can increase but by less than double. If factor inputs are doubled and output increases by more than twice, then this is referred to as *increasing returns to scale*; if factor inputs are doubled and output also doubles, then this is referred to as *constant returns to scale*; and, finally, if factor inputs double and output increases but by less than twice as much, then we have *decreasing returns to scale*. Notice in this discussion that all that is being referred to is a relationship between inputs and output. It is purely a technical condition. However, it does have implications for average cost.

To see the effect of returns to scale on long-run average cost, consider a firm which has just two factor inputs: labour (L) and capital (K). Further suppose that both factor inputs are acquired in perfectly competitive factor markets. This means that the firm must accept the ruling wage rate for labour and the price of capital. Let labour have a wage of £3 per unit and capital £2 per unit. If initially the firm is employing 6 units of labour and 1 unit of capital then total cost is $3 \times 6 + 2 \times 1 = £20$. Now let labour and capital double in size to 12 units of labour and 2 units of capital. Since labour and capital are purchased in perfectly competitive factor markets, then their respective prices remain unchanged. It follows, therefore, that total costs simply doubles from £20 to £40. But what about average costs? The result on average cost depends on what has happened to output. Three possibilities are illustrated in Table 12.1.

Table 12.1 Total and average cost for variable output

	(1)	(2)	(3)	(4)
Total cost	20	40	40	40
Output	10	20	40	16
Average cost	2	2	1	2.25

It can be seen from Table 12.1 that if output also doubles, rising from 10 units to 20 units, then average costs remain constant at £2. If, however, output more than doubles (for example rising to 40 units of output) then average costs fall – in this illustration to £1. If, on the other hand, output rises but by less than double, say to 16 units, then average costs rise (here to £2.25). It follows, then, that column (2) represents the effect on long-run average costs of constant returns to scale; column (3) the effect of increasing returns to scale; and, finally, column (4) the effect on long run average costs of decreasing returns to scale.

It must not be assumed from this analysis that the only reason for a U-shaped long-run average cost curve is because of such returns to scale. As will be noted in a moment, there are many factors which affect long-run average costs besides returns to scale. The importance of the present analysis is, however, that these are a major determining factor in the level of long run average cost.

It is worth mentioning at this point that *scale* has two dimensions to it.

1   The rate of output of a product at a particular period of time.
2   The period of time over which the product is produced.

Thus, suppose that an output of 100 units is produced over a period of 5 years. This is equivalent to 500 units per annum for one year. The point is that the manner in which 100 units are produced over a 5 year interval is likely to be different from the way in which 500 units are produced in one year. Put simply, the dimension of scale includes the *rate* of output per period and the *length* of the production run. The higher the rate of output per period the more scope there exists for mechanization to be introduced.

Economies of scale

Economies of scale are distinguished from returns to scale in so far as the former are concerned solely with the effect on the long-run average cost as the scale of output rises. The latter, as just illustrated in the previous section, is concerned only with the relationship between inputs and output as the scale of production expands.

It is useful to make a further distinction – namely, between real economies and pecuniary economies of scale. Real economies of scale are those associated with a reduction in the physical quantity of inputs: raw materials, various types of labour and capital. Returns to scale belong to this category. Pecuniary economies, on the other hand, are those realized from paying lower prices for factors used in production and distribution of the product. These pecuniary economies do not necessarily imply any actual change in the quantity of physical inputs used, but rather accrue to the firm from lower prices paid for raw materials or lower wages and salaries. In practice it is almost impossible to disentangle pecuniary from real economies, but it is useful to keep them conceptually distinct.

There are basically five sources of pecuniary economies of scale. These are:

1   Lower price for raw material bought at special discount from suppliers.
2   Lower costs of external finance, e.g., favourable loan terms from banks.
3   Lower advertising prices for large-scale advertising.
4   Lower transportation charges for large amounts transported.
5   Possibly, but not likely in the UK, lower wage rates (although possibly higher take-home pay).

The more important economies of scale, however, are on the real side. These fall into five categories:

1 Production economies.
2 Marketing economies.
3 Managerial economies.
4 Transport and storage economies.
5 Research and development economies.

Each of these will be taken in turn.

Production economies. These arise from three sources: (a) labour economies, (b) technical economies, and (c) inventory economies.

Labour economies are achieved as the scale of output increases and arise from the division of labour and the resultant specialization. Certain degrees of specialization and division of labour are only possible with a certain minimum scale of plant. Furthermore, increased specialization can save time in moving between jobs (although bottlenecks and demarcation disputes may swamp these).

It has long been recognized that with specialization come more specific tools and machines. Such increased mechanization can lead to decreasing costs as the scale of output increases.

Technical economies are those associated with fixed capital. The main economy arises from the specialization of the capital equipment which becomes possible only at large-scale production. Furthermore, the larger the scale the less frequently multi-purpose machinery requires to be set up.

An obvious technical economy arises from the geometric relationship between volume, surface-area and inputs required. This was illustrated above, and they are especially significant in the process industries, such as petroleum refining, steam generation, gas transmissions, and chemical and cement industries.

Another source of technical economy is reserve capacity. With only one large machine, a firm is liable to disruption if it breaks down, and so may have another for reserve. This gives a ratio of 1:1. With a large-scale plant, however, the number in reserve will lead to a much smaller ratio. Thus, if a firm has 4 machines in full-time use it may have one additional machine for emergencies, giving a ratio of 1:4.

Inventory economies have been well investigated, and such studies show that stocks increase less than proportionately with scale.

Marketing economies. Marketing economies are associated with the distribution of the product and arise from a variety of sources. In a situation of largely oligopolistic firms, in other words, a small group of firms for which the reaction of a competitor must be taken into account when taking a decision on such things as output or price, advertising applies to both well-established firms and to new firms. There is general evidence that advertising economies do exist, at least up to a certain level of output. For example, the cost of a television advertisement remains constant regardless of the level of output, and so unit costs of advertising fall. The same applies in general sales promotion, whose costs do not rise in the same proportion to the scale of output.

Marketing economies arise from exclusive agreements made with distributors. This is especially true of car manufacturers and garages, and retail outlets selling agreed brands. One aspect of marketing which is also becoming important is that associated with a change of model or new design. For example, when IBM set a standard for microcomputers many computing firms had to change their microcomputer model design in order to prevent their market share from falling substantially. For instance, different keyboards had to be designed as well as greater memory boards. These can often involve considerable expense. The spreading of such overheads attached to a change in model or new model is lower per unit if the scale of output is large. This also illustrates the link between marketing and the length of the production run, which we referred to above. It could be argued that some advertising is directed at lengthening the production run, while other advertising is directed at increasing the rate of sales per period.

Managerial economies. Managerial costs are a mixture of production and marketing costs. Economies arise from two sources: (a) the specialization of management functions, and (b) the mechanization of managerial functions. The larger the scale the more decision-making is decentralized with specialist management, such as production managers, sales managers and finance managers. Such specialization also allows specialized managerial mechanization, such as the use of microcomputers, telex and data terminal interchange through telecommunications, which speeds up the collection and processing of information. It is such decentralization, however, which may also lead to diseconomies of scale. For instance, more departmental and inter-departmental meetings are necessary and the difficulties of establishing responsibility for particular jobs.

Transport and storage costs. These arise on the production and selling side. Storage costs may fall with size. Whether transport economies exist partly depends upon whether the firm supplies its own transport or whether it uses public transport and outside hauliers.

Research and development economies. Although expensive they may lead to a reduction in unit costs.

Learning curves or experience curves

The learning effect in production was first discovered in the US aircraft industry during the Second World War, when it was found that additional labour hours required to produce aircraft frames fell as the *cumulative* number of planes produced rose. In other words, the more aircraft frames people had worked on

Table 12.2 Data for constructing learning curves

(1) Number of frames	(2) Cumulative number of frames	(3) Additional labour hours	(4) Log of column (3)	(5) Log of column (2)
100	300	6.39	1.85	5.70
200	1100	4.93	1.60	7.00
300	2400	4.22	1.44	7.78
400	4200	3.77	1.33	8.34
500	6500	3.45	1.24	8.78
600	9300	3.22	1.17	9.14
700	12600	3.03	1.11	9.44
800	16400	2.87	1.05	9.71
900	10700	2.74	1.01	9.94
1000	25500	2.63	0.97	10.15

the more experienced they became, and the less time they took to accomplish the same job. This point is illustrated in Table 12.2.

It can be seen from this table that as the cumulative number of frames increases, so the additional hours required declines. Similar information is displayed in Figure 12.1a and b. The difference between Figure 12.1a and 12.1b is that the former plots the actual values, that is columns (2) and (3), while the latter plots the (natural) logarithms of the values, that is columns (4) and (5). As can be seen from Figure 12.1b, the reason for doing this is because the relationship between the logarithm of the cumulative output and the logarithm of the reduction in labour hours is, in this illustration, linear. (A technical reason for doing this is because the slope of the line denotes the percentage change in labour hours divided by the percentage change in the cumulative output. Hence, if the slope is equal to -0.2, which it is in the present example, then a 1 per cent rise in the cumulative output leads to a 0.2 per cent fall in the hours required to produce the same level of output. Put conversely, with slope of -0.2, a doubling of cumulative output leads to costs being 80 per cent of their former value. For this reason the curve is sometimes referred to as 'an 80 per cent curve'.)

A study by the Boston Study Group, which reported to the House of Commons, found that for Japanese Time Recorders (for the period 1962-72) there was 'a 75 per cent curve', whereas for Bottle Caps in West Germany there was 'an 82 per cent curve' and for aircraft frames in the UK there was 'an 80 per cent curve'. In the case of Japanese motor cycles it has been estimated that there is 'a 76 per cent curve' for 126–250cc, 'an 81 per cent curve' for 51–125cc and 'an 88 per cent curve' for less than 50cc bikes. The implication of these results is that unit costs will fall as learning takes place. In terms of simple cost curve analysis, this means that cost curves shift down with cumulative output. The *smaller* the 'per cent curve' the *greater* the reduction in unit costs.

The existence of learning curves has been one argument put forward why some firms who are early in setting up production have a cost advantage over

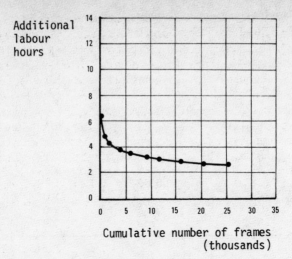

Additional labour hours

Cumulative number of frames (thousands)

Figure 12.1(a)

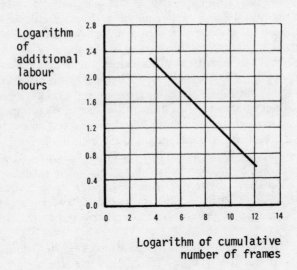

Logarithm of additional labour hours

Logarithm of cumulative number of frames

Figure 12.1(b)

latecomers. Furthermore, it has also been used in discussing the method by which the Japanese have set up new manufacturing. In some industries in Japan production was deliberately restricted by the government to just one (or a few) firms so that experience could be gained and unit costs could fall. Only once such firms have become established are others allowed to enter the industry. This sequencing of production employed by Japan does have the drawback that it gives rise to a temporary monopoly (although this may not be a drawback if the monopoly power, discussed in Chapter 14, is not abused).

'Learning' is by no means the perogative of manual labour. The issue can be put in terms of a question: 'Who learns?' In general terms it would be expected that workers become more proficient in their jobs with experience, that is, 'learning by doing'. This type of learning arises from repetition of the same physical task. This is closely associated with the idea of relating labour hours to the cumulative level of output. On the other hand, some learning is more a question of the length of *time* that has elapsed. This type of learning is more related to the complexity of what is being learnt, and is more typical of managerial learning. For instance, a trainee manager must learn multiple tasks and become proficient at making (quick) decisions, which is related more to the time he or she has spent doing such tasks. Although we have simply referred to labour, it is important to realize that such learning (both of the repetitive type and the complex type) is not independent of capital. A more specific capital item may allow greater repetition and hence a greater possibility of learning, or allow a more complex task to become more manageable. For example, a shorthand typist may do just this type of work and no general office filing. With the growth of microcomputers, some individuals can become experts with word processors, while others can become experts with the use of management software. Neither would be possible without the specialist capital expenditure.

13

Price discrimination

In this chapter we shall consider a monopolist who can divide his market into two distinct groups. Examples of divided markets (although not strictly monopolistic suppliers) are home sales and sales to overseas markets, first-class and second-class passengers, and airline flights during the holiday season and out-of-season. In each of these examples the market demand in each category shows different characteristics. The most obvious difference is that they generally show different price elasticities of demand. For instance, the overseas market shows a greater price elasticity than the home market, because it is likely that there will be more substitutes in the case of overseas demand and because their tastes are not likely to be the same as those in the home market. In other words, for a 1 per cent change in price the quantity demanded falls in the overseas market more than it falls in the home market. If the price of rail tickets for both first and second-class passengers rises by 1 per cent we would expect a greater percentage fall among second-class passengers than we would in first-class passengers. This is because first-class passengers are often businessmen who must undertake such trips and whose tickets are purchased from company funds, while second-class passengers are largely the public who can vary more readily the number of trips they make depending on the price of train tickets relative to other forms of transport. Finally, for a 1 per cent rise in air tickets, we would expect more response from in-season passengers than from out-of-season passengers. This is because out-of-season passengers are making trips for business or specific reasons, while in-season passengers are largely holiday-makers whose choice of taking a holiday is usually quite sensitive to its price. The fact that a commodity or service supplied to two distinct markets can lead to different demand responses raises the question of whether a supplier would raise his level of profits if he charged the same price in the two markets or a different price in the two markets.

Consider a situation where a particular commodity, which is assumed to be wheat, is supplied at home by a single seller, which for illustrative purposes can be thought of as a government agency. The supplier sells wheat both at home and on the 'world' market. The country supplying this commodity is just a small producer as far as the world market is concerned. This is an important assumption because it means that the world price for wheat is determined by world demand and world supply. As Chapter 1 illustrated, demand and supply interact to determine an equilibrium price. In the present example this is the price as

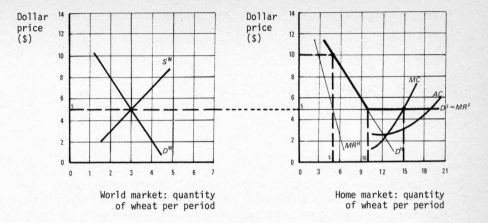

Figure 13.1

determined in the world market for wheat.

The situation is shown in Figure 13.1, where the world market for wheat is shown on the left. The demand and supply of wheat on the world market establishes a world equilibrium price of $5. The situation in the home country is illustrated on the right. The home country has a downward sloping demand curve for wheat, represented by D^H. Associated with this home demand curve is the marginal revenue curve, denoted MR^H. Notice that because the demand curve is downward sloping, then marginal revenue diverges from average revenue.

In Figure 13.1, the home market has in fact two demand curves. There is the home demand curve which is downward sloping, and denoted D^H. But there is also the world demand curve for this country's product, which is denoted D^f. It will be noted that the world demand curve for this country's product is horizontal at the world equilibrium price of $5. Why is this? Since this country is small relative to the world, then it can supply as much as it likes to the world market with no (or virtually no) effect on the world price. Put another way, people abroad are happy to buy any amount of this country's wheat at a price of $5. Hence, the world demand curve, as seen by this country, is horizontal at $5. Also notice that this means that the marginal revenue coincides with average revenue, so that for the world demand as seen by this country,

$$\text{average revenue} = \text{marginal revenue} = \text{price} = \$5.$$

Finally, in terms of Figure 13.1, there are drawn the firm's short-run average cost and marginal cost, which are assumed to be U-shaped.

Given the situation in Figure 13.1, we want to know:

1   What amount of wheat will the home country produce?
2   How much wheat will the home country sell abroad?
3   How much wheat will the country sell at home?
4   Will the price set on the home market also be $5?

In order to obtain answers to these questions, it is necessary first to determine the *total* quantity demanded for each price. In other words, the demand curve for wheat for the *combined* market must be established. At a price of $10 demand for wheat by domestic residents will be 5 units. There will be no overseas demand for the home country's wheat because they can obtain it on world markets for $5. It may be thought that domestic residents too can demand wheat from the world market at the lower price. This would be true, but then the demand would not be for home-produced wheat. It is the combined demand for home-produced wheat that is being considered here. Hence, this combination of price and output represents a point on the combined demand curve. At a price of $6 again there will be a home demand for wheat, this time of 9 units, and no world demand for the home country's wheat. However, once the price reaches $5 there will be a home demand of 10 units plus a very large demand for the home country's wheat from abroad. Since it is being assumed that this country is very small relative to the rest of the world, overseas demand is effectively infinite. There can be no lower price than $5 because at any lower price, although there is a demand, no producer will sell to the home market at such a price when it can receive $5 on the world market. It can be seen, then, that the combined demand curve becomes horizontal at the world price of $5. Hence, the total demand curve is the heavy line shown in Figure 13.1.

Now just as a total demand curve can be constructed, so it is also possible to construct the total marginal revenue curve associated with this total demand (or average revenue) curve. From the analysis so far presented, it should not be difficult to understand that this combined marginal revenue curve is the home country's marginal revenue curve for prices above $5 and becomes the world marginal revenue curve at $5.

It is now possible to answer the four questions listed above. In order to answer question (1) about how much wheat the home country will produce, it is necessary to state the monopolist's objective. It is assumed that the monopolist aims at maximizing its profits. Like the ordinary monopolist, such a firm will maximize profits if it sets marginal revenue equal to marginal cost. The only difference to consider in the present example is that marginal cost is equated with *total* marginal revenue. It can be seen in terms of Figure 13.1 that this will be at an output level of 15 units. At this output level marginal cost is $5 and total marginal revenue is also $5. At any lower level of output, say 10 units of output, marginal cost will be only $1 while marginal revenue will be $5. Hence, an extra unit of output will cost less than the extra revenue that the firm will receive, and it will accordingly be profitable to produce such an extra unit. Beyond 10 units it will cost the firm more to produce the extra unit than it receives from selling such a unit. Hence, profits for the firm will be maximized at output level of 15 units.

Consider now questions (2) and (3) dealing with the distribution of the 15 units between the home market and the overseas market. Having determined the total output level and the marginal cost associated with this output level, it is possible to equate this marginal cost with the marginal revenue in each market and this will give the distribution of output between the two markets. To see that this is truly the situation, look again at Figure 13.1. At a marginal cost of $5, if this is equated with the *home* marginal revenue, then sales at home are 5 units, and the remaining 10 units are sold abroad. The reasoning behind this is not too difficult to understand. Having determined this profit maximizing output level and established that this has a marginal cost of $5, then sales in each market will be raised/lowered until the extra revenue from the sale is just equal to the marginal cost. If this is not done, then profits cannot have been maximized.

Finally, at what price is wheat sold in the home market? This is readily established from Figure 13.1. Since 5 units are sold in the home market, then the domestic price of wheat is read off the home demand curve, which is a home price of wheat of $10.

It is to be noted that the higher price is charged in the market with the smallest (absolute) price elasticity of demand. With a downward sloping demand curve, the (absolute) price elasticity at sales of 5 units and price of $10 must be less than infinity. (In fact, given the figures, the slope of the demand curve is $-(5/5) = -1$ and so the price elasticity of demand at sales of 5 units is $-(1) \times (10/5) = -2$. It should be appreciated that this result is general for discriminating monopoly. Namely, *the higher price is charged in the market with the lower (absolute) price elasticity of demand.*

In the examples given at the beginning of this chapter, the analysis shows why the price in the home market is higher than the price of the same commodity when sold abroad; why first-class fares are higher than second-class fares; and why in-season flights are more expensive than out-of-season flights.

However, for discriminating monopoly to operate, the two markets must be quite distinct and no re-sale must occur. To see why this is so, suppose wheat is sold abroad for $5 and at home for $10, as discussed in the above illustration. It might then be possible for overseas buyers to re-sell the goods which they have purchased in the home country for, say $7, so undercutting the home supplier by $3, and they in turn making a profit of $2 – a process referred to as *dumping* (and which is banned by the General Agreement on Tariffs and Trade). In the case of in-season and out-of-season holidays, there is no problem because they are at different times of the year. With first and second-class passengers, re-sale is avoided by making the first class service better than for second-class passengers.

14

Arguments about monopolies

Many western countries have some form of legislation to control firms which have large shares of the markets in which they operate. In the United Kingdom, for example, the government defines as a 'monopoly' any firm with a market share of 40 per cent or more, and has the power (exercised with the help of the Monopolies and Mergers Commission) to regulate the prices set by such 'monopolies', and also the power to vet and, if it wishes, to prevent any mergers which would create a new 'monopoly' or extend an existing one. Inverted commas are used for these 'monopolies' since the term here is used in a looser sense than elsewhere in this book, where it refers to firms with 100 per cent of their markets. Incidentally, the UK legislation gives the government powers over both national and local 'monopolies'.

This chapter builds on the theory of the firm outlined in Chapter 10 to show why firms with large market shares may give cause for concern. The next two sections outline the major worries by comparing monopolists with perfect competitors; there follows a section to see how far similar worries are applicable to oligopolists. Between them, these three sections outline the main arguments against 'monopolies'. However, it is sometimes possible to produce arguments in favour of them, and a further section presents those arguments. It is because arguments can be made on both sides that each 'monopoly' or merger needs to be examined on its merits, and the chapter concludes with some further observations on the task of those concerned with these examinations.

The price objection to monopoly

Perhaps the most frequently cited concern about mergers is that the new larger firm is likely to use its market power to force up prices and so, in turn, reduce sales to consumers. This process is often illustrated by considering what would happen in an extreme case where all the firms in a perfectly competitive industry merged to form a monopoly. The argument is summed up in Figures 14.1 and 14.2. Figure 14.1 shows the initial market situation with the perfectly competitive industry. D is the market demand curve (shown straight for convenience) and S is the market supply curve, based (it will be recalled from the discussion surrounding Figure 10.8) on the marginal cost curves of the firms in the industry. The two curves intersect at A to give the equilibrium price of £40 and the equilibrium quantity of 4,000 items per week.

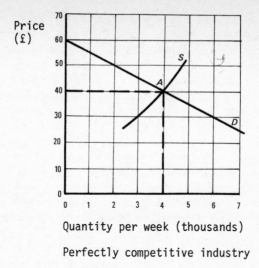

Quantity per week (thousands)

Perfectly competitive industry

Figure 14.1

What happens if the firms merge to form a monopoly is shown in Figure 14.2. This single firm will now face the same demand curve, D, that previously applied to the whole market in Figure 14.1. This curve is reproduced in Figure 14.2 which shows that it will also represent the monopolist's average revenue curve AR (a point explained in connection with Figure 10.5); associated with AR is the monopolist's marginal revenue curve MR. Finally, Figure 14.2 reproduces (in an unbroken line) the supply curve from Figure 14.1 and shows this to form part of the newly-formed monopolist's marginal cost curve MC.

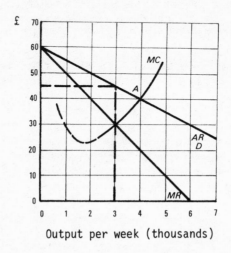

Output per week (thousands)

Figure 14.2

The argument that S in Figure 14.1 forms part of the MC in Figures 14.2 can be explained by showing how any point appearing on the one curve could well appear on the other; this can most conveniently be done with reference to point A which, in Figure 14.1, is the perfectly competitive equilibrium position. Point A shows that the industry output would be 4,000 units per week at a price of £40 per unit. This output might be attributable to 100 firms each producing 40 units per week. Now each of these firms faces the price of £40 per unit, and (as implied by Figure 10.7) each will set its output so that its marginal cost is also £40 per unit. If these firms merged, then each of their premises might be regarded as one plant by the new firm. If this firm set the output of 4,000 units per week, then it might well require each plant to produce 40 units per week. In that case, the firm could produce one more unit by asking any one particular plant to produce the extra unit, and this would cost £40 in the plant concerned. So the monopolist, too, could face an MC of £40 if it set the output of 4,000 units, and hence A lies on its MC curve.

Whilst A may well be a point on the monopolist's MC curve, it is not the point on that curve where it will end up if it seeks maximum profits. As shown in Figure 14.2, it will set its output at 3,000 where MR equals MC; this is below the competitive output of 4,000. The output of 3,000 will be sold at the price £45; this is above the competitive price of £40. Such a rise in price is a powerful argument against mergers (and also a powerful argument for either demerging existing monopolies or requiring them by law to set lower prices). In practice, however, there are circumstances in which a merger of the firms in a competitive industry could eventually lead to a *fall* in price, and these are examined in a later section.

Efficiency objections to monopoly

Quite aside from fears that the merger of a perfectly competitive industry will rapidly lead to a rise in price, it may be opposed on the grounds that a monopolist will be inefficient. Indeed, no less than four different types of inefficiency could appear.

Consider, first, the long-run equilibrium of a typical perfectly competitive firm and a monopolist. The perfect competitor will end up at the bottom of its long-run average cost curve (as at output Q_3 in Figure 10.22) suggesting that it ends up producing its output at the lowest possible cost per unit of output. In contrast, the monopolist is unlikely to end up at the bottom of its long-run average cost curve (as shown by output Q_2 in Figure 10.27) – though it could do by chance – and hence it is unlikely to end up producing its output at the lowest possible unit cost. This point can be summed up by saying the perfect competitor should be as *economically efficient* as possible in the long-run whereas the monopolist is unlikely to be.

A further difference between the long-run equilibrium position of a perfect competitor and a monopolist is that the former will just break even (as in Figure 10.22 where AR' just equals LRAC at Q_3) whilst the latter is likely to make excess profits (as in Figure 10.27 where AR exceeds LRAC at Q_2). This can lead to two further types of inefficiency for the monopolist. For instance, it may lead to what is called *X-inefficiency*, which is really a jargon word for slackness or lack of effort. Thus the management in a monopolist may enjoy late starts to the working day followed by lengthy lunch breaks and early finishes, and it may allow a casual attitude among shopfloor workers. This slackness may effectively raise costs – hence its bad name – and so cut profits a bit, but it need not cause losses and threaten closure. On the other hand, a perfect competitor can at best only just break even in the long-run, and its management is likely to try to prevent any cost increases stemming from slackness, for these would result in losses and eventual closure.

Another possible consequence of long-run excess profits for the monopolist is that it may be lulled by its comfortable situation into doing little R & D (research and development). This means it may eventually be less *technologically efficient* than it might be. In contrast, a perfect competitor has a great incentive to undertake R & D in that if it does little whilst its rivals do a lot, then they might cut their costs and raise their output a little and so force down the market price, and such a fall could drive it from a break-even position to a loss-making one.

The final source of inefficiency associated with monopolies is known as *allocative inefficiency* and stems from the fact that a monopolist's price exceeds its marginal cost. This can be discussed in the context of the short-run equilibrium position, as shown for one monopolist in Figure 14.3 which has settled down with an output of 10 units per week and a price of £50, and hence has a weekly income of £500. Its marginal cost is £30 indicating that it could produce one more unit each week for such an amount. Now the demand curve indicates that 11 units each week could be sold at a price of, say, £48. In other words, there is each week a potential customer who would be prepared to buy an eleventh unit

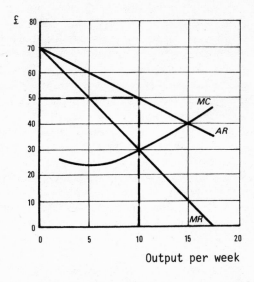

Figure 14.3

for a price of £48 but who will buy nothing so long as the price stays at £50. Now there is clearly something unsatisfactory about an economy where firms refrain from spending £30 on producing items which customers would value at £48 (of course the reason this monopolist refrains is that to sell 11 units each week it would have to set a price of £48 and settle for a total revenue of £528, which means its revenue would rise by £28 a week from its initial level – whereas costs would rise by the £30 needed to produce the eleventh unit – so that profits would fall by £2). In other words, it is unsatisfactory – or inefficient – that resources are not allocated here to producing 11 units a week, or indeed, 15 units a week, since up to that point there are potential customers who would pay more than the extra cost involved. This objection does not apply to perfect competitors, for they settle where price equals marginal cost (as shown in Figure 10.7 where both equal £440 at the chosen output level of 6) rather than where price exceeds it.

Objections to oligopolists

The previous two sections have identified a price objection and four efficiency objections to monopolists. How far do these objections apply also to oligopolists? A detailed answer to this question would require a detailed examination of the various theories of oligopoly which is beyond the scope of this book. However, it is not difficult to give reasons for believing that many of the objections would apply, if perhaps with a shade less force.

Consider the price objection first. Essentially, the argument is this. When there are a large number of perfectly competitive firms, each must accept the competitive industry price (such as the £40 in Figure 14.1) since any firm which seeks a higher price will drive all its customers away; note that its numerous rivals will have no difficulty meeting those customers' requirements. If the firms merged to form a monopoly, then the price could be forced up sharply since there would then be no rivals for the customers to turn to. If, instead, the firms merged to form oligopolies, then individual oligopolists would be wary about putting prices up much, since there would be rivals for their customers to turn to, though they could perhaps raise prices a little in the belief that their rivals could not readily meet all their (numerous) customers' requirements, and in the hope that their many customers would prefer their higher prices to their rivals' queues. Perhaps the greatest worry is that initially each oligopolist would raise its price just a little, and that an initial round of price rises could be followed by further rounds.

Next, consider the efficiency arguments. A perfect competitor is economically efficient in the long-run – that is, it ends up at the bottom of its long-run average cost curve (LRAC) – for two reasons which are reflected in Figure 10.22. First, it is so small relative to the market that it has to accept the market price and so faces a horizontal demand curve; secondly, there is free entry to its industry so that entry continues until the typical firm can just break even at the point where its final demand curve just touches the bottom of the LRAC. Neither reason applies to an oligopolist; such a firm is generally large relative to the market and so is most unlikely to have a horizontal demand curve, and there are generally barriers to entry in its industry (this being a major explanation for the presence of only a few firms). Thus the oligopolist is most unlikely to end up at the bottom of its LRAC and so is unlikely to be economically efficient.

It is because there is free entry to a perfectly competitive industry, and not to a monopolistic one, that perfect competitors break even in the long-run whilst monopolists can earn excess profits. Similarly, barriers to entry in an oligopolistic industry mean oligopolists can earn excess profits in the long-run. In turn, there is the risk of X-inefficiency and technological inefficiency.

Finally, consider allocative efficiency. A firm sets its output where marginal revenue equals marginal cost. Its marginal cost will also equal its price, or average revenue, only if average revenue equals marginal revenue at that point. In turn, this occurs only for firms with horizontal demand curves, for then their average and marginal revenue curves coincide. As noted above, oligopolists will not have horizontal demand curves. Accordingly, their prices will exceed their marginal costs and they could be criticized on grounds of allocative efficiency.

This analysis suggests that all the reasons for concern with monopolists could apply also to oligopolists, though some may have less force. Broadly speaking, the concern with any particular firm will depend on its share of the market, for the greater this share is, the closer it will be to a monopolist. It is for this reason that governments are so concerned when two oligopolists with modest market shares propose to merge to form a new firm with a large share. However, there could be concern with a proposed merger of a number of perfect or monopolistic competitors if this meant several firms with small shares were replaced with one firm with a large share.

The reader may note that some of the objections to monopoly apply also to monopolistic competitors themselves. For instance, they too do not end up at the bottom of their LRAC (as shown in Figure 10.28), and so are arguably economically inefficient, and they, too, end up with prices in excess of marginal cost (as shown in Figure 10.10a) and so are arguably allocatively inefficient. Why, then, does the Monopolies and Mergers Commission pay no attenion to industries characterized by monopolistic competition? The answer is that this form of competition arises in industries – such as the restaurant industry – which display product differentiation. It would be absurd to try to change such an industry into a perfectly competitive one with homogeneous products and uniform prices.

Possible advantages of monopolies

The preceding sections have shown how the merger of a perfectly competitive industry to form a monopoly could lead to price rises and various types of inefficiency, and they have shown that similar problems could arise with mergers which create or extend an oligopoly. However, firms proposing to merge often claim that the merger is, in fact, in the public interest, and such claims frequently persuade the Monopolies and Mergers Commission to sanction them. How can such claims be made?

Essentially, the argument will be that the merged firm will, eventually at least, be able to enjoy very much lower cost curves than those applying to the merging firms. There are two reasons why this might happen. First, the firms might be in an industry with substantial scope for economies of scale; for instance, the firms in a country's steel industry might argue that if a host of small firms each with small furnaces were allowed to merge, then they could in time replace those furnaces with a handful of giant ones and produce steel at a much lower cost. Secondly, they might argue that the merged firms could pool their R & D resources with a much greater chance of producing technological breakthroughs which cut their costs.

To consider the possible effects of a lowering of costs, it is convenient to return to the example examined in Figures 14.1 and 14.2; the essential points are shown again in Figure 14.4 where AR, MR and MC reproduce those in Figure 14.2. It will be recalled that the perfectly competitive industry equilibrium had been at point A with a quantity of 4,000 units a week and a price of £40. After the merger, it was found that if the monopolist used the existing plants, then its MC curve could coincide with the competitive industry's supply curve, so that, for example, the marginal cost when output was 4,000 would be £40. Of course, the monopolist actually settled for the lower output of 3,000 which sold for the higher price of £45. Now suppose that, in time, the many small plants owned by the monopolist were replaced by a few larger and more efficient ones. In this case, the firm would have a new, lower, marginal cost curve, and it would set an output where this cut its marginal revenue curve. If, for example, this fall in costs put it on to MC', then it would result in the monopolist choosing the output 4,000 and selling it at a price £40. In this case, the monopolist would end up with the same price and quantity that operated before the merger; an important point to note is that any more modest fall in costs would result in a marginal cost curve above MC', and, in turn, a lower output and higher price than those before the merger. However, a substantial fall in costs might put the firm on to MC" and result in the output of 5,000 sold at a price of £35; in this case, the result is actually a *higher* output and *lower* price than those before the merger.

If the proponents of a merger can show that it will eventually result in lower prices, then clearly there will be no price objection to it. In turn, the efficiency objections will begin to seem rather pointless; for if the merger eventually results in a higher output at a lower price, then it would be absurd to oppose it on the grounds that the new merged firm would not end up at the lowest point on its LRAC curve, or that it might permit slack, or that it might eventually ease up on R & D, or that its price exceeded its marginal cost.

It follows that those seeking permission to merge are almost sure to base their case on the promise of future cost cuts. To establish this case, they will have first to show that cost cuts are possible, and then to show that they will actively seek them rather then merely enjoying the excess profits which they would probably be able to earn straightaway; certainly they would have a plausible incentive in the form of even bigger profits, and their initial excess profits could well provide the initial finance needed for any cost cutting actions. Next they would have to show that the cost cuts would be large enough to result in a price below the

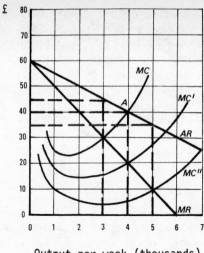

Output per week (thousands)

Figure 14.4

original one. In the case in Figure 14.4, for instance, they would want to show that the new marginal cost curve would be below MC'.

It is worth noting that there are cases where no feasible cost cut would result in a (profit-maximizing) merged firm setting a lower price than the initial price. Figure 14.5 illustrates such a case. Here, again, a perfectly competitive industry merges to form a monopoly. The initial competitive output, Q_C, and

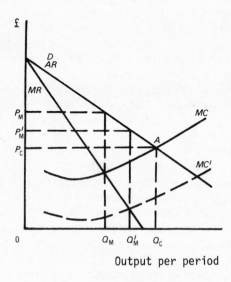

Output per period

Figure 14.5

competitive price, P_C, can, as before, be found at A where the market demand curve D cuts the monopolist's initial MC (which coincides with the previous competitive industry's supply curve). Initially the monopolist fixes its output where MC cuts MR and so produces the monopoly output, Q_M, at the monopoly price, P_M. Suppose, in time, costs fall. The marginal cost curve can hardly fall below the very low one MC′, and with this the firm would produce an output Q_M' at a price P_M', so that its output remains below Q_C and its price remains above P_C. The critical point here is that MR is negative at the output Q_C (which means demand is inelastic at this point); it would need an inconceivable negative marginal cost to persuade a monopolist to produce at this output or at a higher one!

Some further aspects of mergers

This chapter has shown how a merger is likely to result in a higher price and a lower output, at least initially, as well as to various types of inefficiency. However, it has also shown that it could in time lead to a lower price and a higher output than those applying before the merger, and in this case there would be no real concern with any of these types of inefficiency. In examining any proposed merger, the Monopolies and Mergers Commission will clearly be primarily concerned with weighing up all these factors. However, there may be other aspects of the proposals which need to be considered, and some possibilities are considered here.

In some cases, there may be concern that a merger could lead to a monopoly which was able to indulge in price discrimination, that is, the practice of charging different prices to different consumers. The circumstances in which this is possible, and the reasons why it is often felt to be an undesirable practice, were outlined in Chapter 13.

In other cases, there may be concern that the merger will seriously reduce the choice of products available to the consumer. Clearly this would not occur in cases where perfect competitors merged, as they have a homogeneous product anyway, but it could be an important issue in mergers between monopolistic competitors or oligopolists. Ordinarily, such mergers might reasonably be expected to reduce the range of products on offer, but exceptions could arise. The classic example is a country in which there are two competing television companies, each with one channel, which obtain their finance from commercials. The companies will probably find that the amount of money they can squeeze out of advertisers, and in turn their profits, depends largely on the size of their audiences. Accordingly, each company is likely to put on similar programmes of mass appeal; maybe each secures an average audience of, say, 10 million viewers. Now if these companies merged, then the new company might elect to put out programmes of mass appeal on one channel only, and perhaps capture for this channel all the 20 million viewers shared by the previous companies. On the other channel, it might put out programmes of minority interest and secure, say, an average audience of 2 million new viewers. In this case, the merger could be held to have increased the range of products available.

Finally, the Monopolies and Mergers Commission will in most cases consider how large the barriers to entry are in the industry concerned. If the barriers are low, then merged firms with large market shares have some incentive to keep prices low and profits down for fear of enticing new competitors into the industry. If the barriers are high, then there is no such incentive, and the Commission will be inclined to take the prospect of high prices much more seriously.

15

Factor substitution: the case of energy

There has been a rise in the price of many forms of energy, such as gas, coal and oil. Furthermore, the prices of different forms of energy have not risen uniformly and so the relative price of one form of energy as compared to another has changed. In the early 1970s coal prices began to rise relative to other fuels; in the mid 1970s oil prices began to rise; and in the United Kingdom gas prices began to alter also. As one price rose relative to others the question of inter-fuel substitution became important. But since most fuel prices rose, what also became important was the effect on output of such price rises. At the same time, there was a growing concern about the use of fossil fuels, such as coal, oil and natural gas, for purposes of providing energy. These fossil fuels take many years to form and it is questioned whether our use (or even over-use) may be too great; in other words, whether *conservation of energy* is important. These are the types of issues that will be looked into in this chapter. But first it is necessary to provide some general background remarks about energy.

Energy consumption

There has been growing concern about the overuse of energy in the world economy. Energy is usually derived from fossil fuels, such as oil, natural gas and coal, although other forms do exist – most notably atomic energy. As economies become richer, as per capita incomes rise – so does the consumption of energy. In other words, there is a positive relationship between per capita income and per capita energy consumption. Energy is generally measured in terms of British thermal units (Btu's). Thus, what has attracted attention is the ratio of energy (measured in terms of Btu's) to gross domestic product (GDP), that is

Energy/GDP

or what can be labelled as the E/Y ratio. Now although income per capita is a major determinant of energy per capita, it is not the only determinant. The E/Y ratio is variable both over time and across countries, as illustrated in Table 15.1.

In this application only one reason why the E/Y ratio varies will be considered. In doing this attention will be given to *two* forms of substitution. First, the substitution of energy for other factor inputs, such as capital and labour. Second, the substitution of one *form* of energy for another, such as coal for oil

Table 15.1 Energy/GDP ratios in 1973 and 1975

	Primary energy/GDP (10 Btu/$)	
	1973	1975
Canada	81.4	80.5
Germany	43.3	40.9
Japan	41.5	39.9
Netherlands	57.0	53.7
Norway	81.4	72.9
Sweden	48.4	44.8
Switzerland	36.8	38.1
UK	68.2	62.8
USA	64.6	64.6

Source: International Energy Agency Paris, 1976

or atomic energy for oil. The reason for considering the first form of substitution is because the International Energy Agency in Paris is keen to see a reduction in the energy/GDP ratio, and those countries which do reduce this ratio are applauded. But is the reduction in this ratio desirable?

Reducing the energy/GDP ratio

The analysis is presented in terms of Figure 15.1. In Chapter 12 it was explained that a production function denotes the maximum output that results from a given combination of factor inputs, and therefore expresses technical efficiency. Since this chapter is concerned with energy for the economy as a whole, and the level to which it is used within the economy, it is assumed that there are

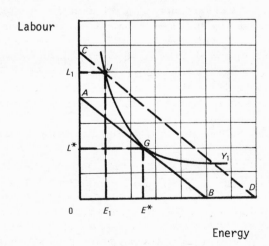

Figure 15.1

two inputs, energy (E) and labour (L), which are used by the economy to produce output (Y). As with the firm, it is assumed that a production function exists relating output to labour and, in this case, energy. It denotes the economy's efficient use, in a technical sense, of energy and labour in producing output. The price of labour, or the wage rate, is given by w and the price of a unit of energy by e, both assumed constant. It is useful to display technical efficiency in the form of an *isoquant* map. An isoquant simply denotes the most efficient combinations of inputs necessary to produce a particular level of output. In Figure 15.1 one such isoquant is drawn through points J and G, and denoted Y_1. This isoquant shows the efficient combinations of energy and labour necessary to produce output level Y_1.

Suppose, then, that real output is given at level Y_1. What is the least-cost use of energy and labour to produce this level of output? The cost of producing output, regardless of the level, is

$$C = wL + eE$$

which can be rearranged in the form,

$$L = (C/w) - (e/w)E$$

This equation represents the isocost line. In other words, all combinations of energy and labour which total in value terms to the same total cost. In Figure 15.1 it is represented by the line AB. The intercept of the line on the labour axis, point A, is given by the term (C/w) while the slope is given by the term $-(e/w)$.

Given the level of output, if the aim is to minimize cost, then it is necessary to find the isocost line nearest to the origin. This is the line tangent to the isoquant Y_1 at the point G, namely AB. At this point, E* units of energy would be used and L* units of labour.

Suppose now that firms were encouraged to use the least energy-intensive method of production, and yet produce the same level of output. Given output is the same, then this would mean a reduction in the E/Y ratio. If output is to remain constant, then production would have to move to a point like point J, so that energy would fall from E* to E_1 and labour input would rise to L_1. Furthermore, the cost of producing Y_1 using E_1 and L_1 units of energy and labour respectively, is given by the isocost line passing through point J and having a slope the same as AB, namely the isocost line CD. The fact that the slope of CD is the same as the slope of AB simply reflects the assumption of no change in factor prices.

Two observations follow immediately from this desire to reduce the level of energy use.

1   It results in a greater use of other factor inputs.
2   It results in an increase in the cost of producing the same level of output.

A rise in the price of energy

In the 1970s OPEC put up the price of oil. This led economists to consider, in particular, the substitutability between energy (oil in this case) and capital.

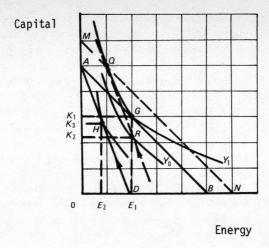

Figure 15.2

Concern here is with the flexibility that exists in firms in dealing with the price rise. If energy and capital have a high degree of substitutability then it is possible that firms could adapt quickly to the rise in energy prices by using more capital and better forms of capital. If, however, such substitution is difficult, then adjustment would be slow and difficult. The situation is shown in Figure 15.2, showing capital on the vertical axis and energy on the horizontal axis and the price of capital (more precisely the rental for capital services) is given by r. In all other respects the analysis is the same as in the previous section.

The initial situation is given by the isocost line AB and output level Y_1, with the cheapest input combination represented by point G, with E_1 units of energy being used and K_1 units of capital. A rise in the price of energy, with the price of capital constant, will change the isocost line to AD. This is because with the price of capital remaining constant the total capital that can be used for a given outlay remains OA. However, now that the price of energy has risen, a smaller amount of energy can be purchased for a given outlay, namely OD rather than OB. Now if output was to remain constant at level Y_1, even at the new factor price ratio, denoted by the *slope* of AD, then the input combination would move to point Q. (The tangent to the isoquant Y_1 at point Q is parallel to AD.) At point Q less than E_1 units of energy but more than K_1 units of capital are used to produce output level Y_1. But consider now the cost of producing output level Y_1 using the input combination shown by point Q. If a given outlay is spent using only capital then the total amount possible is represented by a point on the vertical axis. A greater outlay (a greater total cost) is represented by a point further up the vertical axis, because at the same factor price more capital can now be purchased. It is possible, therefore, to compare the total costs of producing output Y_1 by considering where the isocost line intersects the vertical axis. Since the new price ratio is denoted by the slope of AD and the new input combination is represented by point Q, then a line through Q parallel to AD is drawn, and is shown by the line MN in Figure 15.2. Because OM exceeds OA it follows that the cost of producing Y_1 with input combination represented by point Q is greater than for input combination represented by point G.

However, there is no reason to assume that output would remain constant. If the use of energy could not be reduced in the short run, then output would fall to Y_0. The reason for this is because energy use would remain at E_1. The isocost line is the line tangent to Y_1 at point Q. This isocost line passes through point R so that the cost of producing Y_1 at point Q is the same as producing Y_0 at point R. Hence, output level Y_0 would be produced using the same energy level, E_1, and K_2 units of capital. In this case the use of capital actually falls from K_1 to K_2. Even when adjustment in the use of energy could take place, so moving to a point along the isocost line AD, it is the case that capital use will be K_3, as shown by the input combination at point H. Although K_3 is greater than K_2 it is still less than K_1. Hence, point H also represents a *fall* in the use of capital, as well as energy, in relation to the initial position G. This result of less energy *and* less capital would also arise if capital and energy were in fact *complements* in production. In other words, more sophisticated types of capital equipment are also greater users of energy. As the energy price rises, therefore, the only way firms could cope with the increased costs is for firms to cut back both on energy and capital.

Interfuel substitution

It is, of course, possible that if the price of one form of fuel rises, then firms and consumers will switch to other forms of fuel. If the price of coal rises then firms and consumers may switch out of coal and into electricity. Not only do the different levels of scarcity influence the degree to which one fuel can be substituted for another, but also technical considerations play a part. In Britain when coal and oil prices began to rise there was a move into the use of natural gas as a form of fuel. However, this required more pipes to be laid, especially to fuel gas central heating and domestic cooking in areas which did not have any such pipes laid. For firms, the degree to which one form of fuel can be substituted for another can depend on the product being produced.

In the short-run, most machinery and capital are designed to operate with a certain type of fuel. For example, domestic residents may well have their homes heated by oil central heating. Certain firms, such as the electricity industry, have their whole production line based on coal and oil supply. But suppose there is a sudden rise in the price of oil. A householder will not simply replace his oil central heating, nor will the electricity industry change their whole pattern of production and switch to coal fuel the next day. The point is that in the short-run, the degree of interfuel substitution is very limited indeed. In Figure 15.3 the isoquant Q_S indicates the short-run situation for, say, the electricity industry. In this case the isoquant has a right-angle at the present use of both coal and oil, namely at point R. In other words, the electricity industry is assumed to use coal and oil in a fixed proportion regardless of the level of output. This arises from the nature of the technology. In the short-run this proportion is assumed not to

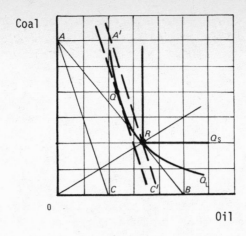

Figure 15.3

be variable. Now suppose the price of oil rises, the price of coal remaining constant. Suppose further that the firm wishes to retain the same level of electricity supply. (Although there is no obvious reason for this – the only point in assuming it is that we can concentrate on the pure substitution effect.) This change in relative prices means that the relevant isocost line changes from AB to A′C′ (which is parallel to AC), leaving the input mix at point R in the short-run. But what about the long-run? In the long-run substitution is possible. This is reflected in the isoquant Q_L. At the relative price A′C′ therefore, the electricity industry will move to point Q, using less oil and more coal and also reducing production costs. In so far as there is an expectation that oil prices will continue to rise, there will be a long-term substitution of coal (or nuclear fuel) for oil in the provision of electricity supply. A similar result arises in the case of home fuel. If oil prices are expected to rise, then there will be a substitution of gas, electricity or even solar energy as a form of household heating.

There have, over the last few years, been major changes taking place in the substitution of one form of fuel for another. Since coal and oil (along with gas) are basically fossil fuels, which are therefore limited in supply, it is not unreasonable to see a search for a fuel which is not based on limited supply. Of course, the difficulty here is that at the present time the most likely candidate is atomic energy. However, atomic energy has major dangers and uncertainties surrounding it. The obvious point to make about interfuel substitution is that as relative prices of the different forms of fuel change, then one energy source will be substituted for another.

Part IV

Firms and their inputs

16

The elements of the theory of input demand

Introduction to marginal product analysis

Part II of this book considered the theory of household behaviour, which can be used to throw light on the factors affecting both demands and supplies made by households. Part III considered the theory of the firm, which concentrates on supplies made by producers. The present, final, part looks at demands made by producers for the inputs they use. The theory developed here is often called the theory of distribution because it was originally felt that it not only explained input demands but also showed how a country's total income would be distributed between wages and salaries on the one hand and profits on the other; however, it is now clear that any explanation of this distribution needs to go far beyond the theory outlined here. Perhaps a more useful title for the theory is marginal product analysis, for, as the following sections make clear, the theory is based on marginal products. These are considered in the following two sections; later sections show how they are used to explain the demand for inputs.

Before proceeding, one important distinction needs to be drawn, namely that between inputs where producers can decide how much to demand without looking very far ahead and inputs where they cannot. The former group can be taken to include pretty well all hired or rented capital, all rented land, all other intermediate goods and services, and all hired labour. Exceptions might be made in any case where the employer has a long-term contract with a supplier or an employee, so these exceptions are included in the latter group along with all owned capital and all owned land; in a slave economy, this group would also include all owned labour! The theory outlined in this chapter shows how a producer could work out its demands for any of the inputs in the former group by considering how much income they would generate and how much they cost to use.

A more complex theory is needed to explain producers' demands for inputs in the latter group. There are several reasons for this. For instance, a firm considering buying some expensive new machinery with a life of 10 years will need to make forecasts of the demand for its output over the next 10 years and will need to assess the risk that demand might fall during that period; and it will have to consider the level of interest rates in the economy, for it will either be borrowing a large sum to finance the machinery (with a view to paying off the loan over a period of years) or it will have saved a large sum from recent profits which it could lend to someone else (for several years) instead of spending on machinery. There are well-established ways of handling these problems, but they are outside the scope of this book.

In considering how much of any input in the former group a firm will wish to purchase, it is necessary to make some assumptions about what the firm is trying to do. As in Chapter 10, it will be supposed that the firm is seeking to maximize its profits. The main shortcomings of this assumption were noted in Part III, and naturally they apply here also. It should be stressed that a profit-maximizing firm will not demand a given input at all unless there is a demand for the output which it helps to produce. For this reason, the demand for inputs is termed a *derived demand*, meaning that it derives from the demand for outputs.

Physical products

Before a firm decides how much of an input such as hired labour to use, it needs to have some idea about how much output it would get from various possible quantities of the input. Consider, for example, the owner of a potato farm wondering how many workers to employ in the forthcoming harvesting season. The quantity of potatoes harvested by any particular number of workers will naturally depend in some measure on the quantity of other inputs used, particularly the hectarage of potato fields, but also the amounts of fertilizer, baskets, tractors and trailers and so on. To simplify matters, suppose for the moment that the quantities of *all* inputs except labour has been fixed in advance: this assumption is a little unrealistic, and it will be released in due course, but for the moment it is assumed there is just one variable input.

On this basis, the firm could predict its total output with varying numbers of workers. This is known as its total physical product (TPP) and is shown in column (1) of Table 16.1. Not surprisingly, perhaps, TPP rises with the number

Table 16.1 Physical and revenue products

Number of workers	(1) Total physical product (TPP) tonnes	(2) Average physical product (APP) tonnes	(3) Marginal physical product (MPP) tonnes	(4) Total revenue product (TRP) £000s	(5) Average revenue product (ARP) £000s	(6) Marginal revenue product (MRP) £000s
0	0	–		0.0	–	
			30			6.0
1	30	30		6.0	6.0	
			46			9.2
2	76	38		15.2	7.6	
			44			8.8
3	120	40		24.0	8.0	
			36			7.2
4	156	39		31.2	7.8	
			24			4.8
5	180	36		36.0	7.2	
			6			1.2
6	186	31		37.2	6.2	

of workers, though in principle it could stop rising at some point – for instance after whatever number of workers were sufficient to lift every single potato – and at some stage it might conceivably fall – for instance if there were so many workers that they got in each other's way.

Column (2) shows the average physical product (APP) which for any number of workers (say 4) is found by dividing TPP (156 tonnes) by the number of workers (to get 39 tonnes); in effect, this shows how much of the TPP can be attributed to each worker. Column (3) shows the marginal physical product (MPP) which is the change in TPP resulting from a change of one unit in the variable input (all other inputs being held fixed); the MPP numbers are set between the lines of the TPP numbers to show, for example, that if the number of workers changes from 3 to 4 (or 4 to 3) then the TPP changes by 36 tonnes.

It will be seen that the numbers in columns (2) and (3) rise initially and then fall. Why is this? Consider APP first. It is supposed here that as the number of workers rises from (say) one to two, so the prospect of teamwork arises and output more than doubles so that APP rises. However, when the number rises from (say) three to six, it is supposed that there is little scope for extra teamwork, and also so few hectares of potatoes, baskets and so on, that output rises by much less than double, so that APP falls. MPP is affected by the same factors, for the possibility of teamwork means a change in the number of workers from (say) one to two may make more difference to TPP than a change from none to one, so MPP rises to begin with, but before long increases in the number of workers are likely to have less impact on TPP (for reasons just explained), so MPP subsequently falls.

In this example, MPP rose as a result of teamwork being possible and then fell when the ratio of workers to other inputs became progressively more unsatisfactory. In other cases, where teamwork might not be possible, MPP would fall from the start. The tendency for changes in TPP sooner or later to become smaller, and so for MPP to become smaller when successive amounts of a single variable input are added to fixed amounts of all other inputs, is often termed the *law (or hypothesis) of diminishing marginal returns*. Sometimes it is termed the *law of variable proportions* to emphasize the fact that it results from changing the proportion of the amount of the one variable input used to the amounts of the fixed ones used.

Revenue products

Of course, a profit-maximizing firm is interested in figures of physical products chiefly because they enable it to work out how much money would be associated with each possible level of use of the variable input. This section will consider three columns in Table 16.1 (columns (4) to (6)) which relate to the revenue generated by different numbers of workers. The use of these three columns will become clear in the next section.

Suppose, for the moment, that the potato farm considered above is in a perfectly competitive industry. It will face a horizontal demand curve (similar to the one shown in Figure 10.4) and so will be able to sell any number of potatoes at the current market price, say £200 per tonne. This price (P) is also the average revenue (AR) and marginal revenue (MR) that it faces at all output levels (for reasons explained in relation to Figure 10.4).

Column (4) of Table 16.1 shows the total revenue which would be produced by each number of workers. This is termed the total revenue product (TRP) and can readily be found from the figures in column (1). For instance, with five workers TPP is 180 tonnes; at £200 per tonne this gives a TRP of £36,000 (which can in fact be found here from TPP × P, TPP × AR or TPP × MR). Column (5) shows the average revenue product (ARP) which is the TRP divided by the number of workers. This shows how much of the TRP can be attributed to each worker. Thus with five workers producing £36,000, the ARP is £7,200. Note that ARP could instead be found by multiplying the APP of 180 tonnes by £200 (so ARP could be found from APP × P, APP × AR or APP × MR). Column (6) shows the marginal revenue product (MRP) which is the change in TRP when the quantity used of a single variable input changes by one unit. The numbers are placed between the lines of column (4) to show, for example, that if the number of workers changed from 5 to 6 (or 6 to 5) then TRP would change by £1,200. However, MRP could also be found by multiplying the MPP for this change in the number of workers, that is 6 tonnes, by £200 (so MRP here could be found from MPP × P, MPP × AR or MPP × MR).

The firm in this example was a perfect competitor in its output market. Had it been, say, a monopolistic competitor or a monopolist, then it would have faced a downward sloping demand curve (as in Figure 10.5) and hence it would find it

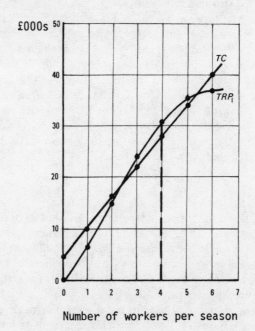

Number of workers per season

Figure 16.1

necessary to cut its price whenever it wished to raise its output. Moreover, at any output level, its price would equal its average revenue but exceed its marginal revenue (see Figure 10.10a where the output is 2, the price and AR are £60 and the MR is £40). Accordingly not all the formulae given above for calculating TRP, ARP and MRP would be applicable. For a given quantity of the variable input, the TRP would clearly equal the TPP times the price obtained for each unit of its product at that output level; thus TRP would equal TPP × P or TPP × AR (but would now exceed TPP × MR); and the ARP would clearly equal the APP times the price obtained and so equal APP × P or APP × AR (but exceed APP × MR). But what about MRP? As it happens, this would be given by MPP × MR alone. To see why, suppose a firm took on an extra employee and thereby raised its weekly output by one tonne from 100 to 101 tonnes; and suppose it had to cut its price from £1,000 per tonne to £995 per tonne to sell this higher weekly output. Its revenue would rise from £100,000 (100 tonnes at £1,000) to £100,495 (101 tonnes at £995). Thus the change in revenue produced by one extra tonne (that is MR) is just £495, which is well below the new price of £995 since selling the 101st tonne also means selling the first 100 tonnes each week for a little less than before. In turn, the extra revenue from the extra worker in his MPP (here 1 tonne) multiplied by the MR (£495). The MRP in this example is £495 and is not given by MPP × P or MPP × AR, each of which will equal £995, but is given by MPP × MR.

One can plot a curve for Table 16.1's TRP (as in Figure 16.1) and curves for ARP and MRP (as in Figure 16.2). The subscripts I show that these curves relate

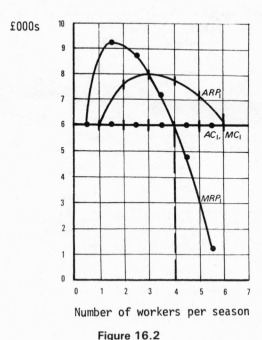

Figure 16.2

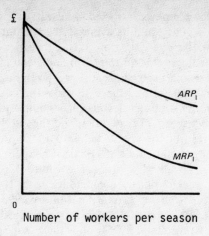

Figure 16.3

to a particular input. In this example, the possibility of teamwork means APP and MPP initially rise and then fall; in turn ARP and MRP rise and then fall. Had there been no scope for teamwork, then each curve would have fallen all the way as in Figure 16.3. Notice that in both Figures 16.2 and 16.3 the MRP curve meets the ARP curve at its highest point. The reason is that when an extra worker adds more to revenue than the average generated by the previous workers (that is when MRP exceeds ARP), then the average will rise (so ARP slopes up); conversely, when he adds less, so the average falls. Accordingly, MRP is above ARP when ARP rises and below it when it falls, so it coincides with ARP at the highest point where ARP is neither rising nor falling.

Maximizing profits

Once any firm's revenue product figures have been derived, it becomes possible to move on to decide what level of the one variable input will yield the highest profit, though to do so requires some information about the cost of the input. At this point it is necessary to distinguish between perfect and imperfect input markets. In a perfect input market, a firm is able to buy as much of the input as it wishes at the present price of the input; in other words, the firm is too small to affect this input price. This applies broadly to many input markets – such as electricity, office space, hired photocopiers or lorry drivers' services – even when the purchasing firms may be far from perfectly competitive in their output markets. It is this situation which will be assumed until the final section of the chapter. That section will consider what happens when an input is purchased by a firm which *is* large enough to affect its price. That situation might well occur with some inputs when the purchasing firm is a monopolist in its output market, for then it might well buy some special inputs which are bought by no one else; but it could also occur when the purchasing firm is a perfect competitor, as might be the case for a potato farmer on a small offshore island who sells his

Table 16.2 Maximizing profits with a variable input

Number of workers	(1) Total cost of variable input (TC_1) £000s	(2) Average cost of variable input (AC_1) £000s	(3) Marginal cost of variable input (MC_1) £000s	(4) Total revenue product (TRP) £000s	(5) Total cost of all inputs (TC) £000s	(6) Profit £000s
0	0.0	–		0.0	4.0	−4.0
			6.0			
1	6.0	6.0		6.0	10.0	−4.0
			6.0			
2	12.0	6.0		15.2	16.0	−0.8
			6.0			
3	18.0	6.0		24.0	22.0	2.0
			6.0			
4	24.0	6.0		31.2	28.0	3.2
			6.0			
5	30.0	6.0		36.0	34.0	2.0
			6.0			
6	36.0	6.0		37.2	40.0	−2.8

products in mainland markets where he faces a fixed market price, but is dependent on his few fellow islanders for labour and finds he must raise sharply the wages he offers each time he wants an extra worker.

For the moment, though, it will be assumed that firms face a fixed input price, and in the case of the potato farm considered earlier it will be supposed this is the (princely!) sum of £6,000 for a worker for a season. From this information, it is easy to calculate the total cost of this variable input (TC_1) for each number of workers as in column (1) of Table 16.2. The average cost (AC_1) is shown in column (2), and is always £6,000; this is TC_1 divided by the number of workers to show how much of the TC_1 is attributable to each worker. Column (3) shows the marginal cost of this input (MC_1) which is how much TC_1 changes when the amount of the input used changes by one unit. The numbers are placed between the lines of the TC_1 column and show, for example, that when the number of workers changes from 3 to 4 (or 4 to 3) then TC_1 changes by £6,000.

The most straightforward way of illustrating the profit-maximizing number of workers is to see which number produces the greatest difference between total revenue product and total costs. The total revenue product figures are shown in column (4) of Table 16.2 and reproduce those shown in column (4) of Table 16.1. In order to calculate total costs, it is necessary to allow for the cost of all the fixed inputs as well as labour. Suppose the combined cost of these fixed inputs is a mere £4,000. In that case, the total cost (TC) associated with any number of workers will be £4,000 more than the TC_1 shown in column (1), and will be as shown by the figure shown in column (5). The difference between the column (4) and (5) figures in any row of the table is the excess profit for the number of workers represented by that row, and the profit for each number of workers is shown in column (6) (where negative figures indicate a loss). The highest number shown there, £3,200, appears with four workers. However, the firm might wonder if it could get a little more profit with, say, 3.9 workers (that is, three workers for a whole season and one for 0.9 of a season), or 4.1 workers. To investigate this, it might add to Figure 16.1 a curve for the total cost (TC) associated with each number of workers as shown in column (5). The gap between the TRP_I and TC curves represents the total profit for varying number of workers, and does indeed seem to be greatest when there are just 4 workers. Even so, a diagram like this, where it is necessary to find the greatest gap between two curves, is not very convenient. It is preferable to use a figure where two curves cross at the critical profit-maximizing point, and it is in order to construct such a figure that all the average and marginal figures so far encountered have been calculated.

The ARP_I and MRP_I curves in Figure 16.2 have already been mentioned. A single horizontal line can be added to represent the AC_I and MC_I figures in Table 16.2. This line intersects the MRP_I line precisely at the profit-maximizing point and shows this to be precisely 4 workers rather than 4.1 or 3.9. Why is this the profit-maximizing point? It is because MRP_I and MC_I must be equal at that point. To the left, with say 2 workers, MRP_I exceeds MC_I indicating that a rise in the number would raise TRP_I more than TC_I and hence raise profits; indeed, the MRP_I curve shows that a rise from 2 workers to 3 would raise TRP_I by £8,800 while the MC_I curve shows that it would raise TC_I by £6,000. So it is sensible to expand the number of workers if MRP_I exceeds MC_I. To the right of the optimum point with, say, 6 workers, MRP_I is below MC_I indicating that a cut in the number would cut TRP_I less than it would cut TC_I and hence raise profits; indeed, MRP_I shows a cut from 6 to 5 would cut TRP_I by £1,200 and MC_I shows it would cut TC_I by £6,000. So it is sensible to cut the number of workers if MRP_I is below MC_I. It follows that profit-maximization occurs when MRP_I equals MC_I. (Actually, this happens at two numbers of workers, 0.5 – one picker for half a season – and 4. Readers should refer to the discussion of the related situation in Figure 10.7 and convince themselves that profit-maximization occurs at the right-hand intersection; the left-hand one is the profit-minimizing or loss-maximizing point).

If MRP_I and MC_I cut at the optimum point, then it may be wondered why ARP_I and AC_I are included in the figure. The reason is that they enable the TRP_I and TC_I at the optimum point to be calculated. For example, with 4 workers, the ARP_I can be estimated from the ARP_I curve as £7,800 – indicating a TRP_I of £31,200 (4 multiplied by £7,800) – and the AC_I can be read off the AC_I curve as £6,000 – indicating a TC_I of £24,000 (4 multiplied by £6,000). In turn, it is possible to estimate the total profit by finding the difference between these two figures, that is £7,200, and then deducting the cost of the fixed inputs, £4,000, to reach a final profit figure of £3,200, though this step cannot be represented on the figure itself.

The demand for inputs

A demand curve for an input: stage 1

It is possible to draw a figure analogous to Figure 16.2 for any firm which purchases a single variable input in a perfect input market – that is to say at a market-determined price which is not affected by the amount the firm buys – to see what is the profit-maximizing amount to buy. This is where MRP_I equals MC_I. The only difference between firms which are perfect competitors in their output markets and firms which are not was explained earlier, and lies in the choice of formulae that may be used in calculating the numbers on which their MRP_I and (if required) ARP_I curves are based.

It is now possible to extend the analysis to see how much of the input the firm would buy at each of a range of possible input prices and hence derive the firm's demand curve from that input. A common approach to this problem is to look at a figure like Figure 16.2 and suppose the input price had been something different. With a wage of, say, £3,000 per season, the curve representing AC_I and MC_I would have been a horizontal line at the £3,000 level and would cut MRP_I at around 5 workers. With a wage of, say, £7,000, the AC_I and MC_I line would have been horizontal at the £7,000 level and would cut MRP_I at around 3.5 workers (obtainable by hiring 3 workers for the whole season and one for half). Indeed, it seems that to find the optimum number of workers at any wage level it is necessary only to look at the MRP_I curve and read off the number of workers at that level. In turn, the MRP_I curve can be regarded as representing the firm's demand curve. Note that this demand curve would stop where MRP_I is cut by ARP_I. At higher wage rates, say £8,800, the AC_I and MC_I line would be horizontal at the £8,800 level and its intersection with MRP_I might suggest the firm should employ some 2.5 workers; but in this case, AC_I would be £8,800, which exceeds the ARP_I of under £8,000 at this employment level, so indicating that the firm would not cover the cost of its sole variable input. In these circumstances (for reasons explained in connection with Figure 10.10f), the firm would be better advised to shut down at once and purchase no variable inputs at all.

A demand curve for an input: stage 2

The analysis of the previous section suggests that a firm's MPR_I curve for an input (up to its intersection with the ARP_I curve) can be used as its demand curve for that input. However, such a demand curve embodies two unrealistic assumptions. Attention has already been drawn to the first, namely that the analysis so far has assumed a single variable input. It is now necessary to point out the second. Suppose the firm in Figure 16.2 did initially face a wage rate of £6,000 per season and employ four workers. Then suppose that just as the potato-lifting season started, the wage rate fell to £3,000. Would the firm now want 5 workers and seek to employ an extra worker for the whole season? It certainly would if its MRP_I curve stayed put, but this would happen only of none of its rivals reacted to the wage cut by raising their employment and output levels.

To see why the MRP_I curve is likely to shift, recall from column (1) of Table 16.1 that if the firm raised the number of workers from, say, 4 to 5 then it would produce 24 extra tonnes of potatoes. So long as these fetch a price of £200 a tonne, the MRP resulting from raising the number of workers from 4 to 5 would be £4,800 as indicated by MRP_I in Figure 16.2. Now suppose wage rates fall from £6,000 to £3,000. If the firm's rivals ignore the change and keep their employment and output levels constant, then potato prices will stay at £200 a tonne (as the firm is considered too small to affect the market price, and so the demand curve and MR curve it faces, by changing its own output level), and so the firm's MRP_l if it raised employment from 4 to 5 would still be £4,800; likewise, the MRP_l for any other change by one in the number of workers employed would stay at its original number so the whole MRP_l curve shown would still apply. But in reality, the firm's rivals would take on more workers and so raise their output levels and sell more potatoes, so in turn causing a fall in potato prices. Suppose potato prices fell to £150 per tonne. In that case, the firm in Table 16.1 would find its MRP_l if it raised the number of workers from, say, 4 to 5 would be only £3,600 (that is 24 tonnes extra output sold at only £150 per tonne); likewise, the MRP_l for any other change by one in the number of workers would now be lower than before, so the whole MRP_l curve would shift down. This means the firm's employment level at the new wage would have to be read off its new lower MRP_l curve. The old MRP_l curve could not be used for this purpose and so would *not* be its demand curve. (Incidentally, this second objection to using the initial MRP_l curve as a demand curve applies to all types of firms except monopolists who have no rivals.)

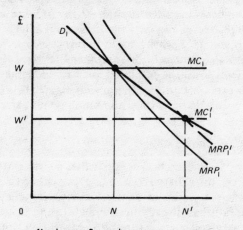

Figure 16.4

It is necessary, therefore, to see how a demand curve can be derived in a realistic world for a firm which has more than one variable input and rivals who do react to changes in input prices. The way in which this is done is shown in Figures 16.4 and 16.5. Suppose these relate to labour demanded by a potato farm which initially faces the wage rate W, giving rise to the MC_l curve shown, and suppose, too, it initially has the MRP_l shown. It will settle down employing N workers.

Now suppose the wage rate falls to W'giving rise to the new marginal cost

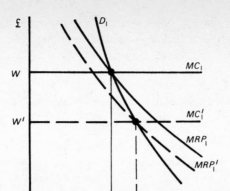

Number of workers per season

Figure 16.5

curve for the input labelled MC_I'. The firm will *not* settle where MC_I' cuts MRP_I, for forces are now at work to give it a different marginal revenue product curve from MRP_I. One force, indicated in the last paragraph, is that its rivals will expand, forcing potato prices down and putting downward pressure on the firm's marginal revenue product curve. However, there will be other forces at work putting upward pressure on this curve, provided only that the firm has some variable inputs besides labour. In practice, as a fall in wage rates is likely to cause the firm to take on more labour, it will probably also take on more complementary inputs – such as baskets and tractors – and fewer substitute inputs – such as potato-harvesting machines. These changes serve to increase the productivity of its workers since they now have more equipment to use, and fewer potatoes will have been removed by the harvesting machines before the workers reach them. The effects of such changes can be readily seen in the case of the firm considered in Table 16.1. The TPP figures shown there were calculated on the basis of a given number of complementary and substitute inputs for labour. If the number of complementary inputs rose and the number of substitute inputs fell, then these original TPP figures would become inapplicable. Suppose they were replaced by new numbers which were all 25 per cent larger; then, for example, the TPP would be 195 tonnes with 4 workers (instead of 156) and 225 with 5 (instead of 180). As a result, the MPP as the number rose from 4 to 5 would be 30 instead of 24; likewise, all the other MPP figures in column (3) would also be larger.

It is now possible to see what might happen to the firm's MRP_I curve when the wage rate falls. The MRP_I at any point – say when the number of workers changes from 4 to 5 – is the MPP resulting from the extra worker multiplied by the MR of an extra unit of output. By encouraging an expansion in the industry's output, the falling wage rate depresses potato prices so that the MR

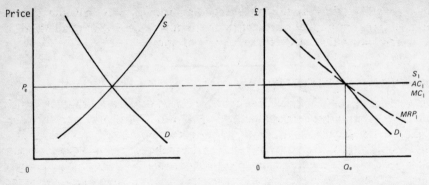

Input market: quantity per period   Typical buyer: quantity per period

Figure 16.6

from selling an extra tonne of potatoes falls; but by changing the amount of other inputs used by a typical firm, the falling wage rate raises the MPP resulting from the extra worker. In turn, the new MRP_I may be higher or lower at this point. Likewise, it could be higher or lower at any other point. In turn, the whole MRP_I curve can settle in either a higher or lower position than the original one. These two possibilities are shown in Figure 16.4 and 16.5 respectively. In each case, the optimum amount of labour to employ at the new wage rate W' is N' where the new MC_I' curve with the new MRP_I'. In each figure, then, the firm originally took on N workers when the wage was W, and it now takes on N' when it is W'. This information indicates two points on the firm's demand curve for the input, and these are marked by large dots in the figures. By finding the number of workers wanted at other wage rates, it would be possible to trace out the whole demand curve, and this is shown by the curve D_I in each figure.

For any particular input where usage can readily be varied, each firm has a demand curve which could in principle be found like D_I in Figures 16.4 and 16.5. By using the information in the demand curves of all the firms purchasing that input, and seeing how much each would want at each price, it is possible to work out how much they would want between them at each price and so derive the market demand curve for it. Suppose this market demand curve is represented by D in the left-hand part of Figure 16.6. The equilibrium market price (P_e) for this input would be fixed where D met the market supply curve. This price would be faced by all buyers and so presents a horizontal supply (S_I) curve to a typical buying firm (which can buy as much as it desires at this price) as indicated in the right-hand part of Figure 16.6 (where the horizontal axis is drawn to a different scale from that used in the left-hand figure); this S_I curve is also the buyer's AC_I and MC_I curve for this input. The firm concerned will buy Q_e units of the input (in each period of time) as this is where MC_I cuts its own demand curve D_I. It will also settle down with a MRP_I curve which passes through the same point, just as the firms in Figures 16.4 and 16.5 found MRP_I passing the point where MC_I cut D_I when the wage was W, and MRP'_I passing the point where MC'_I cuts D_I when the wage was W'. So, despite adding in some realism, this section has not altered the main earlier result, namely that firms settle down where MC_l equals MRP_l; it has merely shown that MRP_l curves may jump about!

Changes in the demand for inputs

The analysis of the last section can readily be used to show four factors which could cause the market demand for an input to shift. Consider why this demand might rise. It could be caused, first, by a rise in the number of firms using the input. Secondly, it could occur if there were a rise in the price of a substitute input, and hence a fall in the quantity of the substitute used. Thirdly, it could occur if there were a fall in the price of a complementary input, and hence a rise in the amount of the complement used. For instance, it was shown in the last section that the MPP (and hence the MRP) of potato harvest workers would rise if either fewer harvesting machines were used or more baskets and tractors were used. So, for example, the firm in Figure 16.4 might find that if wages stayed at W, then a rise in the price of harvesting machines and a fall in the price of baskets would cause the MRP of workers to shift from MRP_l to MRP'_l. Consequently, the number of workers employed at W would rise from N to the number where MC_l cut MRP'_l. Similarly, the number of workers which would be employed at any other wage would also rise, so the firm's demand curve for this input would shift to the right.

Fourthly, market demand could rise if the productivity of the input rose without any change in the amount of other inputs used; for instance, workers might agree to organize their time more effectively. Such an agreement would tend to raise the TPP of any number of workers and also the MPP from taking on one more at any starting level. However, if the productivity improved in all firms in an industry, then the supply of that industry's output could rise dramatically and hence the output price would fall. This means the MR from selling an extra unit of output would also fall. Consequently, each firm's initial MRP curve (on which each point is given by MPP × MR) could rise or fall depending on whether MPP rose proportiotely more or less than MR fell; in turn, each firm's D_l could also rise or fall, as would the market demand curve.

Imperfect input markets

This chapter is concluded by considering what happens with firms which are so large relative to the market for some inputs they use that their use of those inputs affects their prices. The analysis of this situation is often discussed in the context of monopsonistic demand where one firm is the sole user of an input, but it can be applied in any situation where a firm can affect an input's price. The critical point is that the firm will no longer face a horizontal supply curve (like S_l in the right hand part of Figure 16.6) but an upward sloping one like S_l in Figure 16.7 which assumes the input is labour. This shows the wage the firm must pay for each possible size of labour force, and hence the AC_l for each possible level. For instance, it would have to pay the wage of £100 per week to obtain 5 workers, so

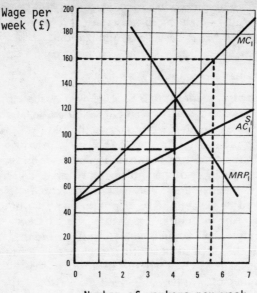

Wage per week (£)

Number of workers per week

Figure 16.7

£100 would be the average cost of each unit of input if it did indeed employ 5. In this situation, the MC_I curve no longer coincides with AC_I. Suppose, for instance, that the firm initially employed 5 workers at £100 each, and so paid £500 in all, and then decided to employ 6 workers. S_I shows that it would have to raise the wage it offers to £110. The total wage bill would rise to £660, that is by £160. Thus the MC_I shows that total labour costs rise by £160 when the labour force changes from 5 to 6. Other points on MC_I could be found in a similar way, and it would be found that MC_I starts at the same point as AC_I but is otherwise above it. (It can be shown that if AC_I is straight, then MC_I passes points half-way between AC_I and the vertical axis).

To see how much input the firm will use, suppose its labour force has the MRP_I curve shown. Then, like any profit-maximizing firm, it will seek to have the labour force size where MRP_I equals MC_I which here is with 4 workers. Notice that to obtain 4 workers, the wage offered has to be £90 as shown by S_I. It should be mentioned that it is not possible to derive a demand curve here. A demand curve would imply that at any particular price there was one quantity of labour which the firm would seek. However, changes in the shape and position of S_I (and hence MC_I) mean that even if MRP_I were constant, the firm might end up wanting, say, a different number of workers at the same wage (£90). This happens in Figure 16.8 where the new MC_I' cuts MRP_I with a labour force of 3 workers which the new S_I' shows can be obtained here with a wage rate of £90. Incidentally, the shape and position of the supply curve of labour to this firm could be affected by such factors as changes in the wage rates paid in other

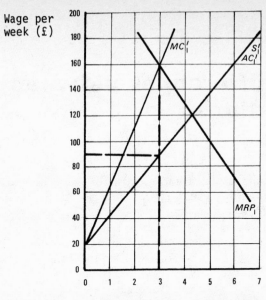

Wage per week (£)

Number of workers per week

Figure 16.8

similar jobs, the level of unemployment and tastes of employees.

Although the analysis embodied in Figures 16.7 and 16.8 is rather different from that of earlier sections, which assumed a perfect input market, the equilibrium positions here will be affected by the same demand-side factors as before. Thus a rise in the demand for the firm's output will tend to raise its price, and hence the marginal revenue obtained from selling an extra unit; this will put upwards pressure on the curve for the MRP of labour shown in the figures and so will tend to lead to a rise in both the firm's employment level and its wage rate. Similar results would follow if (for reasons explained earlier) the MRP schedule was to rise following a fall in the price (and so a rise in the use) of complementary inputs, or a rise in the price (and so a fall in the uses) of substitute inputs. On the other hand (again for reasons already outlined) a rise in the productivity of labour whilst the amount of other inputs used remained constant could cause the MRP curve to rise or to fall and could lead to a rise or to a fall in both employment levels and wage rates.

17

Wage differences between occupations

It was explained in Chapter 1 that the forces of supply and demand determine the equilibrium price in any market where there are many buyers and sellers of a homogeneous product. The markets for different types of labour approximate to this situation, though in these markets it is usual to use the term wage rate – often for an hour's or a week's labour – instead of the term price. Different occupations often command very different prices or wage rates, and the following sections consider in turn various factors which cause wage rates to vary from labour market to labour market.

Before considering these factors, it is useful to make some general points about labour markets, and these are illustrated in Figure 17.1, which may be taken to apply to shoe shop assistants in a modest sized market town. Suppose this market has settled at the equilibrium position where the demand curve for the labour concerned cuts the supply curve (regarded for convenience as a straight line). In this situation, the wage rate will be £120 per week and the

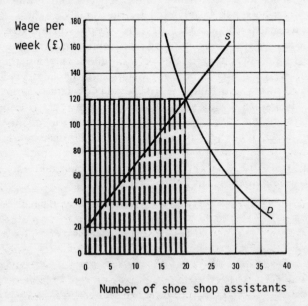

Figure 17.1

number of assistants will be 20, so the total weekly wage bill will be £2,400. Notice, first, that the demand curve slopes downwards; the last chapter explained why firms are likely to employ more of an input when its price falls. Notice, secondly, that the supply curve slopes upwards. Broadly speaking, this indicates that the higher the wage for this occupation, the more people will offer their services to it. An upward sloping supply curve is likely in all occupations. It should be stressed that this result assumes constant wage rates in all other occupations. Clearly, if wage rates rose in this market whilst wage rates also rose in all other markets, then this occupation would not become more attractive relative to the others, so the number of people willing to work in it might not rise.

There are further implications of an upward sloping supply curve. Looking towards the left-hand end of the supply curve, it can be seen that if the wage were £20, then no one would work as a shoe shop assistant in this town. However, if the wage were some £25, then just one person would be willing to be a shoe shop assistant. Put another way, the curve indicates that there is one person in this town who would be an assistant at that wage, though if the wage fell below that level, then even that person would refuse this type of work. It is said that this person has *transfer earnings* of £25 – represented by the dashed line above the first employee – this being the wage necessary to persuade that person not to transfer from this labour market to another. The remaining vertical dashed lines in the figure show that the transfer earnings for the second person might be about £30, for the third about £35 and so on; the transfer earnings for the twentieth person are just £120. The total transfer earnings for the whole market are given by the quadrilateral occupied by these dashed lines and actually equal £1,450.

In practice, all the 20 employees will be paid the present wage of £120 a week. It follows that all except the twentieth are paid more than their transfer earnings. The excess is known as *economic rent*. The economic rent is some £95 for the first person and is represented by the continuous line above that person (running from £25 up to the wage of £120). The economic rent is £90 for the second, £85 for the third and so on, as represented by the remaining continuous vertical lines. The total economic rent in this market is given by the triangle occupied by these vertical lines and actually equals £950. Added to the £1,450 for transfer earnings, this naturally gives a figure of £2,400 which equals the total earnings in this market.

The 20 assistants may be employed by perhaps eight shops. One shop might employ three assistants whose transfer earnings happen to be, say, £50, £70 and £85. It is tempting to suppose that the shop's owners would seek to pay them those wages respectively, instead of paying them all the going wage of £120, but there are two reasons why the owners could not do this. First, they would not know what the individual employees' transfer earnings were. Secondly – and perhaps more importantly – they would find that any cut in those employees' wages would lead them to seek work at other shoe shops which were paying the market wage rate of £120. This emphasizes an important feature of the definition of transfer earnings, which is that it shows how much people must be paid to stay in their present labour market but *not* how much they must be paid to stay with their present employer within that market. The three employees considered here might not be willing to take up another form of employment altogether unless shoe shop assistants wages fell sharply, but they might well leave their present shoe shop for another one if their present employer made the slightest cut in their pay.

Compensating (or equalizing) differences

The eighteenth-century Scottish economist Adam Smith approached the analysis of wage differences by arguing that one might expect workers to leave low paid jobs for high paid jobs, so reducing the supply of labour in the former and raising it in the latter. This should raise wages in the former and cut them in the latter, and it might be supposed that the process would continue until the wages in each job were the same. If differences persisted, however, then it seemed that many people were not willing to forsake the low paid jobs for the high paid ones. Smith suggested that reluctance to make these moves would arise if there was some *non-pecuniary disadvantage* attached to the high paid jobs or some *non-pecuniary advantage* attached to the low paid one. This reluctance might appear, for example, between North Sea divers (working from oil rigs) and bartenders, and could cause the situation shown in Figures 17.2 and 17.3. Figure 17.2 shows the market for bartenders and how its equilibrium position is at a presumably modest wage W_B with N_B workers; many people are prepared to work at W_B since they regard the surroundings, the company and the occasional liquid gratuity as making up for the low pay. Notice that it would be possible to get some bartenders at a wage of W_A or a shade more. In contrast, Figure 17.3 shows that a high wage, W_C, is needed before anyone would be a diver, for at lower wages no one would be willing to accept this work, which is dangerous and also means spending so much time away from home; in fact this

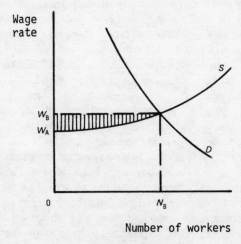

Number of workers

Figure 17.2

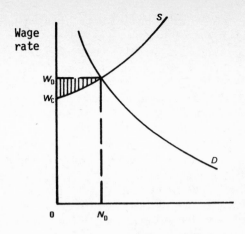

Figure 17.3

market has its equilibrium at wage W_D with N_D employees. Notice that the amount of economic rent (shown by the shaded areas in the figures) is fairly modest in each case here. This may seem surprising in the case of the divers as they are paid a high wage, but, of course, their transfer earnings are also high.

Smith argued that when people decide what jobs to take, they weigh up both pecuniary factors (that is the wage rates) and non-pecuniary factors. Differences in wage rates are needed to compensate for any differences in the non-pecuniary factors, and these wage rate differences have sometimes been termed *compensating differences* or *equalizing differences*. Taking both pecuniary and non-pecuniary factors into account, the overall attractions or *net advantages* of many jobs may be similar.

It should be pointed out that non-pecuniary disadvantages may include periods of training on low incomes. The situations shown in Figures 17.2 and 17.3 could apply, for example, to bank clerks and dentists respectively. Bank clerks need a fairly short training period during which they get paid (albeit at trainee wage rates), and this means some people would take these jobs even at a modest wage, W_A, though the market settles down into an equilibrium wage of W_B. By contrast, dentists need a long training period (during which they survive chiefly on student grants) and this means that a high wage, W_C, is needed to tempt anyone to consider such an occupation, though the market actually settles into an equilibrium wage of W_D. Economists argue that when people train they are investing in *human capital*, and many will do so only if the jobs for which they train offer a wage high enough to yield a reasonable return on (or compensation for) that investment.

Differences in innate ability

Important as they are, compensating differences are not the only factors to cause wage differences. A further factor will be discussed here, and two others in the sections which follow. This section concerns differences which arise from the high wages paid to those people with some innate skills; this term is used to distinguish these skills from those which can be acquired by training, like those of the dentists considered in the last section (though it should be stressed that people with innate skills often improve them with instruction and practice).

Figures 17.4 and 17.5 depict respectively the markets for footballers in the English first and second divisions. The supply curve in Figure 17.4 has been drawn to suggest that suitable players will not offer their services in the first division for a wage below A which equals the wage (W_2) shown in Figure 17.5 to be the one presently applying in the second. However the critical feature here is that the supply curve (S_1) of highly skilled players for the first division rapidly becomes very inelastic, for there is a very limited number of suitable players who can make their services available, no matter how high the pay, since such people are scarce. This supply curve interacts with a somewhat higher demand curve (D_1) than the second division one (D_2); D_1 is higher than D_2 because first division clubs typically have larger grounds than second division clubs and can charge higher ticket prices, so the marginal revenue products of their players (on which their demand curves are based) are higher than those of second division players. The upshot is that the first division wage (W_1) greatly exceeds the second division wage (W_2).

As drawn, Figure 17.4 depicts economic rent (shown by the shaded area) as being relatively high in the first division. This is certainly plausible, for most of the players there might be willing to do the same job for any wage which exceeds W_2. It is often the case that people with innate skills command high wages much of which represents economic rent, for they would often be prepared to work in the same job at much lower wages since the alternative jobs they would consider might not require their own particular skill (or any other) in any great degree and so might not be especially well paid.

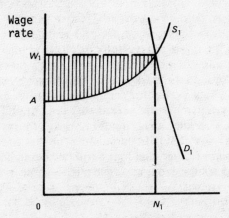

Number of first division players

Figure 17.4

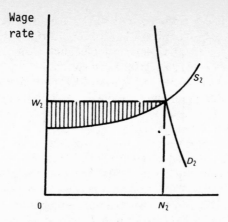

Number of second division players

Figure 17.5

Differences caused by sudden changes in demand

Wage differences which stem from differences in non-pecuniary factors or from differences in the degree of scarce innate skills involved in different jobs may well persist indefinitely. For this reason, such differences are sometimes termed *equilibrium differences*. However, sometimes wage differences between different jobs appear fairly suddenly and then in time disappear once more. These differences are sometimes termed *dynamic differences*.

Dynamic differences arise as a result of changes in the pattern of demand for different types of labour, especially sudden changes. This pattern is liable to change as a result of changes in technology, which may mean machines reduce the need for some types of worker, or as a result of changes in the pattern of demand for the goods and services that different types of labour are used to produce. Consider, for example, the markets for the labour of workers in cotton mills and television factories after World War II. Perhaps the initial demand and supply in each case was as shown respectively in Figures 17.6 and 17.7 by D_1 and S_1. For simplicity, it will be assumed that there were no non-pecuniary factors favouring either job and that their wage rates (W_C and W_T) were equal, though there were more workers in cotton mills (N_C) than TV factories (N_T). It will also be assumed for simplicity that there is no tendency for wages to rise over time as a result of inflation or economic growth.

Now the development of man-made fibres on the one hand and regular TV broadcasts on the other caused a fall in the demand for cotton, and so in the derived demand for cotton mill workers, and a rise in the demand for TVs, and so in the derived demand for TV workers. Perhaps by 1970 the demand curves in the labour markets were those labelled D_2. The result is that wages in cotton mills fell to W_C' (and employment fell to N_C'), whilst wages in TV factories rose to W_T' (and employment rose to N_T'); there is now a difference in wages (equal to W_T'

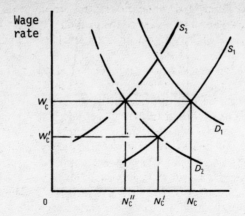

Number of cotton mill workers

Figure 17.6

less W'_C, but this is a dynamic difference which should eventually disappear.

To see why this is so, it is important to understand the nature of the original S_1 supply curves. S_1 in Figure 12.6 shows how many people would want to work in cotton mills at each wage assuming other things stay put; amongst these other things is the wage of TV workers which it is supposed stays put at W_T. When TV workers' wages rise, the supply of cotton mill workers gradually falls so the supply curve for them gradually shifts left. Similarly, the S_1 curve for TV workers in Figure 17.7 assumes wages for cotton mill workers stays put at W_C; when the mill workers' wages fall, the supply of TV workers gradually rises so the supply curve for them gradually shifts right. The two supply curves are likely to continue shifting until they reach positions like those labelled S_2, for

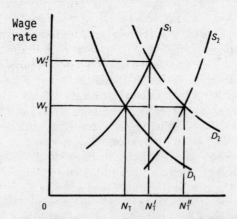

Number of TV factory workers

Figure 17.7

combined with the new D_2 demand curves these result in the two market wages being equal once again, in this case at the original (W_C and W_T) level, though it might have been at a slightly higher or lower level. The final employment levels are N_C'' and N_T''.

It follows that the quicker the supply curves shift, the quicker the dynamic difference disappears. It might be supposed that the supply curves would indeed move quickly, but this is often not the case. Certainly the difference means many cotton mill workers will wish they worked in TV factories; but they will not move quickly since they may be occupationally immobile – that is, unenthusiastic about learning new skills – and geographically immobile – that is, unenthusiastic about moving from a house near a mill to one near a TV factory. It may be that the supply curves shift only as mill workers retire and their children decide to begin their careers working in TV factories. Certainly, the labour force tends to be geographically and occupationally immobile in the short-run but highly mobile in the long-run.

This example may be contrasted with another such as the simultaneous fall in the demand for home coal deliverymen and rise in the demand for home oil deliverymen as more and more households switched from coal fires to oil-fired central heating. It is unlikely that much of a dynamic wage differential appeared. This is partly because the demand changes were not sudden, so the demand curves themselves moved only slowly, and partly because any resulting tendency for even a small wage difference to appear would have been largely offset by fairly quick reactions in the supply curves. The supply curves would react quickly in this example partly because the new skill of delivering oil is readily acquired, and partly because there are oil and coal depots scattered all around the country so that it would almost always be possible for people to change from one occupation to the other without also having to move house.

Trade unions in markets with many buyers

One factor which can affect wage differences is the presence of trades unions. This section considers the effects of unions in labour markets with many buyers, whilst the next looks at their effects in markets with few buyers. Consider, for the moment, two labour markets in a hypothetical country, say shipbuilders and bus drivers, and suppose each group of workers is initially non-unionized. Initially, the supply and demand curves for each market may be as shown by S and D in Figures 17.8 and 17.9 respectively, and wage rates may be similar, as shown in each figure by W. The employment level for shipbuilders is given by N_S and for bus drivers by N_B.

Now suppose one group, shipworkers, forms a union. Suppose, too, they manage to form a closed shop so that shipyards agree to employ union labour only. Next, suppose the workers seek to raise their wage rate. One method is to demand a higher wage, say W', on threat of a strike; this effectively presents the labour market with the new supply curve, S', showing that employers will now have no workers at all if they pay less than W'. Notice that there is a limit (N'_s) – as there was before – on how many people would be prepared to work in

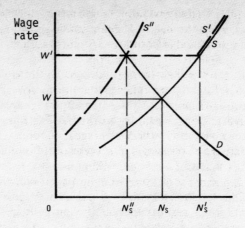

Figure 17.8

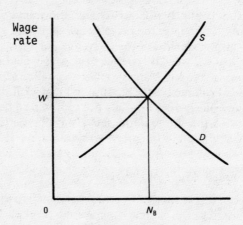

Number of bus drivers

Figure 17.9

shipyards at the wage W' (so beyond this point, the new supply curve coincides with the old one to show that the wage rate would have to exceed W' to secure more than N_S' workers, even if the union was happy for any number of workers to work for W'). Another method of forcing wages up from W is to introduce various conditions for union membership, such as banning women (now an illegal practice in the United Kingdom), insisting on long apprenticeships, or refusing admission to apprentices aged 17 or over; these devices would eventually restrict the number of people offering their services in this market below the previous level and present the labour market with the supply curve shown in Figure 17.8 by S".

Whichever method is used, a new supply curve arises which interacts with D to produce a higher wage. In Figure 17.8, the result is shown for simplicity as a wage of W' with either method as both S' and S" cut D at this level. It will be seen that there is now a difference between shipbuilders' wages of W' and bus drivers' wages of W. Employment in the shipbuilding industry has fallen to N''_s; the union will try to ensure that the fall in the labour force from N_s to N''_s takes place gradually through natural wastage (chiefly as people retire) and not quickly through layoffs. Figure 17.8 shows that if S' is applicable, then more people ($N'_s - N''_s$) want to work at the new wage than there are posts available. The union will have to take care to preserve its closed shop agreement as most of these people who are kept out would be willing for a little less than W' which would encourage employers to take them on in place of union workers (who get paid W') if they could. If S" is applicable, then there may seem less of a problem as the ($N'_s - N''_s$) workers are regarded as being no longer interested in working in the industry; but this is only because they are ineligible for union membership, and once again it will be necessary to preserve the closed shop to prevent employers taking on these people, perhaps for a little less than W', in place of union members.

It is worth concluding this section with three further observations. First, the presence of a closed shop union in a labour market means that the supply of labour is effectively controlled by one supplier, the union. Thus there is a situation of monopolistic supply as opposed to the perfect input markets considered so far, which require many suppliers (as well as many demanders) of the input. Secondly, the typical buyers in these markets will still be faced with a fixed price (now W' instead of W) for labour, and each will settle down with a smaller labour force size such that the marginal revenue product of labour equals the new higher wage rate. Thirdly, the power of any given union to force up wages depends on how far it is able to secure a closed shop, on how inelastic the demand is for its type of labour (for an inelastic demand means large wage rises have little effect on employment levels while an elastic demand curve means wage rises could inevitably lead to rapid and substantial layoffs) and, of course, on how militant its members are if they seek to force wages up with the threat or use of strikes.

Trades unions in markets with few buyers

The last section considered (in Figure 17.8) a labour market which initially had many buyers and sellers. It showed how the formation of a union could raise wages (say from W to W') at the expense of a smaller labour force (say N''_s instead of N_s). This section considers the effects of the formation of a union in a case where there are few buyers and where individual employers generally find themselves having to raise the wage rate they pay each time they want to hire extra employees. It will be seen, once again, that the union is able to raise the wage rate, though this time with more complex and surprising effects on employment levels.

Consider, for example, the employer referred to earlier in Figure 16.7, which

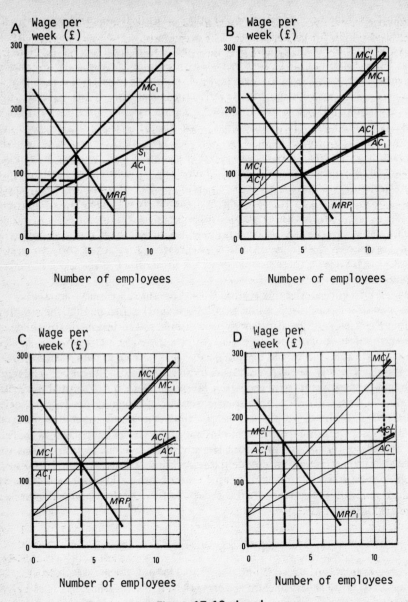

Figure 17.10a,b,c,d

is reproduced in Figure 17.10a. It will be recalled that such an input buyer faces an upward sloping input supply curve (S_l) or average cost curve (AC_l) with a marginal cost curve (MC_l) above it. Initially, the firm selects 4 employees, as at that level the marginal revenue product of labour (MRP_l) equals its marginal cost; and the supply curve shows that a wage of £90 is needed to secure four employers.

Suppose, now, the employees form a union, negotiate a closed shop agreement, and put in for higher wages. The wage rate will be expected to settle at whatever level they agree with the employer, but what will happen to the employment level? To answer this, three possible wage rates, namely £100, £130 and £160, will be taken in turn in Figures 17.b, c and d respectively. In each figure, the original S_I (or AC_I) and MC_I curves are shown in thin lines, and the new ones in thick lines.

The effect of the higher wage on the supply (or average cost) curve is the same as it was in Figure 17.8, that is to make the supply curve mostly horizontal at the new wage rate, showing that the firm will not be able to hire any employees at a lower rate; and the new curves (shown as AC'_I in each of the figures) kink where they join the original curve (AC_I) and coincide with it. In Figure 17.10b, for instance, this is because the original AC_I (or S_I) shows that a maximum of 5 people are willing to work for a wage of £100, and this limit will remain even if the union was happy for any number of employees to be taken on at that wage. So it would still be necessary for the firm to pay more if it wanted more than 5 workers.

Corresponding to the new average cost curves are new marginal cost curves (labelled MC'_I in each case). Each of these is a curve with *two* kinks at the employment level where the relevant AC curve has its one kink. To understand the kinks in the new marginal cost curves, it is necessary to see how these curves relate to the relevant average cost curves. To the right of its kink, each new average cost curve follows AC; accordingly, the right-hand part of the relevant new marginal cost curve follows MC. To the left of its kink, each new average cost curve is horizontal, indicating that extra workers can be hired at the going wage (£100, £130 or £160 as appropriate) so that it is not here necessary to raise the wage rate to get more workers; accordingly, the marginal cost of an extra worker equals the going wage (£100, £130, or £160), a result indicated by the fact that the left-hand part of each new marginal cost curve is horizontal at the appropriate wage level and so coincides with the relevant new average cost curve. It will be seen, then, that each of the new marginal cost curves has two separate parts, and for convenience these are joined (above the average cost curve kink) by a (dashed) vertical line.

With the diagrams complete, it is now possible to see the effects on employment levels. In each case, the employer will set this level at the point where MRP_I cuts the appropriate marginal cost curve (MC'_I), for to the left of this point MRP_I will exceed the marginal cost, indicating that extra workers would add more to revenue than to costs and so raise profits, whilst to the right MRP_I will be below the marginal cost, indicating that laying workers off would cut revenue less than costs and so raise profits. Figure 17.10b shows that when the wage set by the unions is £100, the employment level is 5. In this case, the union finds that raising the wage from £90 actually results in a *rise* in employment levels! This result occurs because MC'_I in Figure 17.10b shows that the cost of raising the employment level from 4 to 5 is now £100 (whereas MC_I shows it was previously £140) which is less than the resulting increase in revenue shown by MRP_I to be £115.

Encouraged by its double success in raising wages and employment, the union may push for a wage of £130 as in Figure 17.10c. However, employment now returns to 4 workers, as MC'_I cuts MRP_I at that level. With the even higher wage of £160, Figure 17.10d shows employment falls to 3 as MC'_I there cuts MRP_I at that level. By studying these figures, and considering other possible wages, the reader will be able to see that, starting with the initial wage of £90 and the initial employment level of 4, the union could raise both, up to £100 and 5 (as in Figure 17.10b) but then finds that all further wage rises are obtained at the cost of falls in employment levels. On its formation, the union may well be tempted to go at once for a wage of £130 (as in Figure 17.10c) as this is a substantial rise from £90 which has no adverse effect on the initial employment level of 4. As there are such temptations, it is highly likely that the wages received by the employees of firms facing upward sloping labour supply curves depend substantially on whether their employees have formed a union and, if so, what wage it is ultimately prepared to press for.

18

Wage subsidies

In Chapter 16 the demand curve for a factor input was discussed. One input of special significance is labour, and in this chapter consideration will be given to the issue of wage subsidies paid by the government. It will be discovered that a large part of the issues surrounding wage subsidies are very much dependent on the demand curve for labour – and most especially on the elasticity of the demand curve for labour.

Wage subsidies have both a microeconomic and a macroeconomic component, but only some of the microeconomic aspects of wage subsidies will be dealt with in this chapter. Of course, one of the main reasons for having wage subsidies is to reduce the level of unemployment. But one feature of wage subsidies is that they can be directed either at certain industries or certain categories of labour. The fact that wage subsidies can be directed at certain groups, such as youth unemployment, means that labour is not necessarily homogeneous. In other words, in earlier chapters labour was treated as a factor input and denoted L, and implicitly it was assumed that all units of labour were the same, that is, were homogeneous. But labour is not all the same, there are different levels of skill, education, age, sex, and so on. In other words, labour is heterogeneous. However, in the first part of the analysis presented in this chapter, the assumption will be made that labour is homogeneous. This is so that attention can be directed at certain features of wage subsidies. Later consideration will be given to how such subsidies can be directed at particular groups of labour.

Basically, wage subsidies can be divided into two types:

1 *Blanket subsidy*, applying to every employee.
2 *Marginal subsidy*, applying only to some of the labour force.

In the case of marginal subsidies two types are important:

(a) *Job-preserving subsidy*, applying to every redundancy that is deferred as a result of the subsidy.
(b) *Job-recruitment subsidy*, applying to every extra recruitment a firm is prepared to take on as a result of the subsidy.

The effect of a wage subsidy

Consider first some features of employment subsidies with the help of Figure

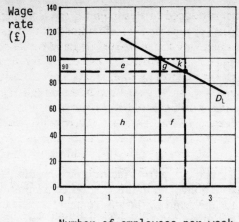

Figure 18.1

18.1. On the vertical axis is the wage rate and on the horizontal axis the amount of labour employed. The firm's demand curve for labour is represented by D_L. Suppose the initial wage is £100 per week and further that at this wage 200 people are employed. Now suppose that the employer receives a subsidy of £10 per worker. Employees still receive a wage of £100, but the employer effectively pays a wage of £90 (£100 – £10). The result of this subsidy is to raise the quantity of labour demanded from 200 units to 250 units.

Figure 18.1 helps to clarify the meaning of a blanket subsidy as distinct from a marginal subsidy. A *blanket* subsidy is paid on all employees, whether newly employed or having been employed before. At the wage £100 Figure 18.1 shows that 200 people are employed. At the subsidized wage of £90 there are 250 people employed. The *employment effect* of the subsidy, then, is to raise employment by 50 people. However, if the subsidy is a blanket subsidy, then it is paid not only on the extra 50 new workers, but also on the previous 200. Hence, the total subsidy payment in this case is £10 × 250 = £2,500, that is the area (e + g + k). A *marginal* subsidy, however, is paid only on the additional labour employed. Since the employment effect is 50 additional units of labour, then the marginal subsidy payment is £10 × 50 = £500, that is the area (g + k). To summarize:

Blanket subsidy = e + g + k = £2,500
Marginal subsidy = g + k = £500

It is clear that the marginal subsidy involves less total subsidy payment than a blanket subsidy for the same employment effect.

What is the net monetary gain to the employer of hiring this additional 50 units of labour? The total revenue received from the sale of goods produced by the increased labour employed is given by the area under the demand curve between 200 units of labour and 250 units of labour. Why is this? To answer this question assume that labour is hired in a perfectly competitive factor market and that the product produced by this labour is sold in a perfectly competitive product market. Finally, assume that the amount of other inputs employed remains constant so that with the short-run, demand for labour is under review. Under these assumptions, a *firm's* demand curve for labour is simply the marginal revenue product curve. In other words, each additional unit of labour employed gives rise to some increase in output (the marginal physical product of labour). This increased output is sold at a fixed price which brings in revenue. This additional revenue is the marginal revenue product. Thus, if labour employed rises by 50 units, and the marginal revenue product is no more than the demand curve for labour, then the total additional revenue received is the area under the demand curve between 200 and 250 units of labour. (For example, suppose the marginal physical product declined from 10 to 8 as result of taking on 1 more worker. Thus, 1 more worker produces 8 additional units of output. If this were sold at £5 per unit then marginal revenue product would be £40. If this is calculated for each of the extra 50 workers then the total additional revenue could be obtained. This represents the area under the demand curve between 200 and 250 units of labour). Hence, the extra revenue received by the employer arising from hiring the additional 50 units of labour is £4,750 (that is, £4,500 + 250 which equals area f + area g). However, this is not the net gain because the employer still has to pay the additional labour. He pays this additional labour £90 per worker, giving rise to an additional wage bill of £4,500 (area f). It follows, then, that the net gain in revenue to the employer from hiring the additional 50 units of labour is £250 (namely, area g).

Figure 18.2 shows the importance of the elasticity of the demand curve. It shows that for a given marginal subsidy, here £10, the more elastic the demand curve for labour then,

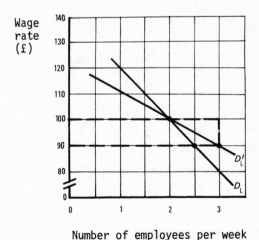

Number of employees per week
(hundreds)

Figure 18.2

1   the greater the employment effect (100 rather than 50);
2   the greater the total subsidy payment (100 × £10 = £1,000 rather than 50 × £10 = £500);
3   the greater the net gain to the employer (½ × 100 × £10 = £500 rather than ½ × 50 × £10 = £250).

Having set out in terms of Figures 18.1 and 18.2 some analytical issues of wage subsidies in general, it is possible now to turn to some specific wage subsidies which have been applied in Britain.

The Temporary Employment Subsidy

The Temporary Employment Subsidy (TES) was introduced in Britain in August 1975 and was the longest running of the special employment measures undertaken by the British Government to deal with the problem of unemployment. It was a job-preserving subsidy. Where redundancies would otherwise occur, the scheme provided a subsidy of £20 per week for each job the employer agreed to keep on. The effect of this particular subsidy is illustrated in Figure 18.3.

The initial wage is £100 at a level of employment of 100 workers on the demand curve D_L. Now assume that there is a fall in the demand for the firm's product. Since labour is a derived demand, then it follows that there will be a fall in the demand for labour also. This is shown by the movement in the demand curve from D_L to D'_L. At a wage of £100 this leads to a new level of employment of 80 workers, and so to 20 redundancies. Now suppose a subsidy of £20 is paid towards the wages of all workers whose redundancies are deferred as a result of the subsidy. This will result in fewer workers being unemployed and so reduce the number of redundancies to 10 rather than 20. In other words, the subsidy has led to 10 deferred redundancies, and this is the employment effect of the subsidy.

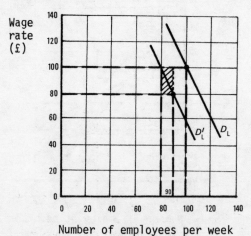

Number of employees per week

Figure 18.3

What is the total subsidy payment? Since the subsidy is paid only on those workers not made redundant solely because of the subsidy, then the total subsidy payment is £20 × 10 = £200 (and is shown by the shaded area in Figure 18.3). It should be noted from Figure 18.3 that the employment effect of TES is *not* dependent on the shift in the demand curve for labour, but rather depends on the level of the wage subsidy and on the elasticity of the demand curve for labour.

There was one feature of TES which is worth investigating. As applied in Britain, the scheme had a 'minimum deferral constraint' – in other words, the subsidy was only given if the number of redundancies deferred was at least 10 in any one establishment. One implication of this is illustrated in Figure 18.4. In this figure it is assumed that the demand curve for labour has shifted to D'_L (the original curve is not shown). In this case, a wage subsidy of £20 on all units of labour not made redundant would have an employment effect of only 8 workers. Since this is below the minimum deferral constraint, then no subsidy will be paid. The question arises as to whether it is worth the employer deciding to retain a total of 10 workers (instead of the 8) in order to qualify for the subsidy. To answer this question it is necessary to consider the total revenue received from the sale of the additional output produced and weigh this against the cost of hiring the additional labour. Suppose the minimum number of redundancies is deferred. The revenue received from the sale of the output produced by these 10 workers is given by the area under the demand curve between 80 workers and 90 workers, that is area (g + f + h). Given the numbers illustrated in Figure 18.4, this amounts to £80 + £640 + £155 = £875. The payment to these workers in wages, however, is simply area (f + h + l). The additional wage bill resulting from keeping them would therefore be £640 + £155 + £5 = £800. It is clear from Figure 18.4 that the net gain in revenue is area (g − l) which, given the numbers in the figure, amounts to £80 − 5 = £75. Thus, so long as area g exceeds area l, it is worthwhile to the firm retaining the specified

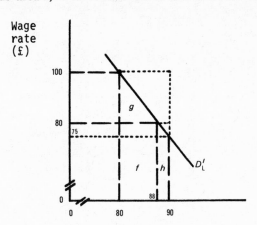

Number of employees per week

Figure 18.4

minimum of redundancies, even though it would prefer to retain fewer if there was no qualifying minimum.

As applied in the United Kingdom, TES was a job-preserving subsidy. In essence, this form of TES induces contracting firms to contract less. But this is one-sided. It seemed to some that what was required was to induce expanding firms to expand more. In other words, the government should implement a wage subsidy which made the stock of unemployed people smaller by creating jobs, rather than preventing the stock of unemployed from getting larger by deferring redundancies. Just such a wage subsidy was suggested by Layard and Nickell.

A simple version of their scheme is illustrated in Figure 18.5. Under this scheme a subsidy of £20 (a figure here used for illustrative purposes only) is paid to the firm for each employee in the current period that is additional to some base period employment level. In other words, some period in the past is chosen as a base, and the number of workers a firm has in that period is calculated. Now consider a subsidy is being considered for the present year. If the level of employment in the current year is greater than in the base period, then a subsidy is given for each such additional worker. Thus, suppose in the base period the demand curve for labour is given by D_b. At a wage of £100 the level of employment is 200 workers. Further suppose the firm is expanding and its demand curve for labour is shifting to the right, as represented by D_1. We now consider D_1 as the *current* period demand curve for labour, and consequently the demand for labour in the current period is 250 workers. If a subsidy of £20 is now paid, then the demand for labour will rise from 250 workers to 300 workers. What is the total subsidy payment to the firm in this case? Although the job-creation effect is 50 (300 − 250), the subsidy is paid on the labour employed beyond the base level, namely 100 workers (300 − 200). Hence, the total subsidy payment is £20 × 100 = £2,000, and is shown by the shaded area in Figure 18.5.

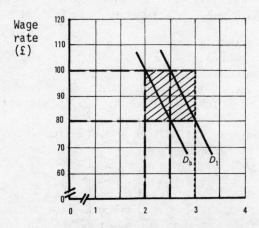

Figure 18.5

It is worth noting that in calculating the total subsidy payment which has to be paid by the administering agency, that the agency only needs to know the current employment level (inclusive of the subsidy), namely 300 workers, and the base level of employment, namely 200 workers. In the job-preserving subsidy, the agency had to know the number of deferred redundancies (10 in Figure 18.3), which would mean it knowing the firm's labour requirement both with and without the subsidy. A further advantage of the Layard and Nickell scheme is that it is not a policy for propping up 'lame ducks' which a job-preserving subsidy may tend to be (or become). There is yet another advantage of the Layard and Nickell scheme, and this is that it can be directed at specific groups of the unemployed, which is not the situation with a job-preserving subsidy. In other words, the subsidy could be placed on expanding industries only if they, say, take on school leavers.

The Regional Employment Premium

In 1957 a Regional Employment Premium (REP) was introduced in the UK and took the form of a wage subsidy in manufacturing industry operating in Development Areas; in other words, it was a spacially limited wage subsidy. For manufacturing firms wholly within the Development Areas a subsidy per worker was given at the rate of £1.50 per man per week, £0.75 for each woman and boy and £0.475 per girl per week. For Development Areas, therefore, REP was a blanket subsidy and by 1974–75 became the most expensive single component of regional policy.

The aim of the policy was to raise employment, which it did in two ways:

1 by lowering unit labour costs in the Development Area, and so attracting new plants; and
2 · by making labour relatively cheaper, and so stimulating labour to be substituted for capital.

The first is illustrated in Figure 18.6a, where perfect competition in both product and labour markets is assumed. The product price is £10. The subsidy lowers the marginal cost curve, resulting in a rise in output from 150 units to 200 units. Assuming the market demand for this product is fixed, then one result of the subsidy is to raise the proportion produced by firms in the Development Areas.

What is the employment effect? This is hard to predict in advance, as will now be shown. The increase in output from 150 to 200 leads to an increase in the demand for labour by existing firms. In addition, the increase in profit margins attracts new firms into the Development Areas.

The substitution effect and the output effect are illustrated with the help of isoquants in Figure 18.6b. Suppose the initial wage rate is £2 per worker and that the rental on capital is £1 per unit. With an outlay by the firm of £5m we have the isocost line denoted AB in Figure 18.6b. Given the isocost line AB, then the maximum output that can be produced is given by the isoquant furthest from the origin subject to having at least one point belonging to the line AB. This is

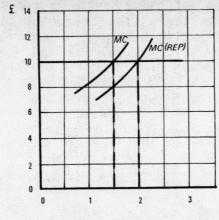

Figure 18.6(a)

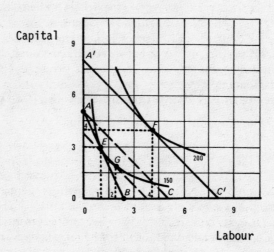

Figure 18.6(b)

shown by the isoquant denoting an output level of 150. The optimal input mix is therefore represented by point E. Hence, the firm will employ 1 unit of labour and 3 units of capital. Now suppose labour is subsidized to the extent of £1 per worker employed. Then the wage rate as seen by the employer is £1 per worker. The slope of the isocost line is, therefore, $-1/1 = -1$ (the slope of AC). The pure substitution effect is shown by a movement around the *original* isoquant but at the new relative price ratio. The new price ratio is given by the line HJ (parallel to AC), and the substitution effect of the subsidy is to raise labour employed from 1 unit to 2 units. Notice that with a subsidy on labour, and with

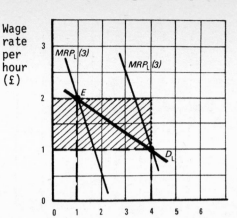

Figure 18.6(c)

the same outlay, the isocost line moves from AB to AC (where AC has a slope of − 1), and that HJ is parallel to AC. However there is also an output effect, as can be seen in terms of Figure 18.6a, which raised output from 150 units to 200 units. This means that at the new price ratio of 1, the cost minimizing input mix necessary to produce output 200 is shown by the isocost line A′C′. The result, then, is for the firm to move to point F, employing 4 units of capital and 4 units of labour. The employment effect of the subsidy is therefore to raise labour employed by 3 units (4 − 1).

What is the total subsidy payment? In establishing this it must be noted in Figure 18.6b that capital has also risen − from 3 units to 4 units. Consequently, this must be taken account of in assessing the extent of the labour subsidy. The situation is illustrated in Figure 18.6c. At the initial wage rate of £1 per worker 1 unit of labour is employed. This is shown by point E on the marginal revenue product of labour curve associated with 3 units of capital, and denoted $MRP_L(3)$. As the wage is reduced to £1 per worker, there is a rise in capital as well as labour. Capital rises to 4 units and so the marginal revenue product of labour curve moves to the right as shown. Hence, at a wage to the employer of £1 then 4 units of labour are employed. The total labour subsidy is £1 × 4 = £4.

It can be seen from this analysis that the *employment effect* of a subsidy, 3 units of labour in this illustration, will be difficult to estimate in practice. This is because it arises from three sources.

1 A rise in output.
2 Substituting labour for capital.
3 A rise in capital.

Furthermore, it is not unusual in practice to have a number of policies applied at the same time, and so it is even more difficult to attribute the change in labour employed to one specific policy.

Further reading

The key theory chapters in this book explain carefully the essential micro-economic theory concepts that first year university students are generally expected to cover. Unlike most textbooks written for these students, this book complements this theoretical core with chapters which show how the theory can be applied; and it does not complement it with more theoretical detail. Students who want a more extensive and detailed theoretical approach at the introductory level will find more theory in Parts 1 to 5 of R.G. Lipsey, *An Introduction to Positive Economics*, 6th edn, 1983, Weidenfeld and Nicolson. At a more intermediate level a useful textbook to consult is D. Laidler, *Introduction to Microeconomics*, 2nd edn, 1981, Philip Allan, which contains a useful elementary introduction to risk under uncertainty – a topic covered in Chapter 9 of this book; another text at this level is J. Hirshleifer, *Price Theory and Applications*, 2nd edn, 1980, Prentice-Hall, although this has a varying level of difficulty. A more applied intermediate textbook is D.N. McCloskey, *The Applied Theory of Price*, 2nd edn, 1985, Collier Macmillan.

On more specific topics the reader might consult the following which are grouped under the four parts of this book.

Part 1
A most useful introduction to the price system is R.A. Radford (1945), 'The Economic Organisation of a POW Camp', reprinted in E Mansfield (ed.), *Economics, Readings, Issues and Cases*, W.W. Norton & Company. A more applied introduction to demand and supply is R. Turvey, *Demand and Supply*, 2nd edn, 1980, Allen & Unwin. One common application of taxes and subsidies is to agriculture. See D. Colemand and J. McInerney, 'The Economics of Agricultural Policy', in R.M. Grant and G.K. Shaw, *Current Issues in Economic Policy*, 2nd edn, 1980, Philip Allan. On tariffs, quotas and flexible exchange rates, which are more specialist topics, see Bo Sodersten, *International Economics*, 2nd edn, 1980, Macmillan. The application of demand and supply is very extensive and it has, for example, been applied to the question of blood donation, see M. Cooper and A. Culyer, *The Price of Blood*, 1968, Hobart Paper No. 41, Institute of Economic Affairs.

Part II
The analysis of labour supply has been extended into directions of taxation and

the shorter working week. On labour supply and taxation see C.V. Brown, *Taxation and the Incentive to Work*, 2nd edn, 1983, Oxford University Press; while on the shorter working week see R. Shone, *Applications in Intermediate Microeconomics*, 1981, Martin Robertson, Chapter A2. Additional information on crime can be obtained from the following: B. Chiplin, 'Crime and Punishment', in *Economic Perspectives on Key Issues*, edited by P. Johnson and B. Thomas, Philip Allan, 1985; D.N. King and R. Shone, 'An Economic Model of Criminal Behaviour' in *Economics*, Vol. XVII, Part 1, No. 73, Spring 1981; D. Pyle 'Crime' in P. Maunder (ed.), *Case Studies in the Economics of Social Issues*, Heinemann Education Books and R.L. Carter, *Theft in the Market Place*, 1974, Hobart Paper No. 60, Institute of Economic Affairs; while the original article on this topic, by I. Ehrlich, 'Participation in Illegitimate Activities: A Theoretical and Empirical Investigation', *Journal of Political Economy*, Vol. 81, 1973, is highly mathematical and the empirical investigation is into crime in the United States of America.

Part III

Additional material on learning curves can be found in R. Shone, *Applications in Intermediate Microeconomics*, Martin Robertson, Chapter A7. On monopolies and mergers see K. Hartley, *Problems of Economic Policy*, 1977, George Allen & Unwin, Chapters 10 and 11 and D. Swann, *Competition and Consumer Protection*, 1979, Penguin (especially Part Two). A useful, although intermediate, textbook on energy is J.M. Griffin and H.B. Steel, *Energy Economics and Policy*, 1986, Academic Press.

Part IV

A number of articles, especially on wage differentials, can be found in J.E. King (ed.), *Readings in Labour Economics*, 1980, Oxford University Press; while a more detailed analysis of wage differentials can be found in H.P. Brown, *Inequality of Pay*, 1977, Oxford University Press. An introduction to the economics of wage subsidies can be found in R. Shone, *Applications in Intermediate Microeconomics*, Martin Robertson, Chapter A8.

Index